Individual learners

The current emphasis in educational discussion is on what is common to learners, whether this is a common curriculum, the assertion that one method of teaching is the best for all, or the belief that differences in educational outcomes reflect the effectiveness of schools rather than differences between students. The issue of personality differences among learners is largely neglected or denied.

Individual Learners redresses the balance by considering significant recent research into the link between personality and learning, and includes discussion of topical and controversial issues such as attention-deficit hyperactivity disorder, Fragile X syndrome, genetic factors in aggression and gender differences in motivation. The book considers fundamental issues in the study of personality and provides an up-to-date review and evaluation of the continuing nature–nurture debate. It then examines five traits that can have an impact upon learning: aggressiveness, anxiety, achievement motivation, self-confidence and shyness.

Individual Learners provides an accessible account of recent research into the links between personality and education and their implications for educational practice. It will be invaluable to all those with an interest in education, whether students, teachers or lecturers.

W. Ray Crozier is Senior Lecturer in Psychology of Education, University of Wales, Cardiff. His previous publications include the edited collection *Shyness and Embarrassment: Perspectives from Social Psychology* (1990) and *Manufactured Pleasures* (1994).

Individual learners

Personality differences in education

W. Ray Crozier

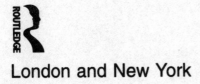

London and New York

First published 1997
by Routledge
11 New Fetter Lane, London EC4P 4EE

Simultaneously published in the USA and Canada
by Routledge
29 West 35th Street, New York, NY 10001

Typeset in Times by Keystroke, Jacaranda Lodge, Wolverhampton
Printed and bound in Great Britain by Mackays of Chatham PLC, Chatham, Kent

British Library Cataloguing in Publication Data
A catalogue record for this book is available from the British Library

Library of Congress Cataloging in Publication Data
Crozier, W. Ray, 1945–
    Individual learners : personality differences in education / Ray
Crozier.
        p.   cm.
    Includes bibliographical references and index.
    1. Students–Psychology. 2. Cognitive styles. 3. Learning,
Psychology of. I. Title.
LB1117.C76 1997
371.8′01′9–dc20   96–43377

ISBN 0–415–13329–7
ISBN 0–415–13330–0 (pbk)

To Sandra, John, and Beth

Contents

Figures and tables

Acknowledgements

Grateful acknowledgement is made to the following for permission to reprint previously published material: Clinical Psychology Publishing Company, Inc. for permission to base Figure 2. 2 in this book upon Figure 1, 'Fragile X syndrome family pedigree', in R. J. Simensen and R. C. Rogers (1989), 'School psychology and medical diagnosis: the Fragile X syndrome', *Psychology in the Schools*, 26: 383; John Murray (Publishers) Ltd for the extracts from 'Summoned by Bells' by John Betjeman; the Powys Society for the extract from *The Joy of It* by Littleton Powys; Bloomsbury Publishing for the extract from *Cat's Eye* (1989) by Margaret Atwood; West Publishing Company and Lawrence Erlbaum Associates, Inc. for permission to base Table 6.1 of this book on material from *Introduction to Social Psychology* (1985) by J. T. Tedeschi, S. Lindskold and P. Rosenfeld, and from E. E. Jones and T. S. Pittman (1982), 'Toward a general theory of strategic self-presentation', in J. Suls (ed.) *Psychological Perspectives on the Self*, vol. 1; The Ciba Foundation for permission to reproduce Table 2.2 of this book from A. Thomas and S. Chess, 'Temperament and follow-up to adulthood', in Ruth Porter and Gerayln M. Collins (eds) *Temperamental Differences in Infants and Young Children: Ciba Foundation Symposium 89*; and Society for Research in Child Development to base Table 2.4 of this book upon Tables 2 and 3 in R. N. Emde, R. Plomin, J. Robinson, R. Corley, J. de Fries, D. W. Fulker, J. S. Reznick, J. Campos, J. Kagan and C. Zahn-Waxler (1992), 'Temperament, emotion and cognition at fourteen months: The MacArthur Longitudinal Twin Study', *Child Development*, 63: 1437–55.

Introduction

A teacher contemplating a new class of students can be confident of one fact – the students will be very different from one another. Some of these differences will suggest themselves at the outset as the teacher looks through the class register, where names will reflect the gender and possibly the ethnic, religious or social class backgrounds of the students. Individual names might trigger expectations if the teacher recognises a child from the reputation he or she has established earlier in the school, or a brother or sister has been in the class, or the family is well known to the school. When the teacher first meets the class, further differences will be apparent: in height and weight, in impressions of neatness or physical attractiveness, in ethnic identity.

The school minimises many of these differences, by grouping pupils according to their age and possibly on the basis of their past academic achievements. Jackson's (1968) description of pupils' experience of school as being a member of a 'crowd' suggests a process of 'de-individuation', that can be seen, for example, in the common requirement for pupils to wear a uniform. Nevertheless, children are very different from one another and older pupils in particular will often put considerable effort and ingenuity into asserting their individuality, perhaps by modifying the uniform. With shirt hanging out over skirt or trousers or tie loosened and hanging over the shoulder, they challenge the school rules.

Differences among children become more salient to the teacher as the class begins its work, attempting tasks that themselves assume a degree of similarity among pupils. Children are typically taught in large classes of 30 or more pupils and, in the main, follow a common curriculum at a similar pace. Very soon, some of the children will be seen to make more rapid progress than others, and may display special talents or aptitudes; the lack of progress of other pupils will become of concern to the teacher, and in some cases additional advice may be sought. Some children will be docile and others difficult, some keen to work, others easily distracted. There will be children who establish effective relationships with the teacher and get on well with each other, but others who are withdrawn, awkward or demanding.

The skilful teacher will search for the individual approach that seems to work with particular students, in gaining their attention and interest, in finding appropriate ways to analyse the tasks they find difficult, in responding to their successes and failures. Of course teachers themselves are just as different from one another as their students. Schools may establish policies for the curriculum and methods of teaching, for discipline and pastoral care, but no two classrooms will be the same, the same class of students will behave in a different way for one teacher than for another, and individual students will behave differently in different classes and with different teachers.

Such variation has always raised controversies in education. There has been a long-running dispute between those who believe that educational provision should be tailored to meet individual needs and those who argue for equality of treatment. This issue was at the heart of the movement to establish a comprehensive system of education in Britain. It is represented in current debates about selection, streaming, and 'mixed ability teaching'.

Psychologists' contributions to these debates have also proved controversial. From the outset, the development of intelligence testing has been linked with the selection of students for different kinds of schools. It was argued that these tests provided a 'scientific' basis for making these selections and, as a measure of the child's 'innate' ability, they would provide a fairer method than school attainment tests. However, arguments about innateness have not fitted easily into a *Zeitgeist* that emphasises equality, and claims that there are differences between ethnic groups in intelligence led to allegations of racism and widespread scepticism about the value of IQ tests.

Psychologists are also involved in decisions about children who have special educational needs or whose behaviour is problematic to the school. The behaviour of a minority of children has always proved unacceptable to schools and they have turned to psychologists for help in diagnosing individual children and providing remedies. Again, their role has often attracted criticism.

From one point of view, they are seen as supporting the school system in stigmatising disadvantaged and ethnic minority children. From another perspective, they are accused of interpreting failure and disaffection as the 'fault' of the individual child without paying sufficient attention to the responsibilities of the educational system or of individual schools. They seem to share the assumption that school is a 'constant' and differences among schools are of negligible importance for understanding the behaviour of their pupils.

This assumption has been undermined by recent research into school effectiveness that shows that schools vary considerably in, for example, the incidence of bullying or truancy and that this variation is associated with factors like the quality of leadership, the school 'climate', and so on. These findings do pose a challenge to personality theories and, as we discuss in Chapter 1, there has been a struggle to conceptualise relationships between individual and contextual factors. Nevertheless, explanation at the level of the school should not lead to concentration upon the average rates of achievement, truancy or bullying, with a consequent neglect of individual differences among pupils. Behaviour reflects an interaction between individual and school factors, although this is, as yet, insufficiently understood.

Despite these controversies, educationalists need to be aware of research into personality because one of the principal goals of education should be the personal and social development of students, and understanding the development of personality is essential if the educational system is to meet its obligations to achieve this goal. Difficulties of adjustment can have serious consequences for the individual as well as for the school, and we see in several places in this volume that problems that are manifest in early childhood do predict problems in later childhood and adulthood.

This volume is concerned with individual differences in personality that are relevant to educational experience. The first part comprises two longer chapters. The first of these considers how personality can be studied. One approach is to start 'in the classroom', identifying individual differences on specific learning tasks and seeking to establish if they are predictive of educational outcomes more generally. An alternative approach is to apply within education personality concepts that have been established elsewhere. We look at examples of both approaches. Chapter 2 considers evidence for the origins of personality differences obtained from investigations of temperamental characteristics, genetic and heritability research, and longitudinal studies of the impact of significant life events. Hopefully, I will convince you that research has moved on from sterile debates about whether genetic or environmental factors are more important. Current thinking emphasises a complex interaction between these factors, and the notion of 'developmental pathways' moves away from simplistic cause and effect explanations.

The second part comprises a set of chapters, each concentrating on one personality trait: aggressiveness, anxiety, motivation, self-confidence, shyness. This particular selection has not been guided by a set of theoretical principles about what constitute the most 'important' traits. For example, I have not set out to examine the 'Big Five' approach to personality traits, as these impinge upon education. This seemed to me to follow a 'top down' model of the psychology of education that informs so many textbooks and that often presents material that is remote from the concerns of those interested in education. Nor did I wish to focus on personality 'problems' as if these could be divorced from the variation in personality that is ubiquitous. Our concern is with the variation that is routinely encountered in the classroom and that can prove challenging to the teacher. The particular set chosen reflects topics that have been the focus of seminar discussions with practising teachers following Masters of Education courses and with undergraduates on psychology of education courses.

The approach taken in these chapters is to review studies that have sought evidence to test theories about individual differences. This book offers a critical evaluation of research literature. This approach requires some justification, as the terms 'theory', 'evidence' and 'research' are now highly controversial within education and, perhaps to a lesser extent, psychology. This is particularly the case if these terms are associated with a view of psychology that is scientific and experimental (or scientist and positivist, to its opponents). There is now considerable interest in exploring alternative conceptions of research, including greater emphasis on personal experience and reliance upon the interpretation of texts of various kinds.

Although I set out to be even-handed in my treatment of psychological approaches (or 'to sit on the fence') I found myself concentrating upon empirical studies, often of a traditional kind. One reason for this, I think, is that the educational debate hears many voices, most of them loud, but it does not often attend to evidence, especially evidence that fails to support the speaker's position. Confident claims are made about how children should be taught, what the curriculum should be, why some students achieve less than others, without very much concern about findings on these questions. If no one else is to be sceptical about claims, then researchers should. I recognise that the forms of debate in themselves are worthy of research and that many qualitative methods are well suited to this.

A further justification is that the research I examined introduced many novel ways of looking at individual differences, and they used empirical methods, often in ingenious ways, to explore these ideas. Experimental methods are typically regarded as devices for finding the holes in theories, but they are also a way of trying out ideas. Studies of intrinsic motivation, test anxiety, self-worth theory, self-handicapping, all illustrate this aspect of empirical research.

Other research seemed exciting because it took on many intractable problems. This is particularly so in studies of the origins and development of personality. For so long, studies relied upon retrospective accounts of early experience but, increasingly, researchers are investing the effort to conduct longitudinal studies that follow people from birth into adulthood. These studies are becoming ever more pertinent as the family structure is changing and raising fundamental questions about the prerequisites for healthy psychological development. Research into genetic influences on personality has also been expanding and has been challenging many long-standing views on development. This research also inevitably raises ethical issues that have yet to be fully discussed.

Psychology is a discipline with many branches, and some of those most central to our concerns – developmental and social psychology, and personality, have been the subject of radical criticisms. This 'soul searching' has probably contributed to the changes they have gone through. There is greater emphasis upon phenomenological approaches, and the number of constructs prefixed by 'self' – self-consciousness, self-efficacy, self-esteem, self-presentation, self-regulation, self-serving bias, self-worth – emphasises not only the importance for understanding behaviour of how the individual perceives him or herself, but also agency. The person is not the passive product of genes or environment but strives to make sense of his or her experiences and acts in the light of expectations of the future. This view of the person provides the framework for our interpretation of research into personality factors in education.

Part I

Describing and explaining individual differences

Chapter 1

The reality of personality

DEFINITIONS

The aim of this volume is to provide an overview of research into personality as it impinges upon learning. The term 'personality' is open to many interpretations. We have in mind differences between students in personal characteristics other than intelligence, but we now attempt to define the term more carefully. The word itself derives from *persona*, which has its origins in Latin, referring to the actor's mask and to a character in a dramatic performance. The Concise Oxford Dictionary gives two meanings: (1) being a person; personal existence or identity; (2) distinctive personal character. Within psychology, Allport (1937: 48) has defined personality as:

> The dynamic organisation within the individual of those psychophysical systems that determine his unique adjustments to his environment.

Child (1968: 83) provides the following definition:

> More or less stable internal factors that make one person's behaviour consistent from one time to another and different from the behaviour other people would manifest in comparable situations.

There are similarities between these two definitions and also differences of emphasis. Both agree that personality is an internal factor that exerts a causal effect upon behaviour. The person acts upon, or adjusts to, the environment, but his or her behaviour is not a product of environmental forces. Both definitions refer to variation, to differences between people. Both refer to the distinctiveness of an individual's response to the environment. Hampson construes this in terms of a comparison with the behaviour of other people whereas Allport emphasises the unique constellation of psychological systems within the individual. Finally, Hampson makes more explicit reference to stability and consistency.

Two of the central elements of these definitions, that personality is a causal factor and that it produces stability in behaviour, have been challenged in recent years. There has also been a dispute between those psychologists who prefer to identify the important ways in which people are different from one another and those who argue that each person is an individual and that, although people can be described in terms that are not unique in themselves, 'clever' or 'conscientious', the person is more than the sum of these descriptions.

Before we discuss these issues, we consider empirical approaches to the study of personality. Educationalists suspect that there are important differences between students, but how are these to be identified and studied? This chapter adopts the following approach. We illustrate the investigation of individual variation, first by discussing a classification derived from the study of approaches to learning. Next we consider the example of field-independence, a trait which arose in the identification of individual variation in a specific perceptual task but which has been shown to have much wider implications. We then consider personality traits, both in ordinary language and in psychological theory. We look in greater detail at Eysenck's account of extraversion as an example of an explanatory theory. Having reviewed this research, we turn to a critical examination of its assumptions.

THE STUDY OF INDIVIDUAL DIFFERENCES IN LEARNING

Approaches to learning

A useful starting point for consideration of individual differences in learning is an investigation of college students' approaches to reading .academic articles reported by Marton and Säljö (1976). Students read lengthy excerpts from an article and were subsequently posed questions about details in the article and asked to explain to the researcher what it was about. They were also interviewed about how they had set about this task, and the researchers were able to use answers to these questions to identify two approaches, which they labelled as a deep-level and a surface-level approach.

In the former, the student aimed to understand what the article was about, looked for its main points, and analysed the relationships between its arguments and evidence. To quote two of the students, 'I tried to look for . . . you know, the principal ideas'; 'I tried to think what it was all about . . . I thought about how he [the author] had built up the whole thing.' Students adopting a surface approach devoted their attention to the details of the text, often attempting to learn it by rote: 'Well, I just concentrated on trying to remember as much as possible'; 'I remembered . . . but, I'd sort of memorized everything I'd read . . . no, not everything, but more or less' (p. 9). There was evidence that deep processing led to superior comprehension of the material, a finding that is not surprising given what psychological research has established about the superiority of active and meaningful learning over a passive and rote approach, the facilitation of memorising provided by strategies that make use of elaboration and organization of material, and the beneficial effects of prior knowledge and interest upon the acquisition of new information.

It is useful to know something about differences among students in the ways that they read articles, take notes in lectures or while they are reading, or memorise material, because these are all valued skills in education, but the distinction between deep and surface approaches raises further questions for psychologists. Do these different approaches constitute *styles*, in the sense that students have a tendency to utilise them across a range of different learning tasks? Are these styles associated with other characteristics of students? What factors influence a student to adopt a particular approach? What are the long-term consequences?

Psychologists have found it useful to tackle these questions by devising questionnaire measures of the extent to which an individual adopts a deep or a surface approach in addition to inferring their approach from interviews with students in a learning situation. The reasons are largely pragmatic. It is very time-consuming to categorise learners on the basis of personal interviews and, accordingly, there is a risk that these studies are conducted with small numbers of participants who may be an unrepresentative sample of the student population. On the other hand, this research has the advantage of looking directly at fairly realistic learning tasks of the kinds that students routinely encounter (although written tests of understanding may be more commonly experienced than interviews), whereas questionnaires are at one remove from these tasks and ask students to describe how they typically behave.

This raises the question of the validity of questionnaire measures: is it legitimate to infer learning styles from students' self-descriptions of their study behaviour? The use of questionnaires in research into personality is ubiquitous and remains controversial. Respondents might be 'economical with the truth', try to create a good impression upon the researcher, deceive themselves, lack insight into their behaviour, be subject to biases in the way they answer questions, or might answer in an entirely superficial way. Those more sanguine about questionnaires argue that if you want to find out something about somebody why not just ask them, why reject in advance what they have to say? The view taken here is that a single study using one questionnaire does not tell us very much. Questionnaire responses need to be compared with other kinds of information about learning styles, and many studies have done this (e.g. Entwistle and Ramsden, 1983). But more important, researchers should undertake a series of studies which approach the behaviours of interest in different ways in order to put together an intelligible account of individual differences in learning. If this account provides a sound grasp of these matters, then this should be reflected across the measures taken, even measures which may vary among themselves in their sensitivity or validity.

Motivation and learning styles

What other characteristics of students are associated with the tendency to adopt a deep or a surface approach? Students' educational goals turn out to be important. Biggs (1978) identified associations among students' beliefs that education is a means of self-development, their interest in learning for its own sake (intrinsic motivation) and learning strategies that were associated with a search for personal meaning. On the other hand, a surface approach was associated with instrumental goals, where courses are regarded as means of obtaining qualifications, and also with students' fear of failure. Entwistle and Ramsden (1983) similarly found that a deep approach was associated with intrinsic motivation, whereas a surface approach was associated with extrinsic motivation and fear of failing. Nolen (1988) reported similar findings. Deep processing was correlated with *task orientation*, which reflects students' goals, specifically their commitment to learning for its own sake, and their beliefs about the causes of success, in particular the belief that success depends on hard work and understanding and not simply memorising material. Finally, Schiefele (1996) found that students who were interested in the topic under consideration were more likely to achieve a deeper level of text comprehension and less likely to have a superficial grasp of the text, when their comprehension of the topic material was assessed by recognition tests.

These studies report further links between learning styles and motivation. A cluster of items that recurs in several investigations identifies well-organised students who adopt effective study methods, who have a strong motive to succeed, and who are very competitive. It should be noted that these factors are clusters of several items, and thus the meanings of deep and surface have widened from classifications of approaches to a specific learning task to labels that summarise a set of correlated approaches to a range of tasks. Thus, for example, a deep approach is not incompatible with the simple rote learning of material, since that type of learning might have a valuable, albeit limited place within an approach that is predominantly concerned with a search for meaning.

These constellations of motives and approaches to learning are correlated with student attainments. In British universities and colleges measures of student motives and learning styles are at least as successful at predicting degree class in the humanities and social sciences as are A-level grades (Entwistle and Wilson, 1977). The tendency to adopt a deep approach is positively associated with progress in university whereas students who adopt a surface approach tend to make less progress. High scores on surface approach items were associated with lower grades. Schmeck (1983) reported that scales of 'deep and elaborative processing' were associated with higher grade point averages among American students. Finally, Nolen (1988) reported significant negative correlations between course grades and measures of belief in the value of surface level strategies and of their reported use among a sample of 14-year-old students.

It has to be admitted that the values of these correlation coefficients are small. There are several reasons why low correlations are unavoidable. For example, students in British higher education are a relatively homogeneous group in terms of their achievements, given that they have already undergone a selection process on the basis of their A-level grades (this presumably contributes to the very low correlations reported between A-level grades and degree class, at least in arts and social science subjects, reported by Entwistle and Wilson, 1977). Also, the measures being compared are rather crude and, in the psychometric sense, unreliable. A single questionnaire that takes only a few minutes to complete may not be an adequate measure of the underlying concepts of learning style or motivation; examination performance might be a poor indication of the outcomes of learning, since it is influenced on the one hand by individual differences in students' anxiety and examination techniques, and on the other hand by their tutors' inconsistency in marking essay-type answers.

The fact that these differences in attainment are small should not be taken to imply that they are unimportant. It does mean that we cannot predict with very much confidence any individual student's achievements on the basis of his or her score on a learning style questionnaire. However, we are able to make statements about trends among the student population. On average, adopting a deep approach results in higher achievement and adopting a surface approach is an impediment to such achievement. To express this in a different way, it is unlikely that among those graduates with first class degrees one would find many students who have reported that they have relied upon a surface approach to their learning.

However, it must be recognised that studies which rely upon correlational methods cannot provide conclusions about the causal relationships between learning styles and achievement. The significant correlations between adopting a surface approach and poor achievement may reflect different mechanisms. It might be that a surface strategy produces poor learning outcomes; alternatively, weak students might tend to favour that strategy. It is interesting in this respect to observe that Nolen (1988) found a significant correlation between students' perceptions that they lacked ability and their beliefs in the value of a surface approach. Again, correlations do not prove the causal relationship. Students who have come to rely upon a surface strategy might find that their attainments are poor but, in the absence of any insight into their strategy, they might attribute these to their lack of ability. Or it could be that students in difficulties with a course fall back upon a surface approach: because they don't understand the material they adopt a rote learning approach in the hope of fulfilling minimum course requirements.

Biggs (1993) has argued that although clusters of associated motives and strategies may characterise students across a range of learning tasks, these clusters may also be sensitive to the context of learning. For example, undergraduates often are more interested in or have particular goals concerning some parts of their course than for others. Contemporary modular degree courses are often wide-ranging in their subject matter and in the skills that students are taught – abnormal psychology might hold greater interest for some students than cognitive psychology, or children's literature be more attractive than Chaucer – and students might adopt different learning approaches for particular parts of their course. Students might also change their strategy within a given course as they come to perceive the course differently, perhaps when they come to appreciate its relevance, or else a boost in confidence when they receive good grades reduces their fear of failure. The schedule of assessment of a course – the relative salience of unseen examinations, multiple choice tests, essays, project work, group activities – and the tutor's teaching style are further contextual factors that may influence the adoption of particular learning styles.

We complete this section on learning styles by considering the implications of this approach to the study of individual differences. Psychologists seek to identify such differences among students by setting them learning tasks and talking to them about the approach that they have adopted. Once a potentially significant dimension of difference has been detected, there is an attempt to develop a method for measuring this. In this case, the preferred method is the questionnaire, and statistical analysis has shown that there is considerable similarity among the measures. A sceptical reader might dispute the significance of this level of consensus, given that most of the questionnaires drew upon others in their construction. Nevertheless, it is safe to conclude that independent researchers in different countries can reach similar conclusions about self-reported learning styles. These styles do relate to students' motivations for learning and to their achievements in the educational system. Teachers 'know' that their students are different, but educationalists are not always clear on the nature or extent of these differences and have not approached in any systematic way the task of arranging teaching and assessment methods that would reflect this variation. The research we have summarised begins to address these questions.

The findings about the correlations between approaches to learning and students' goals caution against any simple idea that one approach is 'best' (best for whom?) or should necessarily be encouraged. Nevertheless, surface, simple reproduction, or rote approaches are unlikely to produce successful outcomes, other than serving as a defensive strategy which is perhaps effective in the short term by helping students cope with fears of failure or the perceived difficulty of the task. Students should be encouraged to reflect on their learning styles, to see where their styles reflect choices that they have made and where they might have trapped themselves.

Cognitive styles

Classifications of learning styles and approaches (Murray-Harvey, 1994) conceive of a continuum from habitual responses to particular learning situations to more stable, personality traits that influence learning across a wide range of tasks. Styles at the latter end of the continuum tend to be classified as cognitive styles, which have been defined as 'characteristic modes of being that show up in perceptual or intellectual activity; they constitute stable, self-consistent forms of adaptation; and they form a link between the cognitive and personal/affective spheres' (Brodzinsky, 1982; cited by Paramo and Tinajero, 1990: 1079). Advocates of the concept have been keen to distinguish cognitive style from ability and to show that there are individual differences in performance on cognitive tasks that cannot simply be reduced to differences in intelligence. They argue that different styles are of equal value or can be equally effective at task performance: the same *level* of performance can be attained in different ways.

Field-independence

The cognitive style that has stimulated most research has been that of field-independence/field-dependence. This was first identified by Witkin when he was assessing subjects' performance on a specific perceptual task, namely their ability to know when they were upright. Judgements of vertical orientation have considerable practical implications, for example, for aircraft pilots. Witkin identified consistent individual differences among people on several tasks (Witkin and Goodenough, 1981). In one of these tasks, the body-adjustment test (BAT) the subject was seated on a chair in a small, specially constructed room. Both the chair and the room could be tilted independently of each other, and the subject's task was to adjust the position of the chair until it was upright. There are two sources of information here for the person who keeps his or her eyes open: visual information from the room and feedback about gravitational pull on the body. Normally, these two sources would supply convergent information, but under these experimental conditions the two sources can be in conflict: for example, the room appears tilted but gravitational cues suggest that one is in an upright position.

Witkin found that some subjects were able to discount visual information and locate the chair in true upright whereas other subjects used cues from the room to align themselves relative to the orientation of the room. There were individual differences on two related tasks, the rod-and-frame test (RFT) and the rotating-room test. In the first of these, subjects are in a darkened room where they are confronted with a luminous square frame and a luminous rod, each of which can be tilted independently of the other. Again, the task is to set the rod in true upright orientation, and subjects tend either to approximate the true upright, ignoring the tilt of the frame, or to align the rod with the orientation of the frame.

The rotating-room test requires more complex equipment, and has been much less studied. Here, the room remains constant but the orientation of the chair can be rotated through 360 degrees, and the subject has to bring his or her position to true upright. Witkin reported that subjects who were influenced by the visual information (the visual field) in any of these tasks were also likely to be so influenced in the other two tasks.

These studies identified individual differences on a perceptual task; for these findings to be considered as evidence for the existence of a cognitive style, it would also have to be shown that these differences were apparent in other kinds of tasks and that they provided a link between cognitive and personality spheres. Evidence for the first condition was reported by Witkin in terms of a correlation between these perceptual tasks and performance on the embedded figures test (EFT). This test is of a kind that has been widely used by psychologists. Subjects are presented with a series of paper and pencil problems, each of which involves a simple geometrical figure and a complex design that contains hidden within it the simple form; the simple figure is removed out of sight and the subject has to find the form in the design. Performance on the EFT is correlated with performance on the perceptual tasks. Witkin argued that effective performance on all these tests requires the person to 'disembed', to analyse and separate out a target object from its context, whether this is the remainder of the design in the EFT or the appearance of the room in the BAT, and to act upon the task, to restructure it and impose an organisation upon it. He characterised this as an 'articulated field approach' and contrasted it with a 'global field approach'.

Witkin argued that these different styles were also evident in personality and social behaviour. People with articulated field style (i.e. who were field-independent) have a greater sense of differentiation between themselves and other people. They tend to keep their feelings and cognitions separate. They are more autonomous and less dependent on other people and they can be demanding, inconsiderate, and manipulative. They do well at science and mathematics and aspire to careers in architecture and engineering. On the other hand, those who are field-dependent and adopt a global field approach are warm, affectionate and tactful, they are effective in personal relationships, and aspire to careers like nurse, social worker or personnel manager.

Individual differences in field-dependence/independence, typically assessed by the EFT or the RFT, have been extensively researched in education. The cognitive style has been related to attainment throughout the school curriculum, to second language learning, ability at art, reading comprehension, understanding of metaphors, use of multimedia and hyper-text, performance on multiple choice tests, and teachers' questioning styles, to select just some of the topics of recent articles. Despite its capacity to generate all this research, Witkin's theory has been heavily criticised on several grounds. One set of criticisms relates to the coherence of the concept of field-independence, and it has been argued that the generalisation from studies of performance on perceptual tasks to personality and social behaviour is unwarranted. Griffiths and Sheen (1992: 136) argue that the extension of the theory to propose that there are generalised articulated and global styles is 'incredible':

> Presuming (perhaps unreasonably) that tight definitions of global and analytical functioning could be agreed, even cursory questioning of the implied relationship between disembedding figures from specific visual displays, and general relating to the 'environment', suggests insurmount-able problems. As meaningless questions defy logical answers, there can simply be no answer to the primary question: what can it possibly mean to consistently approach the environment analytically rather than globally?

Critics of the coherence of the theory also point out that the correlations between the various measures are much lower than they should be, if they are all measuring the same underlying construct. Following a review of relevant studies, Arthur and Day (1991) reported that the correlations between the EFT and the RFT range from 0.28 to 0.60.

A second line of criticism is that tests of field-independence are measuring differences in ability rather than in cognitive style. There are two issues here. The first is that tests like the EFT are similar to many IQ tests. Analyses of IQ tests have identified an ability factor that has been labelled 'spatial ability' or 'general visual perception' and tests of this ability are also similar in item content to the EFT. The definition of articulated field is also similar to definitions of this ability. Many studies have shown that field-independence is correlated with measures of intelligence (Arthur and Day, 1991; McKenna, 1984, 1990). McKenna's (1984) review of the literature showed that the median correlation between the EFT and Raven's Matrices was 0.54. Arthur and Day found that Raven's Matrices correlated 0.62 with EFT and 0.32 with the RFT, and both coefficients were statistically significant. Indeed the correlation between EFT and Matrices was as high as the correlation between the EFT and RFT (0.61). There are also significant correlations between field-independence and school achievement. Paramo and Tinajero (1990) report correlations of 0.39 between EFT and school average grades among 10- to 11-year-olds and 0.23 among 12- to 14-year-olds. Field-independent students had higher achievements in all subjects; indeed Paramo and Tinajero argue that no research studies have ever shown superior school performance among field-dependent students.

These findings call into question the value of the construct as a cognitive style. Fundamental to the notion of style is that there are different ways of achieving the same goal, and this implies that individuals who have the opportunity to study using their preferred style will do as well as other individuals using their preferred style. The 'matching hypothesis' proposes that students perform best when there is a match between the form of instruction and the students' cognitive styles; for example, field-independent students perform to their best when the teaching or instructional method is also field-independent in structure. McKenna (1990) has reviewed studies that have addressed this question and finds little support for the matching hypothesis. The recurrent trend is for field-independent students to do better than field-dependent subjects whether or not they are taught by a field-independent or dependent teacher. Teachers who differ in cognitive style tend to adopt different approaches to instruction; for example, field-independent teachers ask more questions and give more feedback. Some studies have manipulated teaching approaches, emphasising, for example, either discovery or expository methods, but any match between teacher and students is very small relative to the overall superiority of field-independent students. McKenna argues that a more parsimonious account of this pattern of findings is that field-dependence/independence is an ability factor, and that more able students generally perform better than less able students, across a range of teaching methods.

These criticisms of the concept of a global–analytical style have in large part been met by recent developments of the concept. Schmeck (1988: 327) argues that research into cognitive style finds evidence for a global versus analytic dimension. Riding and Cheema (1991) argue for two cognitive styles: (1) verbal–imagery dimension; (2) wholist–analytic dimension. The first style contrasts the ways in which students prefer to process information, whether they rely on verbal means, say, for solving problems, or rely upon visual imagery. The second is similar to Witkin's concept of global and analytical styles, and is assessed by performance on a computer-presented test, the cognitive styles analysis (CSA). This measures response speed on an embedded-figures task and on a task of judging the similarity between two geometric figures.

This approach to cognitive style does not seem to suffer from the disadvantages mentioned above. Unlike Witkin's EFT, scores on the CSA are statistically independent of measures of intelligence (Riding and Pearson, 1994). There is evidence that wholistic learners do better under some circumstances whereas analytic learners do better under others

(Douglas and Riding, 1993). The style is correlated with behaviour other than performance on perceptual tasks and is related to social behaviour, for example, secondary school students' preference for working by themselves or in groups (wholists express greater preference for group work; Riding and Read, 1996). The value of a particular cognitive style for understanding individual differences in learning, and the range of its application, are best established by careful empirical research, rather than by rejecting them as 'incredible'.

We have introduced two approaches to the identification and measurement of individual differences in learning: approaches to learning and cognitive styles. It is clear that questions about specific areas of differences raise much broader issues. Approaches to learning give rise to questions about students' hopes and fears about studying, and the global–analytic dimension relates to perception, learning, thinking, interpersonal relationships, and career aspirations.

THE STRUCTURE OF PERSONALITY

The language of personality

Because differences among people are so conspicuous, one would expect them to become captured in language, and English does indeed have a large trait vocabulary to summarise the impressions that people make on others (Allport, 1937, counted 24,000 trait words in the dictionary). This vocabulary is most evident when we describe someone to a third party, for example when writing a reference to support a candidate's application for a job. The referee writes of the candidate's reliability and honesty, capacity for hard work, ability to form effective relationships with others, and so on. Such language contains many assumptions. Most obviously, to describe someone as, say, honest is to imply a classification of people into honest and not honest; otherwise the term would convey no information. This classification can be modified by the use of adverbs such as somewhat, very, always, etc., and the choice of word can enable the person to make fine distinctions.

A second point arises from the fact that language is not simply a string of words. Its effective use requires a shared understanding about the topic of discourse between speaker or writer and the recipient of the message. Both parties to the discourse must share a common sense theory of traits and of the implications of trait words. When I am informed that someone is conscientious I infer that they are likely to meet deadlines for assignments, that they will finish tasks rather than leave them incomplete, that they will put a certain amount of effort into a task, that they can apply themselves without continuous supervision, and so on. The term implies all of these behaviours and also that they can be expected on more than one occasion.

Referees base their reports on their knowledge of the person as they have come into contact with him or her, and they predict how the person is going to act in the future – they assume that behaviour is predictable and that trait words can both summarise past behaviour and point to the future.

A further implication of the trait vocabulary is that it maps out regularities in human behaviour. The word conscientious was not coined simply to describe the constellations of behaviours that any one person displays. The word is already in the vocabulary of the population and is available to me, or anyone else, to reach the conclusion that it fits, that it serves as a good description of what someone is like. A concrete example might help to illustrate this point. Beynon (1985) studied children who had just made the transition from primary school to secondary school. He adopted an ethnographic approach, that is, he observed the day-to-day activities of pupils and teachers in the classroom and playground. He acted like an anthropologist who goes to live in some exotic culture and who records its customs and mundane activities in order to understand the ways in which that society is organised.

Even though the pupils had only been in the school a matter of months they already used a rich personality language to describe one another and were already categorising each other into types: there were varieties of 'swots' – 'teacher's pets', 'goodies' and 'browners'. There were 'dippoes' and 'weirdos', 'jokers', 'muckers', 'hard nuts', 'radiator kids'. In a school in Lancashire which I knew, children used the expression 'biddies' to taunt children who were poorly dressed, had problems with their hair or were less clean than the others thought they should be: 'I'm not working with him because he's got biddies'; 'He says I've got biddies'. In the boys' grammar school where I was a pupil, the equivalent term was 'mange'. Being overweight or underweight, or a boy regarded as 'effeminate' (poof, fairy) also attract labels. The point I wish to make is that these categories are passed on from generation to generation, and are not invented to fit the characteristics of particular children; rather, children will be fitted to the types. The categorisations have evolved to help children adjust to the many demands of the school and to help them regulate their relationships with each other and with the school.

Factor analysis and personality

Personality theorists have long had the goal of identifying the major ways in which people are different from each other in order to provide a basic classification of personality. At present there is disagreement as to how many basic personality types there are. Most research has been based on factor analysis, and because much of the disagreement concerns the interpretation of the results of this technique, we provide a brief explanation of this difficult topic.

Factor analysis is used where the investigator attempts to identify underlying factors that are common to, or are shared by a set of different variables. A variable is any measure or score that can take different values, like age, attainment test scores, or IQ. In research into personality these variables take different forms: often they are ratings that people make of the degree to which they believe they or other people can be described by trait terms; they can be scores that are assigned to their responses to personality questionnaire items ('I worry about examinations'; 'It is important for me to succeed at whatever I do'); finally, measures may be taken of actual behaviour, for example based on video or audio recordings of interviews or unobtrusive observations.

The method is based on the analysis of the table or 'matrix' of correlations that is produced if scores are collected on a set of variables and the correlations between every pair of variables is computed. Its goal is to find the smallest number of common factors that could reproduce the correlations among these variables. It assumes that the variation in a set of test scores reflects two kinds of factors in addition to the inevitable errors in measurement that are entailed in any test: there are one or more factors that are specific to performance on that test and also one or more factors that are involved in that test and that are also shared by other tests.

Consider, for example, the variation in performance that would be found if one were to assess how good people are at table tennis: there are world champions, national and regional champions, top class club players, junior league players, occasional players, novices, and so on. A player's ability at this game is presumably due to some qualities specific to the game (world table tennis champions aren't usually also world champions at other sports or even especially good at them) and this ability has been shaped by the thousands of hours of practice that are needed for expertise in any endeavour. However, variation in performance might also be influenced by qualities that are not peculiar to table tennis but are shared by other games; for example performance might be associated with general fitness, hand–eye coordination, speed of reflexes, muscular strength, all qualities that will contribute to success in other sports. Imagine further that you are in a position to study a large sample of people and assess how good they are at a number of sports, and you calculate the correlations between these assessments of their performance. You might find that the correlations are low, so that ability at table tennis does not predict success at any other sport and, in the terminology of correlational analysis, the percentage of variation in table tennis ability that can be explained by variation in scores on any of these other sports is small.

Alternatively the scores across the range of sports might correlate substantially, and one reasonable interpretation of this would be that all sports share some common quality. The champion table tennis player may not be a champion at golf but would play better than average golf and could also turn in a good sprint time. Factor analysis of the correlation matrix of this set of scores would produce one common factor. Some sports might have a closer relationship with this factor than other sports but all would have some relationship with it. We could conclude that variation in the performance of any one sport, like table tennis, was associated with ability on a factor peculiar to that sport *and* with ability on the factor that is common to all sports – but there would be no other influence on performance and no carry over from any other sport over and above that shared factor.

Other models of performance are possible.[1] Perhaps ability at table tennis correlates with ability at tennis but is independent of ability at hockey, which in turn is correlated with lacrosse or soccer. One might find that there is no common factor but several factors related to different groups of sports. There might be one factor that is common to sprinting and long-jumping, one common to netball, lacrosse and hockey, one common to weight lifting, wrestling and rugby, and so on. We would be tempted to assign names to those factors ('speed', 'ball skills', 'muscular strength') in the belief that we had identified abilities that were shared by some sports but less relevant to others. Factor analysis could be applied to produce a score for each sport to show its involvement on any particular factor. A high score (a high *loading*, in the terminology of factor analysis) means that this factor is strongly involved in that sport, a low loading means that the factor makes little contribution to that sport. Ability at table tennis might be predicted by a factor peculiar to that sport and also by several factors to varying degrees; there is not just one common factor but several common factors.

If these measures of performance were taken across a representative range of sports, the researcher might conclude that he or she had discovered something important about sporting performance by showing that this could be divided into two or three factors (or whatever number of factors had been found). The researcher would have to convince us that the selection of tests and of athletes was representative; it might for example be possible to bias the results in favour of some pre-existing theory by means of a careful selection of which tests to include and which to leave out. Furthermore, the claims that the researcher is making are about sport in general and are not restricted to describing the particular sample of athletes that has been assembled. Critics would want to be assured that the size and nature of this sample permit generalisation to all athletes; ideally the study should be repeated and comparable results obtained with a fresh sample. A critic might also point out that the researcher might have made a good job of classifying the sports but was still not in a position to *explain* the structure that had been found: what physiological or psychological aptitudes or training experiences or interests underlie this structure? It is all very well to label a factor 'ball skills' but, in the absence of other kinds

of corroborative evidence, how do we know that this is what in fact under-
lies these correlations in test performance?

Factor analysis has proved a very powerful tool in psychology. It has
been applied for many years to investigate the structure of intelligence and
to underpin different theories of its structure. It has proved fruitful in the
construction of tests of personality. Issues that preoccupy test constructors
such as whether a given test is measuring one trait or a number of different
traits have lent themselves to this technique, and it has also been useful in
selecting items for inclusion in tests, since items that have little in common
with the majority of items can be discarded.

We encounter factor analysis at several junctures in this book where it
has been used to look for order and structure among a large set of variables.
A typical use is demonstrated by the attempt to classify children's emotional and behaviour problems. In a study by Achenbach *et al.* (1991)
parents were presented with a list of descriptions of behaviour and asked
to rate whether each of these was characteristic of their child during the
previous two months. Parents made their judgements about the frequency
of these behaviours on a 4-point scale that ranged from 'never or not at all
true' which was assigned the value 0, and 'very often or very much' which
was assigned the value 3. Typical items were: 'absentminded or forgets
easily', 'bites fingernails', 'can't concentrate', 'deliberately annoys others',
'excitable', 'fears going to school', 'gets angry if routines are disrupted', 'has
a hard time making friends', and so on. Ratings were collected from a large
number of parents.

The question addressed by the researchers is whether there is a discernible pattern in these ratings. Across the sample as a whole, are children
who tend to be absentminded also more likely to bite their fingernails? Is
a child who has difficulty in making friends also more likely to annoy
others? Some of these behaviours will tend to occur with each other
whereas others will not. It should be noted that the researcher is not
asking parents whether *they* think particular behaviours go together and
they are only asked to comment on their child. Any associations between
behaviours will be characteristic of the sample as a whole, not necessarily
the case for individual children.

This is precisely the issue that factor analysis has evolved to deal with.
A correlation can be computed for any pair of items to provide an index
of the co-variation between the items. A matrix can be drawn up compris-
ing the correlations between every pair of items, and a computer program
can find a solution to the number of factors that are to be found in the data.
Achenbach *et al.'s* (1991) monograph identified eight factors, which the
authors labelled on the basis of the content of items with highest loadings
on the factor:

Withdrawn (loading on items to do with looking unhappy and preference
   to be alone)

Anxious/depressed (lonely, cries without good reason)
Somatic complaints (headaches, pains)
Social problems (acts too young for age, doesn't get along with others)
Thought problems (can't get mind off thoughts)
Attention problems (impulsive, can't concentrate)
Delinquent behaviour (cheats, lies, plays truant)
Aggressive behaviour (bullies, is destructive).

These factors are themselves inter-correlated and can in turn be factor-analysed. This produces two second-order factors, the first labelled *Internalising*, defined by factors 'withdrawn', 'somatic complaints' and 'anxious/depressed'; and the second *Externalising*, defined by factors 'aggressive behaviour' and 'delinquent behaviour'.

The two second-order factors to emerge from this study are similar to the distinction that has been made by clinicians between personality problems and behaviour or conduct problems. The study shows that these distinctions underlie parents' judgements of their children's behaviour, and this analysis has provided the framework for the development of tests to identify children's problems. It shows how factor analysis can find structure in a large body of measurements and produce a solution that is psychologically meaningful.

However, many researchers into personality have felt that the potential of factor analysis has not been realised and have become disillusioned, and there is as yet no consensus among personality theorists equivalent to that which apparently obtains in the field of intelligence. Why is this? In order to summarise the basis of factor analysis I have had to simplify my account, and I have allowed the impression that the question of how many factors there are that can account for the correlations in any given matrix is a straightforward one, but unfortunately this turns out not to be the case. Factor analysis is not a single method but is a family of methods, all of which make different assumptions which can lead to different solutions for a given set of data.

Two key issues in particular divide psychologists. How many factors constitute the minimum necessary to reproduce the correlations among variables? On what criteria can the researcher choose between different factor solutions, all of which are compatible with the data? To return to my example of the assessment of sporting abilities, the fundamental question of how many such abilities there are does not have one clearcut answer; and, even if one reaches agreement about this number, the nature of the factors is open to interpretation. We may agree that the data are best described by three factors rather than one, two or four factors. The three factors may be identified as speed, muscular strength and ball skills, with particular sports having specific loadings on these factors; but, on the other hand, a different factor analysis of the same data might interpret the factors as flexibility, stamina and reaction time, with the various sports now having different patterns of loadings. How is the researcher to choose between these two possible explanations of the data? Is there a mathematical solution to this, are there grounds other than mathematics for reaching a decision, or is the decision subjective and a matter of taste? One common solution has to appeal to the principle of parsimony that is argued to be a feature of good scientific practice. The best solution is the simplest one or the one that makes fewest assumptions about the data.

Factor analysis is applied to quantitative data, and such data may be less easily obtained in the field of personality than in the field of intelligence, where the number of correct answers obtained on a test or the time taken to complete a set of items seem appropriate measures of intelligence. It is, of course, possible to obtain quantitative measures in personality, especially with the widespread use of questionnaires and rating scales. Factor analysis requires the data to be in a particular form, and the implications of this are not always made explicit. The analysis is based upon a data matrix which includes scores from all of the participants on all the items. Incomplete matrices create problems; for example, missing data may result in a participant's responses being excluded from the analysis. All items are given equal weight. The relationships which are found hold for the whole set of data.

However, many important relationships in personality do not take this form. A syndrome which is characteristic of a small number of people might involve items which are inter-correlated for that group but which are not correlated in the sample as a whole or in the general population which is being sampled. For example, Kagan *et al.* (1993: 26) draw attention to the following finding about infant temperament:

> Only a small proportion of infants – about 10% – show a combination of high motor activity and frequent crying at four months, high fear in the second year, and large cardiac accelerations to psychological stress. These variables are not positively correlated in a large unselected sample, only in a small group of individuals who inherit a particular temperamental profile.

A further example is Fragile X syndrome, which has been identified as an important genetic cause of learning difficulties, with an estimated incidence of one per 1000 of the population (Hagerman, 1992). Eighty percent of males who are affected show a cluster of physical features – large or prominent ears, a long face and large testicles – which are associated with low IQ. These characteristics are correlated within this small selected sample of the population, but there is no implication that they would be correlated in an unselected sample.

Both examples involve categories. One is either a member of the category, and shares qualities with other members, or one is not a member, in which case one may or may not have these qualities or share them with others. The point is that inter-correlations which are computed across all cases may give a misleading picture of the relationships that exist in the population. Types and categories are common in personality theories. Studies of lay theories of personality also provide evidence of categorical thinking. We have looked at one example in Beynon's ethnographic study. Categories cannot be captured by factor analysis. They can and do emerge in qualitative studies, and in studies using methods like cluster analysis that focus on features of similarity. Factor analysis has its uses but reliance upon it can provide a biased and incomplete picture of personality.

The search for the core factors of personality

We now briefly review some of the most influential approaches to identifying the fundamental personality traits, noting their dependence upon factor analysis and the disagreement among them as to the number and nature of the factors of personality. For many years the study of personality traits was dominated by the theories and research programmes of Raymond Cattell and Hans Eysenck, and by a longstanding dispute between them as to which of their explanations of the structure of personality is the correct one.

Each of these theories arrived at a set of fundamental personality traits or dimensions by the application of factor analytical techniques. Cattell applied this technique to measures of individual differences in performance on laboratory tasks; people's self-reports on questionnaires, and ratings that people make of people whom they know well. Although the same factors did not emerge in all these types of data, Cattell identified 16 factors that can be identified in ratings and self-report questionnaire data (Cattell *et al.*, 1976). A number of self-report questionnaires, including the 16PF, the High School Personality Questionnaire (HSPQ), and the Children's Personality Questionnaire (CPQ) for adults, older children and younger children respectively, have been constructed to measure the source traits and have been widely applied in research and for professional purposes such as job selection.

Eysenck's research has its origins in attempts to devise brief screening measures for service personnel who were presenting psychiatric problems in London during the Second World War. Self-report checklists were devised for reaching decisions about individuals' needs for more intensive psychiatric investigation. Factor analysis of these checklists identified two factors: severity of neurotic condition, and a second factor reflecting type of condition, which Eysenck labelled as a dimension with extraversion and introversion as its poles (he prefers to write about personality *types*, but he treats them as continuous dimensions rather than as discrete categories and we shall refer to them here as dimensions). Various self-report questionnaires have been constructed, including the Eysenck Personality Inventory

(EPI) and a version for children, the Junior Eysenck Personality Inventory (JEPI). These questionnaires measure two orthogonal personality dimensions, extraversion–introversion and neuroticism. Subsequently Eysenck added a third dimension, psychoticism, and the Eysenck Personality Questionnaire has been devised to measure these three dimensions.

Is personality better described by 16 factors or three dimensions? This question has been the subject of controversy for many years. This has largely concerned disagreements about the use of factor analysis. As we discussed above, there is no mathematical answer to the questions of how many factors to extract from a matrix of correlations and which of the possible solutions to adopt. Convention, as reflected in the default values of most computer programs, has been to extract as many factors as have eigenvalues greater than unity and to rotate these factors to simple structure using either an orthogonal rotation method or an oblique, correlated rotation.

Cattell has argued that the eigenvalues criterion extracts too few factors and provides no objective basis for reaching a decision about the number of factors to extract. The methods he recommends produce substantially more factors than reliance on eigenvalues. He argues that too few factors enter the next stage of analysis, that is, the rotation of factors to simple structure, and hence, the interpretation of these factors will be biased, because traits that contribute in a meaningful way to the variation in the data have been omitted. Furthermore, Cattell maintains that researchers who rely solely upon the rotation solutions provided by computer programs fail to ensure that a simpler solution cannot be found for their particular data set, that is, the factor solution can be further rotated to maximise the separation of factors.

Both orthogonal and oblique solutions are available to the researcher, and there are no mathematical grounds for preferring one over the other. One of the arguments for oblique solutions is that many phenomena in the domain of personality are presumably correlated rather than independent. Environmental disadvantages are usually correlated. Although there are different kinds of behaviour disorders they all have in common that they *are* disorders and lead to problems for the individual or the school. One consequence of choosing an oblique solution is that the ensuing factors are themselves correlated and hence scores on these factors can themselves be analysed to produce further, higher-order factors. Factor analysis of Cattell's oblique factors produces eight second-order factors, and the two most studied of these have been exvia and anxiety. These bear considerable resemblance to Eysenck's dimensions.

In recent years there have been claims that the issue of the number of basic factors has been resolved: there are five core traits rather than Cattell's 16 or Eysenck's three. The set of fundamental traits that has been proposed is familiarly known as the 'Big Five' because adherents of this position argue that factor analysis of personality data has converged on five factors: 'openness', 'conscientiousness', 'extraversion', 'agreeableness' and 'neuroticism'. Adjectives that define these factors as outlined by McCrae and John (1992) appear in Table 1.1.

This theory of five basic traits has seemed to some psychologists as a milestone in research and has provided a breakthrough in finding the important factors of personality. What is meant by 'important' factors? One interpretation is that the diversity of human personality can be reduced to five factors and the five are these and not any other set. This finding would be worthwhile in itself and would have strong implications for educational research methods, particularly for the very many studies that search for correlations between measures of behaviour at school and traits like self-esteem, locus of control, impulsiveness, aggressiveness, test anxiety and so on.

This research has always been open to the argument that the obtained correlations may be influenced by further variables that have not been included in the study. Thus it is known that self-esteem is correlated with neuroticism, and perhaps it is neuroticism that predicts low attainment, and self-esteem only appears to do so because it too shares aspects of neuroticism. Of course it can always be argued that any researcher has omitted important factors, but one implication of the Big Five is that if the researcher can show that his or her measures are predictive after their relationship with these factors has been taken into account then he or she can be confident that their findings are not due to important unmeasured variables.

Table 1.1 The 'Big Five' traits, descriptive attitudes and correlations with grade point average

Trait	Descriptive adjectives	Correlation with GPA
Openness	Artistic, curious, imaginative, insightful, original, wide interests	0.10
Conscientiousness	Efficient, organised, planful, reliable, responsible, thorough	0.34*
Extraversion	Active, assertive, energetic, enthusiastic, outgoing, talkative	−0.10
Agreeableness	Appreciative, forgiving, generous, kind, sympathetic, trusting	−0.14
Neuroticism	Anxious, self-pitying, tense, touchy, unstable, worrying	−0.02

Note: * $p < 0.01$
Sources: of descriptive adjectives – McCrae and John (1992: 178–9); of correlations with GPA – Wolfe and Johnson (1995).

However, if the goal is to predict how someone will behave in a specific situation, to predict their educational attainments or how well they adjust to school, then these five traits may not be the best at this, since they have resulted from a data reduction process that produces some distance from actual situations.

Personality and educational attainment

The empirical question as to which theory makes the best predictions in the educational sphere is not straightforward to answer. Personality traits taken in combination do add significantly to our ability to predict scores on tests of educational achievement and confirm that personality factors are at least as important as intelligence for influencing attainment. For example, in a study of school children that predicted achievement test scores from the HSPQ, intelligence correlated 0.50 with achievement. Adding the personality factors to the equation raised the multiple correlation to 0.79, and the percentage of variation in test scores explained from 25 percent to 62 percent (Cattell *et al.*, 1966). On the other hand, the predictive value of individual traits is very limited, and the correlations between scores on Cattell's traits and attainment are typically very low. The correlations between the Big Five and attainment are also very small (with the exception of conscientiousness; see Table 1.1).

However, the relevance of personality factors to attainment should not be dismissed solely on the basis of small correlation coefficients. Small coefficients might obscure trends that are important. Furthermore, the pattern of correlations might be informative about the influence of personality in education. We support these points with evidence from two very large-scale studies that correlated JEPI scores with attainment. These were carried out in the 1960s in Aberdeen, with 13-year-old children, and in Staffordshire, with 11-year-old children (see Eysenck, 1978, or Entwistle, 1988, for details).

The findings from these studies suggest that at primary school extraverts have somewhat higher attainments but this superiority has disappeared and is reversed by the time they are at secondary school. The Aberdeen study showed a very clear and consistent relationship with low scores on neuroticism (N); the Staffordshire study also found a relationship between neuroticism and achievement, although there was a suggestion that high and low levels of N were associated with higher attainment and intermediate scores on N associated with lower attainment. The correlation coefficients can be significantly greater than zero, in terms of statistical tests, but are small in value. However, Entwistle (1988: 190–1) cautions against using low values of correlation coefficients as an argument to dismiss findings as educationally irrelevant. He has reanalysed the results of girls in both studies by dividing the sample into nine groups, three levels of extraversion cross-tabulated with three levels of neuroticism, and then looked at the average attainment of each group.

Seen in this light, the differences are striking. High N girls can be as much as eight months behind low N girls in attainment. Pass rates in the eleven-plus examination are also influenced by scores on both personality dimensions. In the Staffordshire sample, girls with high scores on N were less likely to pass than girls low in N, but this relationship was strongly influenced by extraversion. Only 9 percent of girls who were both introverted and high in N passed the examination, compared with 23 percent of their peers who were extraverted as well as high in N. There were no equivalent differences among girls low in N, where 25 percent of extraverts and 22 percent of introverts were successful. The data are not presented for boys, and we might expect a different pattern given the finding that there are gender differences in the relationship between extraversion and attainment, and given also that the criterion for a pass might be set at a different level for boys and girls. Some of the most telling arguments against the eleven-plus were made by sociologists drawing upon research which found that the pass rates were very much lower among working-class pupils than among middle-class pupils. Mauger (1972) reported that 54 percent of upper middle-class children and 11 percent of lower manual working-class children attended grammar school, a ratio of about 5:1. This can be compared with a personality difference ratio that can reach nearly 3:1, showing that personality was a significant, if rarely recognised, source of inequality.

In secondary school and at university introverts and students low in neuroticism have superior attainments, whether these are defined in terms of GCSE grades, degree class, or rates of failure and withdrawal from courses (Eysenck, 1978; Entwistle, 1988; Corulla and Coghill, 1991). For example, neurotic extraverts have the smallest share of first-class honours degrees. EPI norms report that, on average, students are higher in neuroticism than young people who are not in higher education, and one implication of this, taken in conjunction with the findings of variation within the university population, is that there might be a non-linear relationship between neuroticism and achievement, with those of higher levels of N and possibly those of lower levels of N achieving more than students with intermediate levels. There are theoretical reasons why this might be the case, an issue to which we return.

There is also evidence of an association between personality and the kinds of courses that students prefer to follow. Students on university arts courses are somewhat high in introversion and in neuroticism, and arts students tend to have higher N scores than science students (Corulla and Coghill, 1991). Eysenck (1978) argues that extraverts and students high in N are attracted to 'people-oriented courses', extraverts and those low in N to more practical courses, and introverted students to 'theoretical' courses.

Students of fine art – painting and sculpture – tend to score higher than other students on introversion and neuroticism; for example, Götz and Götz (1973) found that art students rated by their teachers as more gifted scored significantly higher on introversion and neuroticism on the EPI than less gifted art students, whose scores were close to the overall student norms.

Do these findings have any practical educational implications? Eysenck has argued for what he calls 'personality-teaching method interaction'. This seems to be equivalent to aptitude–instruction interaction, a concept devised by researchers into the relationships between cognitive factors and learning. They have attempted to show that particular methods of instruction are more appropriate for some aptitudes than for others and have argued that a range of methods should be available to enable individual students to find the one best suited to them.

Eysenck extends this idea to personality trait factors. He rejects the idea that students should be 'streamed' on the basis of their personality, but proposes that schools should offer a wide range of teaching strategies and should look carefully at individual students' progress with different teaching programmes. What kinds of variation in strategies are relevant?

The relative superiority of extraverted children in primary school might offer a clue to the identification of relevant teaching strategies, although there are too many factors here to be easily disentangled. These research studies continued the nomothetic tradition of treating personality in isolation from its school context so we have no indication what methods were used or whether teaching in primary school was similar then to now. Primary classes have invariably been different from secondary classes, even when they have included examination work, in that they involve more frequent teacher–pupil and pupil–pupil interactions, a closer relationship between teacher and child, more practical activities, and more group work.

Learning at the secondary level, on the other hand, involves more distant relationships between pupils and teachers, interaction with many specialist teachers rather than one class teacher, less group work and practical activities, more reading, and more solitary homework and preparation. Are these relevant factors in the extravert's better performance at the primary stage, or does schoolwork simply become more complex and demand the kind of concentration and docility that typifies the introvert, and places the more restless and impulsive extravert at a disadvantage? Or is an age change in extraversion, where the population mean for extraversion declines as children grow older, sufficient in itself to explain these trends?

Eysenck summarises several studies which claim to show that students respond differently to different teaching styles. For example, Leith (1974; cited by Eysenck, 1978) tested 200 college students after they had been taught a course in genetics under different conditions. Extraverts performed much better when they had been taught by 'discovery methods', characterised by discovery, tolerance for uncertainty and tolerance of errors whereas introverts made better progress with a direct teaching (reception learning) method.

Bennett (1976) found that some personalities were more susceptible than others to the influence of variation in teaching style: unmotivated stable extraverts did much better in formal and much worse in informal classes, whereas timid pupils were relatively impervious to classroom style. Bennett (1976: 147) provides a detailed summary of the interaction between teaching style and neuroticism:

> The level of neuroticism . . . has a markedly discrepant effect depending upon which type of teacher the pupil finds himself with. In informal classrooms pupils with a high neuroticism score spent half as much time on work activity as those with a lower neuroticism score. They spent more time chatting to other pupils and behaved in a negative manner more frequently . . . These differences do not appear in formal classes.

McCord and Wakefield (1981) reported an interaction between extraversion–introversion and teachers' use of reward and punishment among fourth and fifth grade American children. Extraverts tended to perform better in mathematics when teachers used rewards more whereas introverts tended to do better when teachers used punishment more.

Extraverts seek out activity and change; they look for excitement and an opportunity to interact with other people. Schools tend to discourage these kinds of behaviour within the classroom, but there is suggestive evidence that extraverts do achieve more if the opportunity is provided to learn in this kind of way, by doing rather than reading about doing, by experimenting rather than following routine procedures. The evidence for this isn't overwhelming, but perhaps it doesn't have to be. Any reliable evidence that learners with particular personalities routinely under-achieve and can improve when taught in particular ways should lead to reflection about reliance on specific teaching strategies even if the differences in achievement and the improvements are relatively small. One problem is that we don't have many studies of individual differences in students' responses to classroom teaching strategies of different kinds. The trends in research into classroom management and achievement emphasise a well-structured, carefully planned, direct-instruction approach, and although there are many studies of the effectiveness of this, there is less interest in whether this suits some students better than others. For example, Kaplan (1990, chapter 11) provides an overview of empirical studies of effective teaching. Variation in the teaching approach is recommended as an important element in the teaching strategy. However, the effectiveness of methods is assessed in terms of the attainments of the class as a whole, with no attention to the possibility that some students might do better under some conditions than under others. Personality psychologists are inevitably suspicious of approaches that neglect individual differences, but more research evidence is needed on the joint influence of teaching style and personality on individual achievement.

EXPLAINING INDIVIDUAL DIFFERENCES: EXTRAVERSION

Extraversion has emerged as an important concept in all three theories of personality but Eysenck is unique in the attention he has paid to formulating and testing an explanation of individual differences on this dimension. Learning plays a pivotal role in this theory and, since attempts to test the theory have involved studies of performance on academic tasks, they deserve our attention here. At the risk of oversimplification of a complex set of propositions, Eysenck's account of individual variation along the extraversion–introversion dimension can be summarised as follows. The ascending reticular activating system (ARAS) is part of the mid-brain that functions to activate the cells of the cortex. It conveys specific sensory information to the cortex and also sends non-specific impulses that raise the general activation level of the cortex. Thus the ARAS controls levels of alertness, wakefulness or arousal in the cortex. Suppression of its activity by anaesthetics has the effect of reducing wakefulness. Drugs like caffeine, which increases alertness, and alcohol, which reduces it, have their effects on the ARAS. Eysenck has proposed that there is individual variation in baseline levels of arousal in the ARAS, and that in particular the introvert is characterised by relatively high baseline levels and the extravert by relatively low levels.

It is a short step to imagine this difference being translated into motivational terms and think of the extravert as perpetually trying to raise his or her baseline measures by seeking additional sources of arousal. Research also suggests that extraverts perform less well on tasks that require sustained concentration, such as vigilance tasks, where the person has to be alert to the possibility of receiving information, as in car driving, say, or operating machines. Drugs like caffeine that raise levels of arousal in the ARAS should alter behaviour in an introverted direction and those, like alcohol, that lower levels should make people behave in a more extraverted fashion. Drinking coffee as I write this in the evening, at the same time hearing the laughter and shouting from the pub along the road, suggests that this is not a finding confined to the laboratory. A large body of research has tested predictions from this theory and offers broad support although many issues of detail remain to be examined. One important aspect of this research is that it moves beyond reliance upon self-report questionnaires to look at differences in how people actually behave.

Extraversion is clearly to do with craving excitement, but an account in these terms does not make a convincing explanation of all aspects of sociability and uninhibited behaviour. Eysenck proposes that socialisation involves learning, particularly learning restrictions on the expression of impulses, and the high levels of arousal in the introvert facilitate learning. Thus the introvert is relatively over-socialised and the extravert under-socialised. Predictions about learning were framed by Eysenck in terms of conditioning, which was the dominant approach to understanding learning processes at the time when the theory was constructed. The role of conditioning in the theory remains controversial, but we will not explore this issue further here, and we direct our attention to more recent research that investigates the impact of extraversion upon learning conceptualised in terms of information processing.

Are introverts superior on memorising tasks? The answer is that it depends on the nature of the task. Extraverts are poorer at long-term memory tasks but perform better on short-term memory tasks. For example, if the task is to commit a list of words to memory, extraverts perform better than introverts if the test of recall is given immediately after learning but perform less well if the test takes place after 30 minutes (Howarth and Eysenck, 1968). Humphreys and Revelle (1984) distinguish between short-term memory tasks and information transfer tasks. An example of the former is 'digit recall', where the subject has to repeat back to the experimenter a list of digits that he or she has just heard. Transfer tasks include speed of reaction to a signal, vigilance, and letter cancellation. Here the subject is given a page containing letters of the alphabet in random order, and has to read through the page, crossing out every instance of a particular letter. These are labelled *transfer* tasks under the assumption that they involve the ability to transfer information between components of the information processing system, between attention, short-term memory and long-term memory components. The prediction is that arousal facilitates transfer but impedes short-term memory and thus introverts who have a higher baseline level of arousal should be superior on the transfer tasks but inferior on short-term memory tasks. Further support comes from experiments that show that extraverts show greater incidental learning, when they are instructed to attend to one dimension but are given an unexpected test on another. Also, if they have to retrieve information from long-term memory, for example by being asked to produce as many words as they can beginning with a particular letter, extraverts produce more words within the time limit. Alternative explanations of these findings are possible. Perhaps introverts are more cautious in responding, or they focus on the more accessible words and find it hard to generate other words (Eysenck, 1977, has proposed that the high arousal characteristic of introverts can lead to a narrowing of attention).

Notwithstanding this pattern of results, findings on personality differences in information processing can present a complex picture. Attempts to understand this tend to be framed in terms of the concept of arousal and its influence upon task performance. So far we have considered arousal as a base level of the nervous system, but it is important to recognise that variation in levels of arousal is not only a characteristic of individuals but is affected by a range of environmental events. As we have seen, drugs act directly on arousal levels of the ARAS. Levels of arousal also vary throughout the day, on a diurnal rhythm, with average levels of arousal increasing from the morning until they reach a peak and then decline. There are indications from measures of body temperature that this pattern is not the same for different personalities: introverts reach their peak arousal level some hours before extraverts, in early afternoon as opposed to early evening. Task characteristics also affect arousal. Simple or highly familiar tasks produce lower levels of arousal than difficult or novel tasks; pressure to complete a task, or instructions that emphasise the need to perform well or that draw attention to the serious consequences of failure, also increase arousal.

How does level of arousal affect learning? One widely accepted view is that moderate levels of arousal are associated with optimal task performance, whereas low levels of arousal or high levels are associated with poor performance – in common sense terms, either lack of interest or high agitation produces less effective learning. This view has attained the status of a law in psychology, named after a study of discrimination learning in mice reported by Yerkes and Dodson in 1908 (see Teigen, 1994). In this experiment the difficulty of the task was manipulated, as was the severity of punishment for failing to make the discrimination. Learning was best at an intermediate level of punishment, but the optimal level of punishment was a function of the difficulty of the discrimination. Teigen has traced the subsequent history of this account of relationships among task difficulty, emotion and performance. The account became associated with the proposal that the relationship between arousal and performance could be described by an inverted-U function, and this has now become established as one of the fundamental 'laws' of personality and learning. We encounter it at several places in this volume.

Making predictions about the achievements of introverts and extraverts is clearly going to be complex, as their performance will depend on the time of day of testing and on the level of difficulty of the task. Revelle et al. (1980) tested the hypothesis that increasing the level of arousal of students by giving them caffeine would hinder introverts, who already have higher levels of arousal, but would help extraverts, by raising their low levels of arousal. That is, among introverts, the increased arousal induced by caffeine would shift their arousal level *away* from the optimal level for a particular task, but this increase would shift extraverts *towards* the optimal level. However, this prediction will apply only to tasks of a certain level of difficulty and at certain times of day. An intake of caffeine would improve the learning of both introverts and extraverts on a very easy task and would hinder the learning of both personality types on a very difficult task, although the rate of change would not be the same for both because of their different baseline levels of arousal. Introverts would show relatively greater improvement on the very easy task and a relatively larger decline on the very difficult task. Finally, all these relationships would depend on what time of day the tasks were carried out.

Revelle *et al.* tested these predictions, assessing students' personality and testing them under two conditions: a caffeine condition where subjects ingested 200 mg of caffeine mixed in a drink of Tang (a typical cup of coffee contains 75 mg; Tang is a bitter-tasting soft beverage which serves to disguise the caffeine), and a placebo condition where the subjects simply drank the Tang. The task was a difficult academic test, the American Graduate Record Examination, and this was completed at either 10.00 or 19.00. The average test results of the placebo group at different times of day show that, as predicted, introverts scored higher than extraverts in the morning, whereas extraverts scored slightly higher in the evening, although this finding was only true for the impulsiveness and not for the sociability component of extraversion–introversion. Adding the caffeine improved the performance of high impulsives and slightly decreased the performance of low impulsives, but only when tested in the morning. In the evening, low impulsives (introverts) improved slightly and impulsives decreased slightly. This pattern of results could be explained by assuming that introverts are close to their optimal level of arousal in the morning (and the caffeine pushes them over the optimal) whereas the extraverts are at a lower than optimal level in the morning and the caffeine provides a boost to their performance. The opposite is true in the evening when extraverts are at their peak and the introverts under-aroused. The results are complex, and open to different interpretations (Eysenck and Folkard, 1980). Matthews (1989) has reported a similar interaction between extraversion–introversion, time of day, and arousal on a vigilance task.

To summarise, performance on tasks ranging from laboratory tests of attention and memory to intelligence tests and university entrance examinations is influenced by students' personality. Introverts are not invariably better at these tasks and are out-performed by extraverts at some tasks or under certain conditions. This may help to explain why the correlations between personality and attainments in school and university are only moderate at best, as these learning experiences involve many different abilities and can be approached using different strategies. Eysenck (1978: 169) has argued that 'Both [extraverts and introverts] have strengths and weaknesses which could, with skilful guidance, be used or obviated. The known factors will suggest to the ingenious teacher many ways in which this knowledge can be used.' We are still, perhaps, a long way from applying in the classroom the experimental findings on personality, but further study is surely a promising direction to take in pursuit of the goal of understanding individual differences in academic achievement. Psychological arousal is a general term that refers to the effects of a range of phenomena, and we see in later chapters that students do differ in motivation and in their response to the stresses that school activities and examinations can produce.

The influence of time of day is one that has been little explored in education, particularly in the context of examinations. Research has established that time of day does affect performance. Questionnaire studies (e.g. Horne and Ostberg, 1976) have established that people can be categorised according to their tendencies to be more alert and active in the morning or the evening. May *et al.* (1993) report the following percentages of different types in a sample of students: 'definitely evening' – 7 percent; 'moderately evening' – 37 percent; 'neutral' – 50 percent; 'moderately morning' – 6 percent; 'definitely morning' – 0 percent. A very different distribution was found among a sample of older people, aged 66 to 78 years; there were no evening types and 74 percent were in the two morning categories. Whatever their age, the groups tended to perform best at their preferred time.

In addition to age differences, there is substantial evidence, as we have suggested, that time of day is also related to personality. Any effects of these trends on classroom activities are presumably cancelled by the fact that the school day spreads across both morning and afternoon, but it would be interesting to see whether time of day affected examination performance and also revision practices. Since examinations are both cognitively demanding and anxiety-creating, levels of arousal inherent in the task are high, and this should interact with the arousal associated with time of day and extraversion–introversion to influence student performance.

CRITICAL PERSPECTIVES

The language of traits and types is pervasive in explaining why people behave as they do. We have seen, for example, that children categorise each other after a brief acquaintance. Classification is also central to the endeavours of personality theorists and although there remains disagreement as to which system of classification is best, the traits of extraversion and neuroticism/anxiety are regularly found in research. The status of these traits as explanatory concepts remains unresolved. There is a clear risk of circular reasoning – the trait is inferred from behaviour and is then used to explain that behaviour. Eysenck has avoided this risk by proposing a reductionist explanation in terms of psychobiological processes, and his theory has given rise to a substantial body of research. This research has added to understanding of the processes of learning and has identified a regular pattern of individual differences in learning, but this has yet to lead to any educational applications.

Other arguments for traits are based upon construct validity. The researcher makes inferences from behaviour and the value of those inferences is tested by their capacity to bring order to phenomena and to make predictions. Contemporary research focuses on the Big Five model but although this has brought order to the field of personality it remains remote from educational concerns. This is a recurrent problem in personality research. When we considered the trait vocabulary of the school it seemed natural to ask what functions this language served. The pupils were 'scientists' in the sense that they were seeking to make their experience intelligible. But they also used that language to manage their social relationships. The arcane terminology of, say, Cattell's theory, its appeal to the minutiae of mathematical models and its nomothetic approach to predicting attainment serve to confine much research to the scholarly journals.

However, we do not believe that this is an inevitable consequence of a scientific approach. In the second part of this volume we consider traits like self-esteem, anxiety and aggression that are more closely related to the experience of school. In part, this is because the questions that are investigated arise in the school, whereas much of the research summarised here seeks to apply concepts that have been developed elsewhere.

The research we have discussed has been concerned with questions of classification: how many approaches to learning or personality traits can be identified. The emphasis has been on assessing variation and little attention has been paid to uniqueness. For example, research is concerned with making generalisations about the population of students as a whole and is not interested in the characteristics of any of the particular individuals who participated in the studies. Findings from studies carried out in Sweden are compared with findings from Britain or the USA without seeing any need to take into account particulars of the respective educational systems.

The measures that are taken of personality are assumed to be reliable. Someone who is field-independent today is expected to show those characteristics tomorrow, otherwise it is difficult to attach much significance to the research findings. It is worthwhile reflecting upon the assumptions underlying this approach. First, some aspect of a person's psychological functioning can be isolated and quantified, and in particular it can be assigned a number that can be used to compare one individual with another. Second, these measures are relative, not absolute. An individual's score on the measure only has meaning in the context of the scores that are obtained by other people. Third, a stable characteristic of the person is identified; the whole point of test scores is that predictions can be made about the individual's future performance, their ability to cope with tasks they have yet to face.

Finally, this research assigns a causal role to the factors that it isolates. At one level, the research could be viewed as entirely descriptive. Students who are afraid that they will fail their course are likely to adopt a surface approach to learning. Students who obtain high scores on the embedded figures test are more likely to prefer to work on their own than those who obtain low scores. However, it is clear that psychologists would not be satisfied with description and see their goals as understanding and explaining individual differences. Field-independence and extraversion are intended to be explanatory concepts.

We examine these issues in turn. In the remainder of this chapter we consider whether it is appropriate to study personality by isolating aspects of psychological functioning from their context and then ask whether stability of personality is found in practice.

Nomothetic and idiographic approaches

Psychologists draw a distinction between two broad approaches to the study of personality – the idiographic and the nomothetic. Stated briefly, the idiographic approach involves the intensive study of individuals, whereas the nomothetic approach is a search for general laws by combining data from many individuals. Simonton (1990: 3–4) amplifies the distinction:

> the crucial characteristic of truly nomothetic statements is that any restrictions on their applicability ... do not entail specific tags that identify persons ... At the other extreme, we possess idiographic propositions that make no sense without specific names, dates, and places attached ... the explanation is bound intimately to a special person, place, and time, even if some general law is evoked to explain the unique event.

The studies we have reviewed have taken a nomothetic approach. They offer generalisations about approaches to learning, motivation or cognitive styles among the population of students on the basis of a sample of observations. The goal of this kind of investigation is theory building. When the investigator obtains support for predictions derived from the theory then understanding will be achieved. It should be noted that there are no *persons* in this research. The investigator abstracts some aspect of personality in order to turn it into a datum, and takes no further interest in that person except as a source for any other aspects that may be abstracted for measurement. The person remains anonymous and is one of many subjects in the research. The investigator also sets aside his or her own individuality to become a detached, objective collector of data.

Supporters of the nomothetic approach have argued that this represents the classic scientific method but in recent years there have been claims that this argument is based on an inadequate conception of the scientific method and that the idiographic approach is more compatible with criteria of scientific research. For example, Bromley (1986: ix) argues that 'the individual case study . . . is the bedrock of the scientific method'. One way of accommodating these positions is to suggest that the two approaches emphasise different aspects of the phenomena of personality. The idiographic approach is concerned with individuality whereas the nomothetic approach lends itself to the study of individual variation and consistency.

It can also be argued that the difference between the approaches has been exaggerated. The nomothetic approach concentrates on universals, the idiographic on particulars. But how universal is the nomothetic and how particular is the idiographic? Are there principles of mother–infant social interaction or 'mothering' behaviours that transcend particular cultural practices? Researchers carrying out longitudinal studies of child development are conscious of the difficulties of comparing one cohort with another because of the confounding effects of the continuing changes in society. Children of different generations are born into somewhat different worlds. For example, consider the changes that have occurred within one generation in attitudes towards illegitimacy or schoolgirl mothers and the implications that these changed attitudes might have for child rearing practices.

The idiographic approach studies particulars, but how particular? A school invites an educational psychologist to give advice about an individual pupil, because the school wishes to draw upon the psychologist's expertise. This expertise comprises both knowledge of general principles and the individual psychologist's particular experience. The psychologist will look for signs, say, of personality problems, aware that a particular configuration of behaviours will be presented by this individual pupil that would not be presented by another, but will try to understand and help that individual by drawing upon a body of research which has been established by idiographic and nomothetic methods. There are, to be sure, universals, but not a rigid template into which everyone fits.

Critiques of positivism

This notion that any accommodation can be reached between the two approaches is not accepted by all psychologists. There has been a long tradition of 'humanistic' psychology that disputes the application of positivist and nomothetic methods on both scientific and moral grounds. It asserts that these methods are inadequate for investigating psychological questions, and that they are demeaning, treating people as objects that can be manipulated, and regarding them as lacking responsibility for their actions. There is opposition to the *positivist* approach of science, that regards human behaviour as machine-like, externally caused and obedient to natural laws beyond the actor's control. Finally, there is objection to the strategy of *atomism*, analysing phenomena into parts and treating these parts as if they exist independently of the whole. These aspects of the scientific method have been successful in understanding the natural world, but they won't do for the human world. People, it is argued, are *agents*. They do not act blindly or in reaction to external events but they initiate actions and take responsibility for them. The predictability of their behaviour should be understood in terms of the conscious following of rules or their adherence to standards of conduct, and not in terms of their behaviour being determined by external factors. Researchers, too, are immersed in the world and not detached from their subject matter.

A second critical perspective concerns the role of culture in shaping understanding of personality. This characterises the social constructionist movement, as explained, for example, by Gergen (1985). He sets out a number of assumptions made by this approach. The first is scepticism about the ability of science to reflect reality in any direct way, in conjunction with an awareness that understanding of reality is constrained by linguistic conventions. This represents, of course, a direct challenge to the realist conception of personality, to theorists who regard it as something 'out there' to be measured. A second assumption is that the concepts we have for understanding the world should be seen in their historical context. The concepts of the self, or of childhood, or of emotion, have been very different in the past and vary across cultures. This is in contrast to the dominant view in psychology, which sees itself as an ahistorical discipline, establishing principles that are not constrained by time or place. A third assumption is that explanations of psychological phenomena themselves contribute to social life. For example, Bowlby's theory of maternal deprivation (see Chapter 2) is recruited to support one view of the role of women in society (see also Singer, 1992). If the theory gains wide acceptance, it helps shape the terms in which women view their own lives and the way in which they contribute to raising children; that is, the theory contributes to the state of affairs that it is intended to explain.

The position that is challenged by the social constructionist approach is 'essentialism'. Rather than ask what a 'difficult temperament' is, or what bullying is, this approach asks how are these described, and for what ends. What are the taken-for-granted assumptions in our knowledge of these phenomena? How can these be related to social practices? This approach appeals readily to minority groups within society, for example feminist or black theorising. Many women and blacks believe not only that they are subject to discrimination or victimisation but also that the language which is available to them to analyse their experiences is not their own but reflects the dominant ideology.

These perspectives demand a fresh conceptualisation of personality. This requires that new methods are adopted. Social constructionists draw upon documentary evidence to uncover the history of psychological concepts, for example, the self. Their writings are also replete with references to anthropological studies, and the investigation of common sense accounts of psychological phenomena in different cultures, which can throw the accounts in Western culture into sharp relief. Indeed, the anthropological approach seems to be the model for the social constructionist approach, since it wishes to make the familiar strange, to approach one's own understanding of psychological concepts as if one were a stranger to it. The social constructionist wishes to distance him- or herself from the subject. This can be contrasted with the humanist critique of the dominant psychological perspective. The humanist wishes to get closer to his or her subject, to have empathy with the subject and to see the world through that person's eyes.

There has been a recent surge of interest in qualitative methods. In many cases – the use of interviews, the elicitation of personal constructs, or the content analysis of texts or conversations – these methods are not new and are not incompatible with nomothetic or positivist approaches. Other methods are less compatible. Ethnographic approaches, where the investigator draws upon a range of methods to understand people's experience, challenge the idea of the detached observer: 'the research itself is embedded in the very social world it is seeking to study. Ethnographic researchers thus recognize that they are part of the social world they are studying, and that they cannot avoid having an effect on the social phenomena being studied' (Banister *et al.*, 1994: 36). Discourse analysis focuses on language, spoken and written, but it differs radically from content analysis, not least in the freedom of interpretation it allows the researcher. Consider the following quotations by proponents of discourse analysis:

> The reading I have presented is my own opinion, and I have made no attempt to validate it against other forms of analysis, or even to discover whether the procedure I used is reliable when applied to other texts.
>
> (Banister *et al.*, 1994: 105)

> We argue that the researcher should bracket off the whole issue of the *quality* of accounts as *accurate* or *inaccurate descriptions* of mental states. The problem is being construed at entirely the wrong level. Our focus is entirely on discourse itself: how it is constructed, its functions, and the consequences which arise from different discursive organization.
>
> (Potter and Wetherell, 1987: 178; emphasis in original)

Psychologists working within the dominant paradigm would reject the view that the accuracy of descriptions of mental states is the wrong problem to address, or that understanding behaviour is a matter of understanding discourse. They are wedded to a realist position. Genetic and environmental factors help to shape personality. Factors like the inheritance of Fragile X gene, poverty or inadequate, non-supportive partners are real and not merely the consequences of ways in which discourse is organised. Researchers recognise that these factors do not have a determinist causal relationship with mental states or behaviour. We see throughout this volume that personality researchers have introduced concepts like 'developmental pathways' or 'reciprocal interaction' to accommodate agency. There has been a revival of interest in the self, and theories have a stronger phenomenological emphasis.

Psychological findings and explanations are influenced by the social context in which they are produced and they in turn have an influence upon society.They provide a topic of discourse and this is an important subject for investigation in its own right. Indeed, there is no shortage of discourse in education, and many voices are heard, but much of the discourse is produced by those who are convinced that they have the right answer to questions about individual differences. What psychologists offer are theories that are subject to modification in the light of evidence. They do not claim to provide right answers or infallible evidence, but they take a critical perspective on their research. This is, I think, the problem with an assertion that interpretations require no validation. There is an implicit notion that any 'reading' of a situation is as valid as any other reading, and while this fits with a post-modernist view of research, it is a renunciation of the researchers' responsibilities to those who seek their help.

The consistency of personality

We are most hurt when we are criticised by those closest to us, and the field of personality was devastated by the arguments offered by one of its most distinguished contributors, Walter Mischel, in his book, *Personality and Assessment*, published in 1968. Mischel offered a wide-ranging critique of research into personality but the most telling point was his assertion that there was little empirical evidence that personality traits actually predicted how people behaved. Moss and Shipman (1980: 530) point to the central role of predictability in personality theories:

> Many life decisions and interpersonal actions are predicated on the deep-rooted and universally held conviction that one can anticipate the probable responses and actions of different individuals. Indeed, the very concept of personality implies a differentiated and organised hierarchy of psychological sets and behavioral dispositions that are manifested as consistent patterns in denoting the uniqueness of the individual.

Mischel argued that research had failed to detect any sizeable correlations between measures of personality and measures of actual behaviour. He suggested that correlations were never higher than 0.30, a statistic that he scathingly called the 'personality coefficient', and which implies that differences between individuals in observed behaviour owe very little to differences in their personality. Inconsistency is not, however, true of all approaches to measuring personality. Scores on trait questionnaires often have high correlations with scores on other questionnaires, as we see throughout this volume. Questionnaires are designed to be reliable, that is, an individual should obtain comparable scores on different occasions and, in practice, well-established questionnaires do meet this criterion of consistency. There is also considerable evidence that scores obtained on personality measures can remain unchanged over long periods of time, that is, they show high temporal stability. Moss and Shipman's review of 20 longitudinal studies concluded that there was evidence of considerable stability in personality over many years. Conley (1984) reported findings from assessments of personality obtained 45 years apart. Three hundred married couples had participated in a study of marital compatibility between 1935 and 1938. Between 1979 and 1981, 388 of the original participants could be traced and retested. There were impressive signs of stability. The correlations across time for men were 0.45 for neuroticism and 0.40 for extraversion; among women, the correlations were 0.42 and 0.41 respectively.

It is remarkable that correlations of this magnitude can be obtained, given that there are problems in finding equivalent forms of the personality tests or, indeed, tests where there have not been changes in the meaning of the vocabulary of items (on one well-known extraversion questionnaire items referred to *gay parties*, a term whose connotations have changed somewhat over 45 years). Also, no one doubts that broad cultural factors have an impact upon personality, and there have been marked changes in, for example, the roles and attitudes of women that might be expected to result in pressures towards changes in personality over time. The Fels Research Institute longitudinal study (Moss and Shipman, 1980) found that there was greater temporal stability among the women of their sample than among men in independence, a trend the researchers attributed to differences in cultural expectations, with greater social pressures towards independence among men. It is debatable whether this gender difference is as salient today as it was in 1962, when the study was published. There are thus many factors that would be expected to reduce temporal stability in personality.

The inconsistency alleged by Mischel takes different forms: low correlations between questionnaires and behaviour, variability in the observed behaviour of individuals across different situations, and disagreement between different informants in the ratings they make of individuals. We consider some examples of this third form of inconsistency. Verhulst and Akkerhuis (1989) administered the Child Behaviour Checklist to the parents and teachers of 1161 children aged 4 to 12 years in the Netherlands. Each child was rated by a parent (the mother, in nearly all cases) and by a teacher on a list of behaviour items, and the correlations between the ratings were computed for the sample of children, for each item and for the questionnaire as a whole. Individual item correlations ranged from zero (for item referring to the child's worrying) to 0.58 (being overweight). The highest correlations were for readily observable characteristics such as being overweight, having speech problems or being clumsy. Only 11 out of 400 correlations were greater than 0.40. The average correlations ranged from 0.24 in the ratings of 4- to 5-year-old children, to 0.35 in the ratings of children aged 6 to 12 years.

Achenbach *et al.* (1987) reviewed research of this kind, summarising the findings from 269 studies of children from 119 different countries. The average correlation between the ratings provided by parents and teachers was 0.27 and between parents and mental health workers was 0.24. Children's self-ratings correlated 0.25 with parental ratings, 0.20 with teacher ratings, 0.27 with mental health worker ratings, and 0.26 with ratings made by other children. Mischel's personality coefficient recurs in these studies. Achenbach *et al.* concluded (p. 227):

> The limited correlations between different types of informants pose a challenge for clinical measurement intended to categorise disorders according to fixed rules . . . For most childhood disorders, the rules specify descriptive features that must be judged as present versus absent. Yet our findings indicate that judgments of descriptive features of this sort vary with the informant and situation.

Such findings present no problem to those who argue that behaviour varies from situation to situation, that the child behaves in one way at home, in a different way at school, and perhaps in yet another way with peers. They do present a problem for the advocate of the position that behaviour problems reflect psychological traits which are manifest across different situations, perhaps signs of an underlying conflict or of a disturbed personality. They are also problematic for the psychologist who assumes that ratings are measuring instruments and expects that they should provide reliable measures of an underlying trait. This second position is evident in any discussion of maladjustment or behaviour problems that is not qualified by reference to the specific situations in which the problematic behaviours are observed. Mischel's thesis provided a challenge to that position, a challenge that elicited a number of defences.

One defence was that Mischel was attacking a soft target, challenging a simplistic position that was never adopted by personality theorists. They had always recognised that behaviour in any situation was caused by a host of factors and had never claimed that it could be predicted by personality traits by themselves. Another defence was that the measures of behaviour reported by Mischel were inadequate, particularly the reliance of many studies he cited on measures of behaviour taken on a single occasion. A trait is a behavioural predisposition, that would be likely to be manifest across a range of situations but not necessarily evident on any particular occasion. The child who steals isn't stealing all day long.

Coherence might be a better term than consistency for expressing the link between traits and behaviour, as traits might be more accurately characterised in terms of the equivalence of behaviours rather than their repetition. Thus, aggression might take the form of fighting in the playground and of surliness in the classroom: both behaviours reflect an underlying trait but, superficially, are not similar to each other. A diagnosis of 'conduct disorder' might indeed reflect a general disturbance in the child's behaviour although it is expressed as bullying in school, disobedience at home, and stealing away from home and school. Situations do exert powerful pressures to behave in specified ways and these pressures place constraints on the display of traits, particularly traits that are socially less acceptable. Schools prohibit swearing, but this might be rife beyond the hearing of teachers. Behaviour requires opportunity as well as motive.

The studies cited by Mischel often assessed behaviour by a single-item rating scale, and it has always been recognised by test developers that single items are unreliable in comparison with scores that are aggregated across several items. Researchers would not claim to assess shyness or aggression on the basis of a single question. Inconsistent results might reflect errors in measurement rather than any inherent inconsistency in personality traits. Furthermore, the kinds of studies reported by Mischel are not the best kinds to identify consistency, since they were frequently experiments that were specifically designed to demonstrate changes in behaviour contingent upon changes in the situation.

Parents and teachers might have divergent perceptions of a child but, as Achenbach *et al.* (1987) reported, informants who see the child in the same situation do tend to agree with one another. They found considerable agreement between parents in their ratings of the children, the average parent–parent correlation being 0.59. Fergusson and Horwood (1987) also reported this pattern. There is agreement between pairs of informants who see the child in similar situations, in this case, different teachers of the same child, and disagreement between those who see the child in different contexts, teacher and mother. In their analysis of the assessment of conduct disorders, parent–teacher correlations were of the order of 0.33 to 0.37, but there were also indications that each of these informants was responding to something consistent in the child, in that there was stability in the assessments made by different teachers from one year to the next (the correlation between years was 0.54). Of course, this kind of agreement may occur simply because the two parents or the two teachers discuss the child with each other, and there are presumably pressures upon them to take a common view on the child. Nevertheless, although the ratings vary between informants who have different roles with regard to the child, they are systematic and seldom haphazard.

This finding raises further problems for personality theorists, which can be illustrated by studies reported by Mischel and Peake (1982). They investigated the traits of conscientiousness and friendliness among a sample of 63 university students; we concentrate here, as does the original paper, on conscientiousness. This was assessed by 19 measures proposed by the students themselves – punctuality, personal neatness, neatness of course-work, thoroughness of note-taking, attendance, meeting deadlines for assignments. The correlations between single measures of these behaviours were very small indeed, with an average correlation coefficient close to zero (0.08). This average correlation remained small (0.13) when aggregate measures were taken. The temporal stability of individual behaviours yielded dramatically higher correlation coefficients, of the order of 0.61.

Thus, the findings are compatible with Mischel's claims that traits show little cross-situational consistency (subsequent re-analyses of these data by other researchers argue that it is higher than allowed by Mischel and Peake; see Krahé, 1992: 144). Is conscientiousness a trait? Mischel and Peake asked students to rate how conscientious they were, and also to assess how consistently they demonstrated this. Parents and friends were also asked to rate the students on this trait. The average correlation between the ratings of different informants was 0.52, substantially higher than the index of consistency in behaviours across situations. Among students reporting that they were consistently conscientious, the correlation between informants was 0.68, but among students reporting that they were inconsistent in this trait, the correlation between informants was only 0.22. The puzzle here is that there is considerable agreement in how people perceive those students who see themselves as consistently conscientious, but this agreement is not reflected in any greater likelihood of actually being conscientious in practice.

What are these judgements based upon, and how can they be veridical if there seems to be no basis for them in the actual behaviour of the students? Mischel and Peake's answer draws upon the notion of the *cognitive proto-type*. If a sample of people was asked what a conscientious student was, some characteristics would tend to be elicited first and mentioned frequently whereas other characteristics would be mentioned in a more idiosyncratic way. Working hard, handing in assignments on time, attending lectures, might be most commonly mentioned, that is, they are central to the notion of the conscientious student, whereas neatness of appearance is less central to the notion.

The concept of the prototype implies that membership of the category 'conscientious student' is determined by the tendency of a student to demonstrate some, but not necessarily all central characteristics; there is not a fixed set of characteristics that is shared by all members of the category, and not all characteristics are assigned equal weight. According to this view of personality, traits are not ascribed to people on the basis of an exhaustive assessment of their behaviour but on whether they do demonstrate traits that are implicitly taken to be central to the trait. Mischel and Peake found support for this view when students rated the set of conscientious behaviours in terms of their relevance to the trait of conscientiousness. Students who perceived themselves as consistently conscientious showed greater temporal stability in those behaviours that were rated as most relevant to the prototype of conscientiousness.

Mischel and Peake concluded that variability in behaviour across situations and the existence of enduring dispositions to behave in predictable ways are not incompatible with one another. In order to be effective people have to learn to adapt their behaviour to particular circumstances and, since different situations make different demands, behaviour will be sensitive to its context. However, individuals do develop consistent and distinctive ways of dealing with particular situations, and people who know them pick up on this distinctive behaviour and label it, drawing upon notions of personality that are widely held in the community.

Schools have rules and norms that govern what constitutes acceptable and unacceptable behaviour. Some of these are formal and explicit; others are less formal and implicit. For example, there is a rule that forbids bullying. Until recently, this rule was usually implicit, in that the school dealt with instances of it as they occurred rather than having an explicit policy. One consequence was that there was often uncertainty about just what behaviour did constitute bullying, and there were actions, like teasing or name calling, that were not as central to the prototype as, say, physical aggression. However, these rules coexist with further implicit rules, for example, among pupils the code that you do not tell tales on a fellow pupil, or there is the belief that there is something wrong with someone who cannot solve their own problems. The label 'bully' is not ascribed to a pupil because the teacher or other pupils have noted any cross-situational consistency. One vivid instance of an action that is central to the prototype may be sufficient in itself. The members of the school community observe each other in constrained situations and make their assessments of the personality of each other on the basis of this evidence. Nevertheless, the language that they draw upon is typically highly generalised, with little indication that the traits might be specific to the limited kinds of situations in which people know each other.

What are the implications of the view of personality that has emerged from the person–situation debate? At a theoretical level, the notion that behaviour is a function of both personality and the situation has been replaced by a more complex conceptualisation. Behaviour is a function of a 'dynamic interaction' between personality and situational factors. According to this perspective, personality is sensitive to situational influences and situations are influenced by personality. Bandura (1978) introduced the concept of 'reciprocal determinism', arguing that adherents of the interaction perspective must avoid the mistake of imagining that there is an interaction between two separate entities. The environment does influence behaviour, but this influence is mediated by the individual's goals, plans, and expectancies, and these in turn influence which aspects of the environment will be attended to and the meanings that they will have. The individual can represent the environment symbolically to him- or herself, and mentally try out alternative courses of action. Bandura envisages a three-way interaction among personality, behaviour, and the environment. An individual's personality affects his or her behaviour and makes some of the consequences of that behaviour more likely than others; these consequences, in turn, influence their personality. A situation does not function independently of personality, particular personalities seek out or try to avoid particular kinds of situations. An example of this is provided by under-age gambling. Although it is illegal to sell 'scratch cards' to children under the age of 16, a survey reported by Angela Neustatter (*The Guardian*, 18 October 1995: 14–15) established that young people below that age were able to purchase the cards at 62 percent of outlets that were approached. Particular children *seek out* the excitements offered by gambling despite the constraints. One 17-year-old quoted by Neustatter said of the experience of playing fruit machines:

> When I'm wanting to go there's this uncomfortable restless feeling in my body that won't go away, then when you're on the machine and the lights and then hands are moving it changes and you feel in control. It's exciting because you have to act quickly and there's the atmosphere – being in an arcade is like being in a club.

The notion of a *dynamic* interaction implies that the very nature of the situation is dependent upon personality and the meanings that situations have for individual personalities. Consider a pupil who is anxious about certain kinds of social situations in school, say, who fears being teased, particularly by someone outside her circle of friends. This anxiety might be fundamental to that pupil's experience of school, but in practice that kind of situation might rarely be encountered. However, the 'situation' does not exist independently of the pupil's apprehensions. Any social encounter could change its meaning *to that individual* at any time, as, say, particular individuals leave or join a gathering of pupils, as the topic of conversation changes, or as she is called upon to make a contribution. The girl's anxiety is real and the circumstances that evoke it are predictable, but any measure of cross-situational consistency would reveal considerable variation across situations. The researcher would not be able to classify situations outside the meanings assigned to them by the individual in question. Examples like these push personality research in a more idiographic direction.

A second implication concerns the assessment of personality. Research has shown that assessments are potentially very misleading, particularly if they are based on simple behaviour checklists and rating scales. Kenrick and Funder (1988: 31) concluded on the basis of their review of the consistency controversy:

Systematic sources of judgmental bias, systematic effects of situations, and systematic interactions between persons and situations must be dealt with before we can predict from trait measures ... anyone who seeks predictive validity from trait ratings will do better to use (a) raters who are thoroughly familiar with the person being rated; (b) multiple behavioral observations; (c) multiple observers: (d) dimensions that are publicly observable; and (e) behaviors that are relevant to the dimension in question. On the other hand, one should *not* expect great accuracy when predicting (a) behavior in 'powerful' and clearly normatively scripted situations from trait ratings, and (b) a single behavioral instance from another single behavioral instance.

(emphasis in original)

These lessons are relevant to psychological researchers and to educational psychologists and other professionals who are involved with assessing and making decisions about children and adults. They should lead all of us to reflect upon the judgements that we make about others in the course of our routine encounters with them. We do form impressions about individuals and we share these with others and build up strong expectations about behaviour. It is worth reflecting on the basis upon which we make these. Are we 'writing off' students because we regard them as lazy or difficult or lacking in intelligence? Are we complacent about high-achieving students, assuming them to be confident, or capable in all subjects?

Attempts to resolve the person–situation debate have implications for changing behaviour. The definition of a trait as an enduring personal characteristic that predicts how someone will behave in a given situation leads to the impression that personality is fixed and that little can be done to change ways of behaving that are unacceptable to the community or injurious to the individual. However, the stability in behaviour over time that has been confirmed by this research is tied to particular situations and to the individual's interpretations of those situations. As Mischel and Peake put it, people are sensitive to the contingencies of situations and adapt their behaviour to different contingencies. The implication is that there is scope for change in behaviour if the contingencies in particular situations can be altered. A similar point is fundamental to the behaviourist approach to personality (e.g. Wheldall and Glynn, 1989). This maintains that behaviour in a particular situation is a product of the individual's history of *reinforcement*: in the past, these behaviours have produced consequences for the individual that make them more likely to be repeated. Recurrent features of the situation have become signals – or discriminative stimuli – for that behaviour. For example, the teacher's request for children to get out their books might be the signal for 'messing about' by a particular student who then attracts the censure of the teacher, a reaction that may be reinforcing because it enhances the student's status among his or her peers or because it introduces excitement into the tedium of activities which otherwise hold little interest or reward. The behaviourist's advice to the teacher is to change the contingencies in the situation; to reinforce alternative ways of behaving. Habitual ways of behaving are ingrained and not easy to change, but recent research suggests that there is much more scope for change than was recognised by earlier approaches to personality.

CONCLUSION

The study of traits has a long history in psychology, but in recent years it has been subject to fierce challenges. The inability of many trait measures to predict behaviour and of different observers to agree on whether children displayed particular traits called the whole approach into question. Other psychologists rejected the positivist framework within which this research was conducted and advocated alternative methods of research. Any notion that behaviour is 'caused by' a personality trait seems untenable. However, as we see in the following chapter, regularities in behaviour have been identified by behavioural genetic studies, research into individual differences in infancy, and longitudinal investigations of the influence of life events. These findings have to be accommodated with the recognition that people reflect on their own experiences, take decisions, and try to change the situations in which they find themselves. We reject the view that students fail *because* they lack self-confidence or are not motivated, or believe that they are anxious or aggressive because they have not formed secure attachments with their care-givers. We do believe that students may have a particular temperament or can come from adverse family circumstances, and these influence how they make sense of their experience. It is the sense that they make that guides their actions.

NOTE

1 In fact, research by E. A. Fleishman (see Schmidt, 1982: 405–12) suggests that there is not a general factor of motor ability, and only moderate correlations are found between different skills. Several factors are found to underlie performance on tests measuring control of movements relevant to sports, including 'control precision', as in a golf swing; 'multi-limb coordination', as in juggling; 'reaction time', as in starting a sprint in running or swimming; 'arm–hand steadiness'; 'aiming'; and so on. Other factors represent correlations between measures of physical strength, flexibility, and stamina.

Chapter 2

The origins of personality

TEMPERAMENT

Definitions of temperament

Mothers who have more than one child know how different can be the experiences of confinement and giving birth, and everyone who looks after more than one child knows how differently babies and infants can behave from the very beginning of life. Individual babies have their own patterns of waking and sleeping, of feeding, of cuddling. Systematic observations by psychologists have confirmed this variation. Eisenberg and Marmarou (1981) filmed a sample of infants all less than 90 hours old as they were exposed over a period of one hour to randomly presented repetitions of speech-like sounds and non-speech sounds. There were observed changes in attention ('listening') and activities in response to these sounds, such as active searching for the source of the sound or signs of pleasure or distress. What was striking was evidence of individual differences among babies as young as this and the relationship between the reactions of individual babies and their parents' reports of their typical behaviour (p. 132):

> Indeed, it was our impression, almost from the beginning of the study, that inhibition of crying in order to 'listen' distinguished good natured babies from ill tempered ones. Further, this impression of innate temperamental differences among newborns consistently was supported by parental reports during follow-up procedures: subjects who remained quiet or who cried little during the experiment uniformly were described as 'good' babies, while those who cried long and frequently during the experiment usually were described pejoratively as 'irritable', 'difficult', 'hard to handle', or the like.

Differences have also been identified in newborns' facial expressions in response to pleasant or noxious smells and tastes, and Field (1987: 974) has proposed a basic dimension of expressiveness that contrasts babies who are 'externalizers', whose response to stimulation involves change in facial expression but who are physiologically non-reactive, with other babies ('internalizers') who do have a clear physiological reaction but who nevertheless display little on the face.

Psychologists have elaborated the concept of temperament in order to explain this variation in responses that can be observed so early in life. There exist several definitions of this concept in the literature, as is evident in the following four responses to the question of definition posed in a roundtable discussion of temperament (Goldsmith et al., 1987: 508–10).

> We define temperament as a set of inherited personality traits that appear early in life (Buss and Plomin)

> We conceptualize temperament as the stylistic component of behavior – that is, the *how* of behavior as differentiated from motivation, the *why* of behavior, and abilities, the *what* of behavior (Thomas and Chess; emphasis in original)

> We have defined temperament as relatively stable, primarily biologically based individual differences in reactivity and self-regulation (Rothbart)

> In collaboration with Joseph Campos, I have proposed a definition that identifies temperament as individual differences in the probability of experiencing and expressing the primary emotions and arousal (Goldsmith).

The themes common to these definitions are that temperament refers to individual differences that appear very early in life and that persist over a period of time. The fact that temperamental characteristics appear so early in life distinguishes them from other personality traits. There is also emphasis upon reactions to stimulation rather than searching out and shaping experience. The infant has limited mobility and is heavily dependent upon other people. Nevertheless, the concept refers to what the baby *brings* to any situation rather than what he or she learns from it, and what the baby brings will tend to shape the reactions of others. Babies who have irregular patterns of sleep, who cry a lot, or who who resist being cuddled can be expected to elicit different patterns of reactions from their carers than regular sleepers, settled babies or those who respond positively to being picked up. As carers and infant negotiate these preferences, the infant begins to structure his or her environment, and the outcomes of negotiations will give rise to orientations to experience in terms of recurrent satisfactions, disappointments, frustrations, and so on.

Search for the basic temperaments

The seminal study has been the New York Longitudinal Study, organised by Thomas, Chess, Birch and their colleagues, which began in 1956, and which has followed a sample of 133 individuals from 84 families, from 3 months of age into adulthood (see, for example, Chess and Thomas, 1986). The research began with detailed interviews with the parents of 22 children and on the basis of analysis of the contents of these interviews nine temperaments were identified, as presented in Table 2.1.

These nine temperaments were also organised into three types: the 'easy' child, the 'difficult' child and the 'slow to warm up' child. The easy child has positive mood quality, follows a regular sleep and feeding rhythm, approaches new situations and is adaptable. The difficult child has more intense reactions to stimulation, has negative quality of mood, does not establish regular patterns, withdraws from novel situations and tends not to adapt to change. The slow to warm up child has a low activity level, has less positive moods, withdraws from novel situations, and shows a low intensity reaction to stimulation.

Table 2.1 Thomas, Chess and Birch's nine basic temperaments

Temperament	Characteristics at 2 months
1 Activity level	Moves often in sleep, squirms a lot when being dressed versus passive, immobile
2 Rhythmicity	Regular versus irregular cycle of sleep, feeding and bowel movement
3 Approach or withdrawal	In response to novel situation, e.g. to strangers, new food or toys
4 Adaptability to change	Extent of change in response to new situation, for example, gets used to bathing or to new food
5 Intensity of reaction	The energy level of response, e.g. crying as opposed to whimpering when hungry
6 Sensory threshold	How sensitive the infant is to stimulation such as startle response to a sudden noise
7 Predominant quality of mood	Smiling and enjoyment versus fussy and crying
8 Distractibility	How readily the infant can be distracted, e.g. being picked up and rocked can interrupt her crying
9 Attention span and persistence	How long the infant persists until she gets what she wants

Source: Chess and Thomas (1986).

These temperaments were based on both 'impressionistic' and more systematic analysis of the content of interviews with parents (Goldsmith *et al.*, 1987: 512). Subsequently, a number of parental rating scale measures have been devised, appropriate for different ages from 4 months of age until 12 years (e.g. the Carey Temperament Questionnaire; Carey and McDevitt, 1978). Items on these scales refer to typical behaviours of children, and they yield scores for the nine temperaments and for the easy, difficult, and slow to warm up types. Additional measures have been developed that are based on teacher ratings and, for older children, self-reports on their own behaviour.

Because these scales yield quantitative data they can be statistically analysed to estimate the reliability of the ratings, whether in terms of consistency over time or the degree of parental agreement. Scales can also be inter-correlated and subjected to factor analysis to confirm that the nine temperaments can indeed be reproduced at different ages, providing evidence for the appropriateness of the ratings measures and supporting the theory that individual differences in infants' and children's behaviour can be described along nine dimensions at different ages.

Factor analysis of ratings data provides the foundations for Buss and Plomin's theory of temperament (see Buss and Plomin, 1984). They reviewed studies of rating scales based on the New York Longitudinal Study and concluded that nine different dimensions had not been found in these data. Their revised model proposes three temperaments – emotionality, activity, and sociability – and the EAS ratings scale has been developed to measure them.

Emotionality and activity are, of course, similar to the temperaments proposed in the model of Thomas and Chess. The sociability scale seemed to be a mixture of sociability and shyness. Cheek and Buss (1981) have argued that shyness and sociability should be treated as separate factors rather than being opposite poles of one factor. Shyness is not simply the absence of sociability, and it is possible for someone to be both sociable and shy, desiring the company of others but at the same time being anxious about it. Factor analysis of the EAS (e.g. Boer and Westenberg, 1994) suggests that the test measures shyness rather than sociability.

It would seem that the three basic temperaments found in parental ratings are emotionality, activity and shyness. The first two of these also appear in Thomas and Chess's theory. Shyness is related to their approach/withdrawal temperament, although it refers to withdrawal from new social situations rather than novel situations generally, and is also similar to Kagan's inhibition temperament (see Chapter 7). There is also a considerable degree of conceptual overlap with Eysenck's theory of personality, which assigns important roles to emotionality, sociability and impulsivity, and possibly activity. We should bear in mind the age of the children who are being rated. Consistencies in temperament or personality do seem to emerge around 4 years. The goal of temperament research was to demonstrate stable individual differences long before the fourth year, in early infancy. Variation in the frequency and intensity of emotional reaction, activity levels and tendencies to approach or avoid novel situations can be identified early in life and, conceptually, these are similar to later emotionality, activity and shyness, but longitudinal research has yet to establish stability in temperament from infancy by showing that the emotional, active or shy infant grows into the emotional, active or shy child and adult. The genetic basis of temperament is central to Buss and Plomin's definition. We postpone discussion of this until later in the chapter, when we introduce methods for estimating the contribution of genetic factors to personality.

The difficult temperament

Thomas and Chess defined the difficult child in terms of a profile of five temperaments: quality of mood, approach/withdrawal, rhythmicity, adaptability, and intensity of reaction. However, Bates (1986) has found that these five scales do not always correlate with each other in the expected fashion, and he has argued that this notion rests largely on parental ratings of children's 'frequent and intense expression of negative emotion' (p. 4). Buss and Plomin (1984) also argue that the notion of difficult temperament at 12 and 24 months is essentially equivalent to emotionality. The terms easy and difficult are more value-laden than the objective descriptive language of the nine temperaments, and they refer implicitly to the relationship between infant and carer. Quality of mood can be assessed in terms of rated frequency and intensity of crying, whereas 'difficult' implies difficult for somebody, and what is difficult for one mother may not prove so for another. This gives rise to concern that parental ratings of temperament may be biased such that a mother who is, say, excessively tired or who has emotional problems or great stress in her life may be prone to identify temperamental difficulty in her child. This can to some extent be minimised by avoiding evaluative labels in ratings and interviews, and there are studies (Wolkind and De Salis, 1982; Bates, 1986) that have looked more directly at this issue, concluding that maternal mood does not bias assessments. Reliance upon the notion of difficult temperament has the further disadvantage of losing a great deal of information about the infant, substituting one summary label for a profile on five dimensions. These problems notwithstanding, there is evidence that the difficult child is subsequently more at risk for behaviour problems. We illustrate this point with three studies from the 1982 Ciba Foundation symposium on temperament.

Wolkind and De Salis (1982) studied a sample of mothers in a London antenatal clinic who were interviewed in late pregnancy and when their children were 4, 14, 27 and 42 months. Items from the Carey Temperament

Questionnaire were embedded in interviews, and an index of difficult temperament was constructed on the basis of the correlation matrix of responses to items, with items referring to rhythmicity and quality of mood being most heavily represented on the index. Children with a difficult temperament on this index at age 4 months obtained significantly higher scores on a behaviour problems checklist at 42 months, where the checklist included maternal assessments of sleep disorders, temper tantrums and wetting. Ratings of temperament did not seem to be biased by other characteristics of the mothers, although they were affected by infant temperament, with the mothers of difficult children reporting being physically tired when the children were 4 months and more likely to have developed a depression disorder when the children were 42 months.

Thomas and Chess (1982) reported a follow-up study of the New York sample of 133 subjects when the participants were aged 18 to 22 years. Ratings of the nine temperaments based on parental interview, together with a derived 'difficult temperament' score, were available for each participant for each of the first 5 years of life. The study also included a school adjustment score at 5 years, a composite adult adjustment measure, including assessments of self-evaluation and of family and social relationships, and finally a rating of the presence or absence of a clinical psychiatric diagnosis. The correlations between difficult temperament scores and these assessments are presented in Table 2.2. The sample sizes range from 82 to 84 for school assessments to 115 to 132 for adult assessments, and statistically significant correlations are indicated by an asterisk.

Table 2.2. Childhood temperament and adjustment in school and adulthood: The New York Longitudinal Study

Age of rated difficult temperament	Correlation with		
	School adjustment at age 5	Composite adult adjustment	Clinical diagnosis in adulthood
0–12 months	0.02	0.08	0.03
12–14 months	0.06	−0.09	−0.03
24–36 months	0.02	−0.21*	0.05
36–48 months	−0.30*	−0.32*	0.24*
48–60 months	−0.11	−0.23*	0.19*

Note: * $p < 0.05$
Source: Thomas and Chess (1982: 171).

Difficulty of temperament in childhood is associated with adjustment problems and the presence of psychiatric symptoms in adulthood, but these relationships only become apparent when temperament is assessed from the age of 3 and they only seem to hold for both measures of adult adjustment when assessed at 4 years. The difficulty of making confident predictions about childhood and adulthood from temperament measures made in the first years of life is a consistent finding, and this may reflect a number of factors that are not easy to disentangle. They could simply be due to measurement problems in infancy. Alternatively, they may mean that the experiences which the child has before the age of 4 are less relevant to later adjustment.

Temperaments are, of course, indexed by different behaviours at different ages. Frequency of crying or regularity of the rhythms of sleep, feeding or bowel movements may have little in common with, say, the quality of relationships that children will have with other children. Behaviour in infancy may, however, have an indirect impact on later adjustment by eliciting a pattern of responses from care-givers which in turn might influence the person's self-concept and expectations about how he or she will be treated by others, that is, responses to the infant's temperament may influence the child's internalised working models of relationships. Temperament can interact with other personal qualities and with experiences, and these factors will reduce the ability of making predictions over extended periods of time. Indeed, even the correlations from assessments made later than 4 years are never high.

A difficult temperament at 4 and 5 years has only a moderate correlation with school adjustment at age 5, and this raises questions about the consistency of temperament across different situations. As we discussed in Chapter 1, this is a controversial and complex issue, that raises many questions. For some psychologists, the issue can be resolved by improved measurement techniques, and they regard the low correlations as due to the use of unreliable rating scales in the assessment of temperament and adjustment. Another way to construe this issue is to ask what value of correlation coefficient would be expected given that we had appropriate measures. School makes very different demands from home, and behaviour that would be regarded as 'difficult' in one setting would not necessarily be so regarded in the other. Short attention span and lack of persistence are temperamental qualities that are not usually included in the index of difficult temperament, but they could be expected to lead to problems with adjustment in school. It could be argued that even if temperament could be reliably measured and it were the case that it exerted a powerful influence on behaviour in both home and school, the correlations between behaviour in home and school and between teacher and parent assessments could never be more than moderate.

Keogh (1982) studied the relationship between difficult temperament and teachers' perceptions of children's 'teachability'. Temperament factors were identified by factor analysis of the Thomas and Chess teacher ratings scale. The original set of temperaments was reduced to three factors: 'task orientation', which had highest factor loadings on attention span and persistence, distractibility, and activity items; 'personal social flexibility', with highest loadings on approach/withdrawal, quality of mood, and adaptability items; 'reactivity', with highest loadings on quality of mood, sensory threshold and intensity of reaction. Among a sample of 80 4-year-old children in California, task orientation was significantly correlated ($r = 0.47$) with teacher ratings of the children on a teachability scale and was more closely related to that scale than a measure of the children's cognitive ability. In another study, teachers provided ratings of pupils' temperament together with estimates of their ability. All three temperament factors influenced teachers' judgements of the child's abilities, and indeed teachers tended to over-estimate the abilities of 'easy' pupils relative to their measured IQ. The notion of a 'difficult child' seems to have currency in teachers' perceptions of pupils, and is related to measures of temperament although the notion of difficulty in Keogh's investigations includes temperaments that did not figure strongly in the original definition of that concept by Thomas and Chess.

Taken together, this research suggests that school adjustment is related to difficult temperament, but the definition of difficulty changes from study to study. Further research is needed to identify the specific aspects of difficulty that underlie this relationship. A composite score that is the average of a set of more specific ratings is not helpful in achieving this goal. Reviews of the literature reach opposite conclusions, with Bates (1986: 4) arguing that difficult temperament predicts behaviour problems whereas Buss and Plomin (1984: 25) claim that the evidence points to no relationship. This kind of disagreement is also symptomatic of the absence of a shared definition of the difficult temperament.

Caspi *et al.* (1995) identified three temperaments on the basis of factor analysis of ratings based on observations of children made at ages 3, 5, 7 and 9 years as part of a prospective longitudinal study in New Zealand. *Lack of control* emerged in the responses of the 3-year-old children, loading on items concerning emotional over-reaction to events, restlessness, impulsiveness, and short attention span. Two further factors appeared at each age: 'approach', related to self-confidence, friendliness, approach to new situations; and 'sluggishness', loading on passivity, shyness and fearfulness. Children were subsequently assessed for externalising and internalising behaviour problems at the ages of 9, 11, 13 and 15 years using parents' and teachers' ratings on standard checklists. Correlations that were statistically highly significant (although never greater than 0.30) were found between temperament measures at age 3 and later problems. In particular, lack of control at age 3 was significantly correlated with hyperactivity, inattention and anti-social behaviour at ages 9 and 11, and with attention problems and conduct disorder at ages 13 and 15. Approach at 3 years was negatively correlated with anxiety and withdrawal at ages 13 and 15 among boys, although not among girls. Sluggishness had no significant correlations with behaviour problems among boys and, among girls, correlated only with attention problems at ages 13 and 15. This study demonstrates the advantage of using more specific measures rather than a general measure of difficult temperament. Lack of control was correlated with a range of externalising disorders, whereas low scores on the approach measure were correlated only with internalising disorders.

GENETIC FACTORS IN PERSONALITY

Where are the origins of individual differences in psychological character-istics to be found? Much psychological research and lay discussion alike concentrates on inheritance: personality is formed in the genes. This discussion has usually been a polarisation between two positions: either personality is inherited *or* it is shaped by our environment. Each of these positions tends to be vehemently defended, and each is believed to have obvious social and educational implications. Recent research has rejected this simplistic view and emphasises complex interactions between genetic and environmental influences.

Discussion of genetic factors in human development is highly contro-versial. This is as it should be, I believe, given the evidence of the abuses of genetic experimentation in the concentration camps of the Holocaust, and the implications that are so readily drawn that social issues can somehow be resolved by genetic knowledge. Suggestions that there may be an identifiable genetic basis for predicting intelligence, hyperactivity, learning difficulties, or aggressive behaviour create anxieties, reinforce prejudices, and raise ethical questions that society has scarcely begun to address. To some extent, psychologists have themselves contributed to the unease that often meets dissemination of their findings, and much discussion on the inheritance of intelligence has been unedifying.

Whereas psychological discussion of the genetic factors in human development has attracted mostly scepticism, fundamental research into genetics has become one of the intellectual adventures of our time. The Human Genome Project, which aims to provide a 'map' of the genes and the information that they carry, promises that much of the genetic basis of human life will be understood in awe-inspiring detail.

Of course, there are many reasons why this research should be so much further advanced than psychological studies, not the least being the impossibility of applying experimental methods in psychology, but nevertheless there has been valuable research into the origins of human behaviour that is new and that has challenged many preconceptions, including the assumption that inheritance and environment contribute independently to personality characteristics. There are cases where the genetic factors in psychological characteristics are better understood, and we refer briefly to some of these. There are other cases, where individual differences seem to be associated with biological factors, even if the genetic basis of those factors remains unproven. In most cases, however, the evidence for the role of inheritance is only indirect, and complex behaviour patterns are seen to have complex causes.

It is useful to distinguish two kinds of studies. The first traces the genetic contribution to a particular trait through a combination of pedigree studies and microbiological analysis of genetic material. Its goal is to identify the gene or genes whose action is responsible for the trait. In most cases, this research is concerned with psychological disorders, with trying to find out why development has not followed the normal course. The second kind draws upon studies of family resemblance, particularly the special case of identical twins, and the similarities within families that include adopted children, to estimate the contribution of heredity to the variation in traits between family members.

The nature of genes

Research into the nature of genes has drawn upon many disciplines and techniques and recent advances have been aided by technological developments, for example, in the chemical analysis of DNA. Laboratory research methods vary from counting chromosomes with the aid of a microscope to molecular investigations of specific genetic sequences in DNA. The fact that the complete set of chromosomes is reproduced in all cells (other than germ cells) has proved of enormous importance in decoding the information carried by the DNA, as samples of blood, for example, are readily accessible for genetic research. Much progress has been made by cytogenetic analysis, which involves isolating white blood cells and growing them in a tissue culture, a blend of sterile water, salts, sugars and other ingredients that encourage the cells to grow and divide. Immediately before cell division, the DNA, which had been distributed throughout the cell nucleus, returns to reform the chromosomes which can then be clearly seen through a microscope. A recent and powerful development has been DNA amplification techniques. One of these is *polymerase chain reaction*, where multiple copies of a single piece of DNA can be made by attaching other pieces of DNA to act as primers to stimulate an enzyme, polymerase, that brings about a chain reaction, multiplying the original piece of DNA. This DNA can then be analysed to read off its sequence of bases.

This research relies upon the analysis of human or animal blood cells or tissues. A particularly fruitful approach has combined pedigree studies with biochemical analysis. Pedigree analysis begins with a person (the *propositus*) who displays the phenotype of interest, and traces this characteristic through generations of families, to establish a family tree, pinpointing which individuals display the phenotype.

The principles of reproduction and segregation suggest, at least with the benefit of hindsight, that the chromosomes should be the first place to look for genes, since it was known that they are arranged in pairs and that these pairs separate during cell division. There are two forms of division. The first is *meiosis*. When the father produces sperm, each of the 46 chromosomes in the body's cells is split into two, with one member of each pair going into each sperm. The same is true for the mother's ovum, and during fertilisation the nucleus of the ovum releases 23 chromosomes to pair up with 23 chromosomes from the nucleus of the sperm cell. These 23 pairs constitute the full set of chromosomes. The second kind of division is *mitosis*, and is involved in the multiplication of cells from the original single cell. During cell division, the chromosomes replicate themselves so that a copy of the original chromosome is reproduced in all cells (except in the case of germ cells). These observations imply that the chromosomes are involved in the transmission of characteristics from parent to offspring and also in the construction of the different kinds of cells that constitute the organism.

Research into the molecular structure of the chromosome has shown that it consists of deoxyribonucleic acid (DNA) and protein. Proteins are synthesised from amino acids. There are 20 amino acids and it is the specific combination of these acids that determines which protein is produced. There are thousands of kinds of proteins and they are fundamental to life, as hormones, as antibodies, and as constituents of body structure, such as the skin or the lens of the eye. Specific kinds of proteins, known as enzymes, control the internal chemistry of cells, acting as catalysts that accelerate chemical reactions in the cell. DNA directs the activity of cells by providing the information for the manufacture of specific sequences of amino acids, that is, for the synthesis of proteins.

DNA is composed of four basic molecules called nucleotides which are identical except that each has a different nitrogen base. The sequence of bases provides the code for the production of the amino acids. It is now known that this coding is a two-stage process involving another nucleic acid, ribonucleic acid (RNA). First, a sequence of three DNA bases, or codon, is read into, or transcribed into a sequence of messenger RNA and this is then translated by transfer RNA into the manufacture of protein – DNA makes RNA which makes protein.

Sickle cell anaemia is the most widespread genetic disease in the world, and research established that it is associated with an abnormality in haemoglobin, the major protein involved in red blood cells. Scientists were able to trace this abnormality to a difference in the sequence of amino acids that constitutes haemoglobin. At one part of the sequence valine is found in the blood of those affected by the disease instead of glutamic acid. The DNA codon for glutamic acid is CTT. The DNA codon for valine is CAT. One abnormal codon in DNA produces an abnormal codon in messenger RNA which produces one change in the string of amino acids which form the protein, haemoglobin. The consequences for the affected individual of this small change in DNA can be enormous. The abnormal haemoglobin results in anaemia and ultimately heart failure, and clumping of blood cells that can lead to damage to brain, heart, lungs and kidneys.

The ambition of genetics is to draw up a map of the genes, to show which sequences of DNA on which chromosomes code for particular aspects of human development. For example, children with Down's syndrome nearly always have 47 chromosomes instead of the normal 46, and this extra chromosome is an additional, third copy of chromosome 21 (the technical term for the extra chromosome is *trisomy*). Because Down's syndrome is associated with low IQ, this suggests that genes on chromosome 21 are involved in intelligence. Further analysis can suggest which genes on the arm of the chromosome must be trisomic for the syndrome to occur. Similarly, conditions that are X-linked imply the involvement of the X chromosome. Research into detailed mapping of the genes is proving a very difficult and painstaking task, not only because of the very large number of genes involved, and the possibility that genes may not match with characteristics in a straightforward way, but also because many of the triplets of DNA bases that have been isolated do not seem to code for any particular function.

There is also a logical problem in inferring the genetic basis of behaviour from instances of disorder in that behaviour. An individual's personality is the product of very many genes in interaction with the environment, but it can be severely disrupted by a mutation in one specific gene. It would be as misleading to conclude that this gene controlled that personality characteristic as it would be to conclude that a motor engine was controlled by the battery just because it fails to work when the battery is flat. Very many components need to work together in a precise way for the engine to operate, but there are countless ways in which a breakdown in one component can impede its operation.

Human pedigree studies

Breeding methods have provided a powerful tool in isolating causal factors, but they cannot be applied to the investigation of humans, and psychologists have to rely on the descriptive study of family relationships. There are, of course, many sources of differences within and between families other than genetic ones, and this limits the inferences that can be drawn. The study of family resemblance nevertheless remains fundamental to human genetic research. We consider two examples. Gopnik

(1990) constructed a pedigree for three generations of one family where there was a high incidence of dysphasia, a specific disorder in language among children who develop normally in other respects. Language tests were administered to members of this particular family and revealed evidence of quite specific problems in individuals' performance. Some seemed unable to infer general grammatical rules, like changing the tense of verbs, or forming plurals of nonsense words (such as guessing that 'wugs' is the plural of 'wug').

The distribution of dysphasia across different family members is highly suggestive of a genetic basis (see Figure 2.1). The condition is clearly passed from one generation to the next yet it does not affect all members of the family – siblings raised together do not necessarily share the disorder, a finding which weakens the argument for its origin in shared environmental factors. The appearance of the condition in successive generations – each individual who shows it has at least one parent who also shows it – is characteristic of a single dominant gene.

The fact that the zygote takes half of its set of chromosomes from one parent and half from the other parent is crucial in promoting variation. At the very least, it divides the species into males and females, the division which is fundamental to human reproduction. One of the 23 pairs of chromosomes is the pair of sex chromosomes. The normal female has two large X chromosomes. The normal male has one X chromosome and one, smaller, Y chromosome. Thus, an X chromosome from a female ovum unites with either the X or the Y chromosome from the sperm cell to produce a daughter, in the first case, and a son, in the second case. Certain patterns of family resemblance can be explained by assuming that genes are linked to the sex chromosomes. A characteristic is carried on the X chromosome but its effect may be masked by (be recessive to) an X chromosome that does not carry that characteristic. The inability of the genes on one X chromosome to make a necessary protein may be compensated if the other X chromosome can produce it.

Let us indicate the affected X chromosome as $\bar{X}$. A boy who inherits this gene from his mother will be $\bar{X}Y$ and he will show the characteristic. He will pass it on to any daughter he fathers through his $\bar{X}$ chromosome, but he cannot pass the characteristic on to any son. A girl who inherits this $\bar{X}$ gene will be $\bar{X}X$ and, because X dominates $\bar{X}$, she will not show it. However, she may pass on this characteristic to the next generation, giving birth to either an XX girl, or an $\bar{X}X$ girl, or an XY boy or an $\bar{X}Y$ boy. Only the $\bar{X}Y$ boy will demonstrate the characteristic. This distribution, where the characteristic is passed from one generation to another, but only shows itself in some male offspring, is found, for example, in the blood disorder, haemophilia, in Duchenne's muscular dystrophy, and in some forms of colour blindness. A condition that is transmitted in this way is known as an X-linked disorder. Instances of X-linked disorders are more frequent and

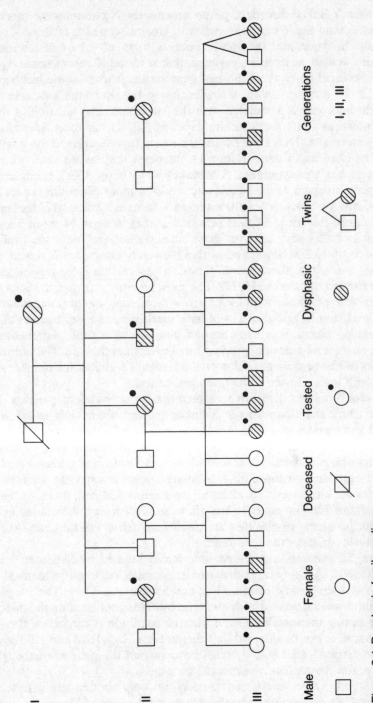

Figure 2.1 Dysphasia family pedigree
Source: Based upon information in Gopnik (1990).

salient than Y-linked disorders, partly because the X chromosome carries more genes than the Y chromosome, with greater scope for error.

Fragile X syndrome, the most common form of inherited learning difficulties, is also, as its name suggests, linked to the X chromosome, and the precise location of the abnormal gene on this chromosome has been identified (Hagerman, 1992). A fragile site on the tip of the long arm of the X chromosome is associated with the syndrome. The location of the gene, known as FMR-1 at this site, labelled Xq27.3, has been identified by cytogenetic and DNA amplification research. Investigation of the fragile site offers clues as to the variation in outcomes that, as we shall see, is characteristic of this syndrome. A triplet of DNA bases, CCG, is adjacent to the gene involved at the fragile site, and the more often this triplet is repeated, the more severe are the symptoms. In an individual who does not have the gene the triple CCG is repeated at that location between 5 and 48 times. In males who carry the gene but show no symptoms, the triplet is repeated up to 200 times, and in those severely affected it is repeated, hundreds, sometimes thousands of times. In general, the more repetitions, the more severe the consequences. The most severely affected males have a distinctive appearance, with long, narrow faces, long and prominent ears, square jaws, and large testicles, and have marked learning difficulties and behaviour problems. It is hypothesised that once this triplet is repeated often enough, it impedes the production of protein at this site. The normal functions of this protein are unknown, although it is found in a number of tissues, with higher levels in the brain and testes.

The syndrome has distinctive characteristics that puzzle geneticists. It does not show the characteristic X-linked pattern where only males are affected and females act as carriers. Some males are themselves unaffected but have inherited the mutation and pass their abnormal gene to their daughters who pass it on to their sons who are often affected. There seem to be three outcomes for those males who are known to carry the abnormal gene: they are either severely affected; moderately affected, that is, if they have average IQ but nevertheless show some learning difficulties and behaviour problems; or else they are unaffected carriers of the gene. Also, some females do show the syndrome.

Figure 2.2 presents a pedigree of a family studied by Simensen and Rogers (1989). Cytogenetic evidence of fragile sites was found in males IV-1 and IV-2, their female cousin, IV-5, and her daughter, V-1. The Fragile X condition was associated with mental retardation only among the males and not among the females. Given that the condition is carried on the X chromosome, it can be inferred that the mothers, II-3, III-2 and III-3, are 'obligate carriers', that is, they must have carried the gene even though they have not themselves revealed the condition.

Girls tend to be unaffected carriers or only moderately affected. Approximately one in three females who carry the Fragile X gene have an

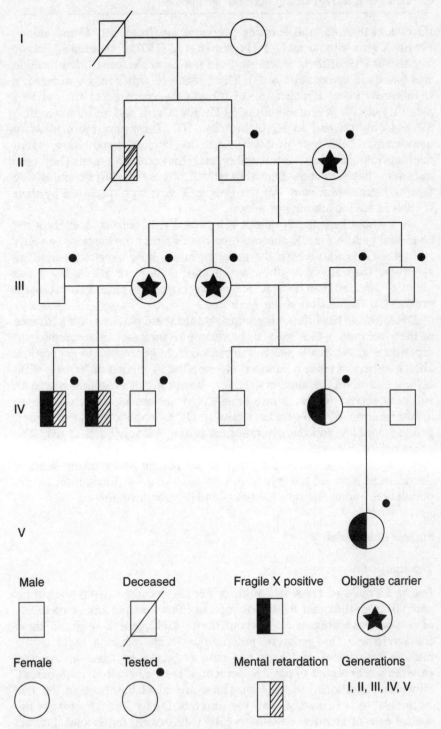

Male

Deceased

Fragile X positive

Obligate carrier

Female

Tested

Mental retardation

Generations

I, II, III, IV, V

Figure 2.2 Fragile X syndrome family pedigree
Source: Simensen and Rogers (1989).

IQ of less than 85, and learning problems are frequently found among Fragile X girls with normal IQ. Hagerman *et al.* (1992) compared 32 Fragile X girls with 19 of their sisters who did not carry the gene (identification was based on cytogenetic tests). The Fragile X girls had, on average, a significantly lower IQ; their mean IQ was 80 compared to their sister's mean IQ of 109. Seventeen out of 32 Fragile X girls had an IQ lower than 85, and only six had an IQ higher than 100. They were more likely to demonstrate behaviour problems, such as shyness, hand-biting, hand-flapping, impulsiveness, distractibility, and short attention span. They were also more likely to show typical Fragile X physical features such as long face and prominent ears. All the Fragile X girls were reported by their schools as having learning problems.

Girls who inherit the Fragile X gene are at risk, but the location of the abnormal gene on the X chromosome has different implications for boys and girls. Girls who inherit the gene are much more likely to escape the syndrome than are boys who carry it and, if they are affected, are less seriously affected than boys; its presence is often only picked up because a brother has demonstrated the syndrome.

DNA testing has offered some insight into these patterns of inheritance of the syndrome, which seem to be related to increases in the number of repetitions as the fragile site is transmitted from generation to generation. High numbers of these repetitions increase the likelihood of learning difficulties, and when the numbers are very large the full Fragile X syndrome will be observed. Research into Fragile X syndrome has been based upon a combination of cytogenetic analysis, DNA amplification techniques, pedigree studies, and the psychological testing of individuals at risk. The relationships between genotype and phenotype are very complex, but they can be unravelled. Rapid progress has been made in recent years in the identification of this syndrome, in assessing its distribution in the population, and in attempts to understand its genetic origins.

Studies of heritability

The study of twins

Because a child receives half of his or her chromosomes from one parent and half from the other the distribution of characteristics among members of a family can provide clues about the possible genetic origin of these characteristics. The genotype inherited by each offspring represents a random assortment of his or her parents' genes so that, on average, children are expected to have 50 percent of their genes from each parent. However, additional sources of clues are available because of two 'accidents', one of nature, and the other of family life. The first is the special case of identical or monozygotic (MZ) twins; the second, the fact that children are frequently separated from their natural parents and brought up in a different family, where the child has no genetic relationship with his or her adoptive parents (this is more characteristic of contemporary, Western nuclear families; in societies where child care is shared among many relatives, the absence of the natural parents through death, illness or moving away would not result so often in such separation from the family).

Identical twins are produced when the fertilised egg, the zygote, is divided to form two zygotes. This is a different phenomenon from the case of fraternal or dizygotic (DZ) twins, where two ova have been fertilised by separate sperm. In the first instance, the MZ twins have identical genetic endowment; in the second case, the DZ twins are genetically no more alike than ordinary siblings. This distinction between the two types is manifest in physical appearance – MZ twins are physically very alike, indeed, it may be difficult to tell one from the other, and they must be, of course, of the same sex. DZ twins can appear quite different from one another and can be of different sex. This distinction suggests different kinds of comparisons that could give insight into the genetic origins of behaviour. For example, one could examine the frequency with which a condition that was true of one MZ twin was also true of the other, on the understanding that a condition that was genetic in origin should be present in both twins or in neither. A comparison of characteristics of MZ twins who have been reared in the same family with those who have been separated for some reason and brought up in different families would also be informative about the relative importance of genetic and child rearing practices. Alternatively, one could try to quantify the genetic influence on a trait that is distributed throughout the population by analysing scores on the trait that are obtained by MZ twins who share 100 percent of their genes, by DZ twins or siblings who share 50 percent of their genes, and by adoptive parents and children who share none of their genes.

We look at a sample of these studies, but first we recognise that they are not experiments, and their results are influenced to an unknown extent by factors outside the control of the researcher. There is the obvious point that MZ twins share a highly similar environment as well as identical genes, and hence we cannot be certain which of these factors is the more influential. Because MZ twins are of the same age and sex and physically alike, they are often treated in very similar ways by their parents and may elicit similar kinds of reactions from friends, other adults, teachers, and all who come into contact with them. Accordingly, the environment that they share may be more similar than that shared by DZ twins and, indeed, some studies of parental ratings which we review later in this chapter suggest that parents may exaggerate the contrast between DZ twins, in that the differences between the correlations of ratings of MZ and DZ twins are often exceptionally large. Children are not simply puppets dancing to the rhythm of their genetic and environmental strings, and the fact of being a twin might in itself influence behaviour. MZ twins might set out to be as similar as possible to each other or they might deliberately copy each other's mannerisms and behaviour – as a child, I had friends who were MZ twins who enjoyed teasing us, each pretending to be the other. Alternatively, some twins might wish to be as different as possible. As one anonymous correspondent wrote to *The Observer* (5 November 1995):

> I always hated being a twin. For most of my formative years my main goal in life was to create an identity for myself, separate from 'the twins'. Any initially tiny difference can be a basis for the twins to work out an unspoken agreement that one is, say, the pretty one, while the other takes on the role of the intelligent one.

On the other hand, no two people are ever exposed to exactly the same conditions, and there may be factors that result in different environments even for identical twins, particularly with respect to experiences between conception and birth when twins share, and perhaps compete for, the same pre-natal resources. For example, MZ twins frequently share a common chorionic membrane which can give rise to an imbalance of placental circulation between the twins. Some indication of these factors is given by the fact that markedly different birth weights are more prevalent among MZ than among DZ twins. A further uncertainty is that MZ twins may not be representative of the population in that they are born nearly a month premature, on average, and have birth weights about 30 percent lower than the average (Emde *et al.*, 1992: 1451). It is not obvious what significance should be attached to this finding as many of the psychological differences between premature and full term infants disappear before school years. On the other hand, shared adverse pre-natal environments might result in a common predisposition to experiencing psychological or physical health problems later in life, and the high coincidence of these problems might lead to the erroneous conclusion that these problems were genetic in origin. Some of these influences may exaggerate genetic factors and others may underestimate them: making inferences from twin studies is not as straightforward as it might first appear.

Other uncertainties surround the case of adopted children. From the point of view of research, good design would assign pairs of twins at random to different environments, but of course the agencies responsible for placing children in new homes have a different agenda, and selective placement policies might mean that a child will go to a family that is similar in important respects to the one he or she has left behind. The age at which children leave their home for another one can also vary considerably, and this might have serious consequences for the design of research if, as is frequently argued, pre-natal and perinatal experiences, child rearing practices, or attachments in infancy are more important than later experiences for personality development. This kind of separation is still relatively unusual in society, which again raises the question of the extent to which findings based on adoption studies can be generalised to the remainder of the population. With these caveats in mind, we now consider the research evidence.

Estimates of heritability

A number of attempts have been made to devise mathematical models that apportion individual differences in personality test scores to genetic and environmental factors. The correlation coefficient plays an important role in these models, and the terminology in this field reflects this. If we have test scores for a sample of pairs of twins, then a high correlation, where scores obtained by one twin co-vary with the scores of the other, that is, the scores of one twin can be predicted with some confidence from the scores obtained by the other twin, then it is said that much of the variation in scores can be explained by this correlation. The goal of this approach is to interpret correlations in such a way that variation can be explained by genetic or different kinds of environmental factors.

For example, consider the relative similarity in the sets of scores obtained by samples of MZ twins and DZ twins, where each of these pairs of twins have been brought up in their own family. MZ twins have 100 percent of their genes in common, DZ twins 50 percent, on average. If we make the assumption that the environments of MZ twins are no more similar than the environments of DZ twins of the same sex (because environmental factors like child rearing practices, parental attitudes, education and income, are common to each member of the pair) then we could argue that because the MZ twins share 100 percent and the DZ twins 50 percent of their genes, the difference in average correlation between the two types of twins should reflect 50 percent of the variability due to genetic factors. Thus, doubling this difference would provide an estimate of the percentage of the variation in scores that was due to genetic factors.

Let us assume, for the sake of exposition, that the average correlation between the scores obtained by a sample of MZ twins on a personality test is 0.50 and the average correlation for a sample of DZ twins is 0.30. Then, according to our simple model, the difference between 0.50 and 0.30, that is, 0.20, provides an estimate of 50 percent of the variability due to genetic factors, and doubling this suggests that the proportion 0.40 (40 percent) of the variability in personality test scores is due to genetic factors, leaving 60 percent due to other factors, including environmental influences. This result would assign a significant role to genetic factors but it would also imply that the larger part of the differences in scores on this test was not due to genetic factors.

This is not to imply that any percentage of an *individual* child's personality is explained in terms of inheritance or environmental factors. The reference is to the population as a whole, and the correlations for any sample of children provide an estimate of the variation in that population that is due to innate or environmental influences. Within any population there will be individual differences and these may be caused by a number of factors, acting in combination. If the environment had a negligible influence on a particular characteristic then most of its variation would be due to non-environmental factors. If genetic factors were irrelevant to the trait then the observed variation would be due to environmental factors. Quite complicated combinations of environmental and genetic factors can be envisaged; for example, the environment might not have a constant effect on the population as a whole but affect only individuals with a particular genetic background. For example, phenylketonuria (PKU) is a metabolic disorder that is genetic in origin. Individuals who carry this gene are unable to cope with a naturally occurring food substance, phenylalanine, and this results in mental impairment which can be severe. If this food is not part of the person's diet they are unaffected, and indeed this disorder can be controlled by dietary means. An environmental factor, like diet, does not affect all individuals alike, and the effects of genes and environment cannot be explained by a simple additive model.

It is possible to extend this simple genetic model to consider different kinds of environmental influences. Researchers in this field have distinguished between *shared family variance* and *non-shared family variance*. The first term refers to variance that reflects the environment of siblings brought up in the same family, and the second term refers to environmental effects that are not due to a shared upbringing. Thus, a strong influence of shared environment would be inferred if there were similarities in personality between two unrelated children brought up together, for example, an adopted child and a natural child of the family. A positive correlation between their test scores would imply that variation was due to their shared environment. A strong influence of shared environment would also be inferred when child rearing practices varied from one family to another, so that children brought up in one family would resemble each other but would be quite different from children brought up in another one. Warmth or hostility within the family would be an example of shared family environment, as would differences between one-parent and two-parent families or differences between families in their socio-economic circumstances.

Several models have been developed to estimate the relative proportion of these influences upon personality. We take the following model from Plomin and Daniels (1987). It assumes that there are three discernible influences on personality – genetic (G), shared environment (SE), and non-shared environment (NSE) – and together these three are sufficient to explain the totality of the variation among people (100 percent or, expressed as a proportion, 1.0). It is assumed that personality can be decomposed into just these three factors. This can be expressed by the equation: $G + SE + NSE = 1.0$. It is further assumed that the correlation between MZ twins (rMZ) reflects only genetic and shared environment because they are brought up together and, thus, there is no non-shared variation. The correlation between DZ twins (rDZ) would reflect a shared environment and 50 percent of the genetic variation (following the reasoning we explained above concerning the genetic difference between MZ and DZ twins). Thus, by the rules of algebra, we can derive equations (see Table 2.3) to estimate G, SE, and NSE. Inserting into the equations the values from our example above, where $rMZ = 0.50$ and $rDZ = 0.30$, $G = 2 (0.50 – 0.30) = 0.40$, $NSE = 0.50$ [because $rMZ = 0.50$], and $SE = 0.10$.

Table 2.3 Estimating the proportion of genetic and shared and non-shared environmental influences upon personality

Equation number	Equation	Explanation of reasoning
1	$G + SE + NSE = 1.0$	
2	$rMZ = G + SE$	Correlation reflects no non-shared variation
3	$rDZ = (0.5) G + SE$	DZ twins share half their genes
4	$rMZ – rDZ =$ $(G + SE) – (0.5G + SE)$ $= 0.5G$	Substituting terms
5	$G = 2 (rMZ – rDZ)$	By cancellation of terms
6	$NSE = 1.0 – rMZ$	Because by equation [2] $rMZ = G + SE$ and by equation [1] $G + SE + NSE = 1.0$. Therefore $rMZ + NSE = 1.0$ and $NSE = 1.0 – rMZ$
7	$SE = 1.0 – G – NSE$	[8] gives an alternative equation
8	$SE = 2rDZ – rMZ$	Adding equations [5] and [6] gives $G + NSE = 2rMZ – 2rDZ + 1.0 – rMZ = 1.0 + rMZ – 2rDZ$ and because $SE = 1.0 – G – NSE$ [1] $SE = 1.0 – 1.0 – rMZ + 2rDZ$

Source: Based on information presented by Plomin and Daniels (1987).

We have a further source of information for estimating shared environment, as this is given by the correlation between unrelated children who
are reared together and who have, across the sample as a whole, no genetic
factors in common.

In this hypothetical example, 40 percent of variation is due to genetic
factors, 10 percent to shared environment, and 50 percent to non-shared
environment. A little school algebra seems to take us a long way, but how
representative are these values of actual data? In fact, they are very close
to the values that have been found across a number of different studies and
across a range of personality traits. Plomin and Daniels (1987) cite correlations of 0.51 and 0.21 for MZ and DZ twins, respectively, on extraversion
and 0.50 and 0.23 for neuroticism, statistics which suggest that heredity
accounts for 60 percent of variation in extraversion and 54 percent of
variation in neuroticism. The average values of correlations over different
traits have been found to be about 0.50 for MZ twins and 0.30 for DZ
twins, suggesting that 40 percent of variation is due to genetic factors, 50
percent due to non-shared environmental factors, and 10 percent due to
shared environmental factors.

There are several published reports of parental ratings of MZ and DZ
twins on measures of temperament. Buss and Plomin (1984: 122) present
average twin correlations from several studies of the EAS, where the
average age of twins was 61 months. The correlations between ratings for
emotionality were 0.63 for MZ twins and 0.12 for DZ twins; for activity
they were 0.62 and –0.13, and for sociability 0.53 and –0.03.

These findings were essentially replicated in a sample of twins aged 14
months participating in the MacArthur Longitudinal Twin Study (Emde
et al., 1992). This programme started in 1986 and is following a sample of
same-sex twin pairs in Colorado who have been assessed at different ages
between 14 and 36 months. Between 86 and 100 children took part in this
investigation. In addition to parental ratings on the Colorado Childhood
Temperament Inventory (CCTI) temperament measures, the children
were visited in their homes and also attended the researchers' laboratory,
and assessments were made of their inhibition and shyness. Inhibition was
assessed on the basis of measures of the amount of time spent close to
mother in the unfamiliar playroom and of how long it took the child to
leave the mother on entering the playroom, to approach the toys in the
room, to approach a stranger, and to approach an unusual object (a large
furry monster). Shyness was assessed on the basis of observations of the
child's reactions to the experimenters in the home visit and when coming
to the laboratory. Correlations and heritability estimates are presented in
Table 2.4. Emde *et al.* (1992) based their estimates of heritability upon
a mathematical model, including a version which was constrained to
produce heritability estimates between zero and 1.0. The assessments of
the children and the parental ratings on the CCTI all indicate a substantial

Table 2.4 Estimates of heritability of temperament from the MacArthur Longitudinal Twin Study

Temperament measure	MZ correlation	DZ correlation	Heritability estimate
Inhibition	0.57	0.26	0.62
Shyness	0.70	0.45	0.50
CCTI Emotionality	0.35	−0.02	0.74
CCTI Activity	0.50	−0.25	1.50
CCTI Attention	0.38	−0.04	0.84
CCTI Shyness	0.38	−0.03	0.82
CCTI Sociability	0.35	0.03	0.64

Source: Emde *et al.* (1992).

genetic factor, but, as was found by Buss and Plomin (1984), many of the DZ correlations based on parental ratings seem to be too low, and in the case of activity there is a substantial negative correlation.

One possibility is that these ratings are subject to bias. Parents may exaggerate the difference between their fraternal twins, seeing them as more different than they actually are. This interpretation is supported by the discrepancy between the significant twin correlations for observed shyness and inhibition and the zero correlation for the corresponding parental ratings of shyness. Different kinds of evidence are needed to resolve this issue but unfortunately it can be difficult to obtain this in studies of young infants. Buss and Plomin (1984) present evidence from studies of the correlations between parents' self-ratings on the EAS and their ratings of their children. They also summarise findings from the Colorado Adoption Project, which is an investigation of the similarities in temperament between adopted children and their biological and adopted parents and a matched group of children living at home with their natural parents. Taken together these studies provide little positive evidence of a genetic component in temperament although the evidence is somewhat stronger in the case of shyness.

Family resemblance

Whatever one's reservations about the validity of isolating genetic and non-genetic influences and assuming that these simply 'add up' to produce personality, there is no doubt that identical twins are much more alike in personality than are fraternal twins or siblings, and that siblings are not very much like each other at all. We shall see that the similarity between identical twins is confirmed in rather striking ways by studies of identical twins who have been separated and have lived most of their lives apart, but we concentrate at this point on the finding that shared family environment apparently has a negligible influence on personality development.

This conclusion is based on the application of mathematical models to twin data as we have described above. Studies which take this approach consistently report that shared environmental effects explain very little of the variation in personality. For example, Scarr (1993) reports statistics of the percentage of variation due to shared environment for the 'Big Five' traits as openness 6 percent, conscientiousness 5 percent, extraversion 2 percent, agreeableness 9 percent, neuroticism 7 percent. Other data support this conclusion. The average correlation in personality test scores between siblings is only around 0.15, with typical figures of 0.25 for extraversion and 0.07 for neuroticism (Dunn and McGuire, 1994). A similar picture emerges in adoption studies: the correlation between pairs of siblings where one of the pair has been adopted is of the order of 0.04 (Plomin and Daniels, 1987).

In one sense, of course, these findings are not at all surprising, as everyday experience shows us how different brothers and sisters can be. A little reflection tells us that these differences could have a genetic explanation. For example, how often do we hear it said that one child is 'the image' of his or her father or takes after his or her mother, or reminds someone of a grandparent? Children inherit an assortment of their genes from their parents, that is, they carry genes that make them different from their siblings as well as genes that make them similar, and there is no reason why an extraverted girl should have an extraverted brother. Nevertheless, it is predicted that if a trait has a genetic basis then, across a large sample of children, the correlation between siblings on a trait should be 0.50. As we have seen, the values of correlations for personality traits are substantially lower than this, indeed they are lower than the correlations found for measures of intelligence – for example, the average correlation in IQ for siblings is 0.54 (Scarr, 1993) and for adoptive siblings is 0.30 (Plomin and Daniels, 1987). These values are in contrast to the figures of 0.15 and 0.04 reported for personality traits.

These differences in correlation between intelligence and personality traits may be due to several factors. One possible source is the phenomenon of assortative mating, that is, the tendency for people to choose as their partner someone similar to themselves on a given trait. For example, people with higher than average IQ might choose a partner who also has higher than average IQ. This is not necessarily, of course, a conscious preference. IQ tends to be associated with differences in socio-economic factors, in educational experience, in educational qualifications, in the likelihood of entry into particular occupations, in attitudes and interests, and so on; all factors that might be thought to influence the choice of a partner, if only in the probabilistic sense of making it more or less likely that one will meet particular others – that one will see a stranger across one particular crowded room rather than across another crowded room. The phenomenon of assortative mating has implications for models of the kind we have outlined which assume that there is no correlation between parents on a given trait. In particular, it would have the effect of raising the correlation between DZ twins, which would obviously make the difference in average correlation between MZ and DZ twins smaller, and so apparently reduce the role of non-shared environment. Thus, one possible explanation of the greater role of shared environment in IQ than in personality traits might be that there are tendencies for parents to be similar in IQ but no equivalent tendencies for them to be similar in personality. It is an empirical question whether these trends are found in choice of partner, although researchers in behavioural genetics do tend to discount assortative mating as a significant factor (Plomin and Daniels, 1987: 3).

Perhaps the finding that shared environment is an important influence on IQ is less surprising because it is compatible with how we tend to think of the environment: we think in terms of social disadvantage, poverty, crowded accommodation, level of parental education, lack of stimulation in the home, and little interest in children's education. Or we think of the influence of dietary deficiencies, drug abuse, smoking during pregnancy, or the stresses experienced by mothers carrying or bringing up their children in adverse circumstances. These problems would tend to be shared by all the children in the family, and the differences between families would be very marked. The fact that shared environment is less important for personality is more puzzling, because many of the favoured explanations of personality also emphasise shared environmental influences: child rearing attitudes and practices, parental warmth or hostility, the quality of relationship between parents, security of attachment, separation of child from mother; all of these too might be thought to affect all of the children within a particular family.

If it is the case that children within the same family are very different from one another, this warns us against ready acceptance of findings from studies that have only looked at one child within a family. For example, a researcher might investigate the characteristics of parents which are associated with high or low self-esteem in the child, and might conclude that parental warmth and acceptance of the child are correlated with high self-esteem. But if only one child from each family is included in the sample, the study would miss those instances where parental warmth was associated with high self-esteem in one child but with low self-esteem in a brother or sister. The implication of behavioural genetic research is that variables like parental warmth might be less important than hitherto recognised. Of course, parents may well treat their children differently, depending on factors like the child's gender (undoubtedly parents do treat boys and girls very differently, although research often controls for this by testing same-sex siblings), birth-order, or the child's temperament. This last factor may turn out to be an important factor in personality development. Variations in temperament can influence responses by children to their parents and by parents to their children, and lead to different relationships between parents and children within the same family.

We can see here important divergence between IQ and personality. Except for cases of very low IQ or learning difficulties, or perhaps of very high IQ, the impact of IQ may be effectively felt only when the child begins to adjust to the demands of school and the parent begins to receive feedback about the child's progress. Here, the child takes on a new role outside the family, and the parent may begin to perceive the child in a fresh light. But the issues of personality feature early and are salient for every parent and child, and 'personality' is negotiated between parent and child and between one child and another. Children who are nervous, shy, boisterous, over-active, hard to settle or to comfort, demanding of attention, or unwilling to concentrate, affect their parents and siblings in different ways. Parents not only respond differentially to these differences, they will try to influence their children, to placate them, to cope with them, to learn which approach works and which doesn't. Thinking of the issue in this way, the notion of shared environment, that can be isolated from genetic endowment or affects all children equally, seems a very static way of construing personality.

Thus, parents might treat their children differently, in part, at least, in reaction to their children's characteristics. Children may be sensitive to these differences and this in turn may influence their personality development. Children also react to their siblings. A child who is the eldest in the family may have different experiences from a child who has an older brother or sister. Perhaps a child whose sibling is shy has different experiences from a child whose sibling is outgoing. The age gap between children might be a factor. Siblings might be close friends or rivals. A child might believe that his or her parents favour their sibling. Daniels and Plomin (1985) invited students to complete a questionnaire to compare their experience with that of a sibling in terms of their perceptions of their treatment by parents, such as parental affection and control, their relationships within and outside the family, their closeness, jealousy, relative popularity, and so on. The results showed that participants reported considerable differences between themselves and their siblings, and the differences were larger for items concerning interaction between siblings and with peer groups than for items reflecting perceptions of parental treatment. The study was able to compare the responses of biological siblings and adoptive siblings, and the differences here were small, suggesting that genetic factors did not play a significant role in explaining different experiences within the family.

A vivid account of differences among siblings is provided in the autobiography of the writer John Cowper Powys, who was the eldest of 11 children. Two of his brothers became highly regarded writers and most of the other children also had significant creative accomplishments. There is evidence in the autobiography of creative play among the children, for example in the construction and elaboration of imaginary worlds. John Cowper describes his invention at the age of 9 of the Volentia Army which he 'forced upon' his brothers and fellow pupils at his preparatory school (Powys, 1934/1967: 62), and he elaborated this into 'the mythology' of an imagined world (p. 64). This activity held no interest for his closest sibling, Littleton, but a younger brother, Theodore (also to become a writer), became involved in his brother's creation and eventually set up his own elaborate imaginary world, as, subsequently, did three much younger children.

In his own autobiography (Powys, 1937: 5), Littleton is explicit about these differences:

> when I read [my brother John Cowper's *Autobiography*] it gave me the greatest interest to see how completely different was the reaction to life of these two little boys, born of the same parents, within eighteen months of each other. The one, myself, unruffled and happy, taking the good things that came, and enjoying them to the full; the other, Johnny, as he was always called in those days, even then made restless by the workings of his powerful and strange imagination, and finding life most difficult.

John Cowper's personality and activities became part of the environment for the later born children, but these reacted differently to him according to their own personalities and interests. He formed different kinds of relationships with his younger siblings, being closer to some than to others, and being close in a different way to one child than to another. Furthermore, the nature of the relationship changes with age, so that, for example, it is several years before he comes to share interests with another brother who was 12 years younger and who was also to become a writer.

Differences between members of the same family, as reflected in the small correlations between the personality scores of fraternal twins, provide many challenges to research. Perhaps environmental factors interact with genetic endowment to reduce the impact of genes. Another possible explanation is that the effects of genes are not additive. When the genes of the mother combine with the genes of the father they may produce traits that cannot be predicted from the original sets of genes – the whole is different from the sum of the parts. This possibility has been explored by researchers involved in the Minnesota Study of Twins Reared Apart, a large-scale investigation of more than 50 pairs of MZ twins who have been separated and brought up in different families, often geographically remote from each other and with little contact since separation. The findings of this research have been dramatic and have attracted considerable attention from the media.

There are remarkable similarities in the lives of these twins (Lykken *et al.*, 1992). For example, one pair of separated male twins turned out to use the same brands of toothpaste, shaving lotion, hair tonic and cigarettes. After their first reunion meeting they sent presents which crossed in the post and which turned out to be identical. One pair of twins had each divorced women named Linda and then married women named Betty. They had both taken their annual holiday for several years on the same stretch of beach in Florida, driving there in the same model of car. Both had given their sons the same name. These similarities were not restricted to anecdotal evidence. There were also marked similarities in performance on psychological tests. EEG measures of brain wave activity showed a mean correlation across frequency bands of 0.80 between MZ twins reared apart. It was possible to isolate a measure of the alpha component that correlated only 0.13 between DZ twins, but 0.80 between MZ twins reared apart.

Scores on personality tests and inventories of interests and talents also showed high MZ correlations and negligible DZ correlations. Lykken *et al.* (1992) suggest that this pattern of results can be explained by assuming that traits might be emergent or configural properties of genes. Because MZ twins inherit the same set of genes they necessarily share these emergent properties. Each child inherits a different set of genes from each parent, and if these interact to produce emergent traits then siblings will have different traits from each other and it is unlikely that they will share these traits with their siblings. These traits will not run in families, but they will nevertheless be genetic in origin. Some traits do seem to be additive – height, for example, is predictable from a simple genetic model – whereas other traits, particularly in the realm of personality, are not so readily predictable.

Lykken and his associates argue that one advantage of the configural model is that it can deal with one of the most puzzling phenomena in the study of individual differences, namely how an outstanding individual can emerge from the most adverse circumstances. One of the earliest studies of individual differences, Francis Galton's *Hereditary Genius* (1869), recognised the significance of this issue and tried to assemble evidence to suggest that genius had an inherited basis. However, there are many documented cases of exceptional achievement by individuals who have no history of such achievement in their family and whose position in life is not conducive to it. James Joyce, who had a profound influence on twentieth-century literature, is a case in point. Born into a family with little education and forced throughout his childhood to move from one house to another because of increasing poverty, he nevertheless proved to be an outstanding student who demonstrated great self-confidence and independence of judgement in pursuing a literary career. There are, of course, many other examples that could be cited.

Exceptional achievements like these are the product of a constellation of traits, rather than one trait. It would also be misleading to imply that creativity is independent of social forces. For example, Simonton (1984) argues that creative development is shaped by factors that include the availability of role-models and exposure to an environment that nourishes divergent thinking, and he proposes that high achievement is influenced by interpersonal relationships within the artistic domain and its broader social context. These influences can be effective at an individual level or at an aggregate level, in terms of the prevailing *Zeitgeist* which can be defined in terms of the number of eminent artists active in a particular place at a given time.

In any human competition someone has to be best. Throughout the country, there are many boys who are very good at football and who have the ambition to be a professional footballer. Only a minority will realise this ambition, and it is often said that factors over and above ability, such as personality, motivation, even luck, contribute to this. It is difficult to predict who will have aptitude at sport and who will go on to have the highest achievements. Most boys will come from families with little record of achievement at football. There are well-known cases where brothers both have high achievements, for example the Charlton brothers in the England team which won the World Cup in 1966, but these are the exception rather than the rule.

Simonton (1984) reported on the low frequency of siblings in his biographical survey of the 772 most eminent artists in history. Only 83 artists (10.75 percent of the sample) had siblings sufficiently eminent to be represented in the sample and the artists of greatest eminence tended not to have siblings who themselves had an artistic reputation. Simonton (1987: 136) summarises the literature: 'Not all siblings from a distinguished family prove equally successful. Relatively few eminent personalities are only children, yet in an overwhelming majority of instances, one son or daughter stands out while their brothers and sisters remain in obscurity.'

At a more mundane level, it is not unusual to find a family where the parents have a firm commitment to high moral standards and their children follow their parents' example except, perhaps, for one child, whose attitudes and behaviour are strikingly different and who may be a source of shame to the family by truanting, being aggressive or breaking the law. Such cases can be inexplicable to the family and all who know them, as they do not seem compatible with common sense notions about how traits run in families or the role of environmental influence upon character.

PERSONALITY AND LIFE EVENTS

The study of life events

An alternative position is that specific life events have a crucial effect upon the development of personality and that any stability in personality is a consequence of the continuity of significant life experiences.

It seems intuitively likely that people can be changed by significant life events, by religious conversion, by 'near death' experiences, or by illness. The more routine stresses of daily life can also have their impact on personality. In one study, Andrews and Brown (1995) investigated the influence of life changes upon changes in self-esteem in a longitudinal study of a sample of women in London. Self-esteem was assessed on the basis of structured interviews where the women were encouraged to talk at length about their life. The interview material was rated by researchers for evidence of positive and negative self-acceptance (e.g. 'I would like to be someone else', 'I'm happy with myself as I am'), and for evaluation of personal attributes (attractiveness, intelligence), and role performance (mother, work role). This method has the advantage that the frequencies of positive self-statements and negative self-statements could be collected for each individual, rather than a single index of self-esteem. The study found that increases in self-esteem were associated with the women's reports of improvements in their own or their partner's work status and improvements in the quality of their relationships with partners and children. However, opportunities for such improvements did depend on more general life stresses: women who had more life difficulties at the time of the first interview were less likely to experience positive changes and hence less likely to have raised self-esteem – 'It is more difficult to be optimistic, when there is overwhelming environmental deprivation' (Andrews and Brown, 1995: 30).

Common sense suggests that the relationships between life events and personality can be complex. The same incident can produce different reactions in different people, and the expression 'the straw that breaks the camel's back' captures the feeling that people can cope with a series of major events until one, apparently minor event can be too much to cope with. What kinds of events do we have in mind? One answer to this question is to consider the kinds of events that have been included in research. A common approach develops a checklist of different kinds of life events to derive a total score of the number of different events experienced within a given time. This score is sometimes weighted according to estimates of the impact of events, and these can also be categorised as positive, negative or neutral in their impact.

This approach was adopted by Sandler and Block (1979). The range of events that comprised their checklist included family loss due to bereavement, divorce or separation; change in family circumstances, such as remarriage of parents, a parent taking or losing a job, or change in economic circumstances; changes in family relationships, such as increases in arguments, and illness of self or family member. The events assigned highest weight were death of a parent, divorce of a parent, marital separation of parents, and child acquiring a visual deformity (all classified as negative events). Children identified by their teachers as maladjusted had higher events score, weighted events score and undesirable events score than a matched control group. Parental ratings of problems of adjustment in the maladjusted group were significantly correlated with the total number of events experienced, the weighted total, and the total number of negative events. It should be noted that the correlations are in the range 0.20 to 0.38.

Brown and Harris (1989) are sceptical of these total events scores, weighted or unweighted, arguing that the significant factor is the *meaning* that events have for individuals. Their measure, the Life Events and Difficulties Scale, comprises an extended interview rather than a questionnaire, and the interviewees' responses are coded to produce an index of number of events of different kinds. Events were included in the interview schedule on the basis of their likelihood of arousing strong emotion in the individual. The interviewer has available a list of events that have been shown to be likely to arouse emotion. Brown and Harris (1989: 22) list the following groups:

1 Changes in a role for the subject, such as changing a job and losing or gaining an opposite-sex friend for the unmarried
2 Major changes in a role for close ties or household members, such as a husband's staying off work because of a strike
3 Major changes in subject's health, including hospital admissions and development of an illness expected to be serious
4 Major changes in health for close ties or family members
5 Residence changes or any marked change in amount of contact with close ties or household members
6 Forecasts of changes, such as being told about being rehoused
7 Fulfilments or disappointments of a valued goal, such as being offered a house to rent at a reasonable price
8 Other dramatic events involving either the subject (e.g. witnessing a serious accident or being stopped by the police while driving) or a close tie (e.g. learning of a brother's arrest).

Of course the intention is not simply to arrive at a checklist by alternative means and the interview allows the researcher to explore the meanings these events have for the individual by asking the respondent further questions about the context in which the event happened, what he or she thought about it at the time, and so on. The measure affords further dimensions for analysis. Short-term threats, like a sudden but brief illness, can be distinguished from long-term threats, like difficulties within a relationship. The degree of threat can be rated.

In a study of the relationship between the onset of depression and specific life events carried out in Camberwell in London, 25 out of 37 women (68 percent) who had an onset of depression during the period studied had experienced a severe event before onset; among the 382 women who did not have an onset of depression 115 (30 percent) experienced a severe event or had a major difficulty. This statistic can be adjusted for the frequency with which women in these social circumstances might be expected to encounter severe events, to estimate the likelihood that the depression was caused by the events. Following these calculations, it was found that the onset of depression among 49 percent of the women was associated with a precipitating event. Only events with marked or moderate long-term threat were associated with the onset of depression. A further significant dimension is that of loss.

In a second study, this time carried out in Islington, London, events categorised as loss of a person (for example, through bereavement or separation) and loss of a 'cherished idea' were both associated with the onset of depression. Loss of a cherished idea includes the experience of being disappointed by someone who was trusted, disappointment in oneself, or a threat to one's view of oneself. The two kinds of loss can be combined, for example one can learn of a partner's infidelity and then be left by the partner, or a close friend might die of Aids.

These studies are clearly important for understanding the onset of depression. From the point of view of this chapter they show that life events, where they are carefully assessed, are associated with psychological outcomes. They also show that an emphasis upon the meaning of events does not result in the influences of events being so personal or subjective that no generalisations can be made. Threatening and loss events do have an impact, even though what is threatening to one person might not be so to another.

Specific events do need to be understood within the context of more cumulative experiences like the effects of social disadvantage or of relationship difficulties within the family. These experiences influence the likelihood of specific incidents such as changing school, or a parent losing a job or leaving home to work, and the psychological impact of these events may be modified by these longlasting experiences. The meanings of events like the departure of a partner might be in confirming an individual's view of him- or herself, or confirming an impression that the negative experience is a recurrent one that he or she is powerless to change. Many of the associations found between indices of stressful life events and personality are only moderate (Dubow et al., 1991). This may be due to inadequacies of measurement, or a statistical artifact of the prevalence of stressful experiences in contemporary life. It might also be because, as

Rutter (1972: 63) wrote about divorce and separation, 'in some cases, the break-up of the home is no more than a minor episode in a long history of family discord and disruption'.

The case of separation experiences

The life event that has attracted most attention has been the separation of a child from his or her mother, particularly if the child is taken into care or placed in an institution. This matter has been the subject of intense public debate since the Second World War and is reflected in current widespread concerns about the family. The focus of these concerns has changed from the immediate post-war period. Women had been employed during the war in traditionally male occupations, and when the war was over, and large numbers of servicemen entered the employment market, there was a movement of women out of those occupations. The extensive state-funded day care provision that had been available during the war rapidly dwindled. These trends coincided with an intense public debate about whether the role of working women was compatible with traditional roles of housewife and mother. Bowlby's theory of maternal deprivation was published in the middle of this debate, and was seized upon by proponents of the argument that a woman's place was at home. It also seemed to address other aspects of the social uncertainties of the time. As Singer (1992: 89) puts it,

> Bowlby's report expressed a great anxiety for the social order in the community, which he felt was being threatened by criminality, anti-social behaviour and psychotic and neurotic personalities . . . Bowlby . . . thought that upbringing was both the cause of, and solution to, social instability at times when the phenomenon was highlighted.

There have been continuing pressures upon women to work, whether or not they have partners. These include the trend towards home ownership based on mortgages, with the consequent pressure for households to have two incomes, and the persistence of low incomes, notwithstanding the general affluence of contemporary society. Concerns are still expressed about the psychological impact upon children of mothers working outside the home, as their numbers continue to rise – over 40 percent of women who have children below school age are at work (29 percent in part-time work and 13 percent in full-time occupation), a figure that has risen from 14 percent in 1965. More generally, the male labour force has remained virtually static whereas the female working force has rapidly increased in absolute numbers and as a proportion of the total workforce.

In recent years, the fear of social chaos has found expression in concerns about single mothers. The numbers of single parents raising a family have risen markedly. Approximately one in five households with dependent children is headed by a single parent, and the 1991 Census showed that 17 percent of all children in Britain were in single-parent families. These statistics are a consequence of many factors, particularly the enormous increase in the frequency of divorce which has followed changes in the law related to divorce. The post-war period has seen parallel changes in social attitudes, where less social stigma is now attached to children born outside marriage. Another relevant trend is the scattering of the traditional extended family.

The changes in the nature of the family during this period have coincided with increases in crime rates, and the links postulated by Bowlby between criminal behaviour and the alleged 'breakdown' of family life have remained at the heart of public debates. An article in *The Guardian* asserted that 80 percent of the prison population were once children in care (8–9 June 1991). A police superintendent in Mansfield commented on eight boys who between them had allegedly been responsible for 500 crimes in under 200 days: 'They're from broken homes, so you could say that this is a cry for help, but some of them are just plain wicked' (quoted in *The Observer*, 29 October 1995).

Bowlby's initial study was of young offenders and described the high frequency in his sample of boys who came from broken homes and who had been taken into care. He proposed an explanation of the association between separation experiences and psychological problems that emphasised that a continuous and unbroken attachment between mother and infant was essential for healthy development. This account – maternal deprivation theory – drew upon theoretical concepts from psychoanalysis and from the study of animal behaviour and was also based upon his reading of research into the effects of short-term and long-term institutional care upon intellectual and emotional development.

Maternal deprivation theory has been heavily criticised by feminist writers who see it as offering an intellectual justification for confining women to traditional subservient roles. The theory also failed to stand up to close empirical scrutiny, and Rutter (1972) pointed out methodological flaws in many of the studies cited by Bowlby, and brought forward further evidence that suggested that the theory was inadequate. Rutter argued that evidence showed that adverse factors that were frequently associated with separation, particularly poor social relationships within the family, were much more significant than the separation *per se*. Research has shown that conflict between the parents is regularly associated with an increased prevalence of behaviour problems in school. The effects of this conflict can be direct, in that the parents provide a model of confrontation and aggression for the child, a model that influences the child's own approach to conflict resolution (Jenkins and Smith, 1991). The effects can also be indirect, by modifying the relationship between parents and child, for example producing greater parental rejection or negligence (Fauber *et al.*, 1990). Jenkins and Smith reported (p. 807) that 'As overt parental conflict increased in this study, children also experienced less parental care and monitoring, and higher levels of physical aggression directed towards them.' Finally, Rutter also disputed the theory's claim that the effects of early experience were irreversible: 'Even markedly adverse experiences in infancy carry few risks for later development if the subsequent rearing environment is a good one' (Rutter, 1989: 24).

Nevertheless, early adverse experiences involving difficulties in family relationships and separation can have longlasting effects, and the question to be asked is what factors make children more or less vulnerable to these experiences? This question can only be answered by longitudinal studies. Bowlby's retrospective identification of an association between separation and criminal behaviour provides only a partial picture, since there is no information about those young people who were separated in childhood but who failed to offend. Nor is there information about those young people who do have a propensity to offend but who have been brought up in an intact family. All Bowlby's juvenile thieves may have had broken homes, but do all broken homes produce thieves? Studies of the effects of institutional care need to follow the children over time after they have left the institution, to see if this experience was modified by subsequent life events; they also need to incorporate control groups: children who were not taken into care, but who were raised in circumstances similar to those of the children who had left the institution.

Tizard and her colleagues have undertaken such a study, following a group of children who had experienced institutional care during the first years of their lives, children who had been separated before the age of 4 months and cared for in residential nurseries (Tizard and Hodges, 1978; Hodges and Tizard, 1989). Although the standards of physical care were good, and certainly better than in the research reviewed by Bowlby, their experiences were similar to early studies in that they were cared for by a large number of the nursery staff rather than being looked after by one or two nurses. Between the ages of 2 and 7 years, some of the children left residential care, either to return to their family (15 children) or to be adopted (24 children). Twenty-five remained in the institution. By adding as a comparison group a sample of 30 children who had never been in care but whose families were similar in socio-economic circumstances to the institutional children, it was possible to trace the development of four groups: 'restored', 'adopted', 'institutional', and 'comparison'.

The children have been assessed at 2 years, 4 years 6 months, 8 years and 16 years. Institutional care had no seriously adverse effects on intellectual development in that IQ scores were comparable across all groups and were close to national test norms. Nevertheless, the adopted children had significantly higher IQ at 4 years 6 months than the children restored to their own family. This trend did not seem to reflect any selective placement of children with higher IQ, in that the groups had been comparable when they had been assessed at 2 years of age. Children who were adopted before the age of 4 years had higher IQ than those adopted after 4 years when IQ was assessed at both 8 and 16 years. There was no equivalent long-term effect of leaving the institution in the case of those children restored to their own home. Tizard's explanation was that these differences reflected the current home circumstances of these two groups of children; in particular, the families to which children were restored continued to experience many problems. Despite these differences, the range of IQs across the groups was within the normal range, so the serious adverse effects originally claimed by Bowlby are not evident in this study.

However, a less sanguine conclusion was drawn by Colton and Heath (1994) following a comparison between a sample of 49 children aged from 8 to 14 years, who had been in foster care for six years on average, with a sample of 58 children who had never been in care but were in families that were receiving support from social services. The performance of both groups on tests of educational attainment were comparable and both were below national norms; the attainments had not improved when the children were tested three years later. This was true even for those children fostered in settled, stable homes and in more favourable economic circumstances than the control group. Children who had been originally taken into care because they had been abused or neglected showed poorer attainments than children taken into care for other reasons, and this latter group performed at a level much closer to national norms.

This study did not have the information on early childhood available in the research conducted by Tizard, and we have no way of knowing that the expectation that this group should be performing at national levels is a realistic one, given that disadvantaged children, in general, have poorer educational achievement, and that children who enter care are, on average, seriously disadvantaged. For example, Bebbington and Miles (1989) found that the families of 66 percent of children taken into care were receiving Supplementary Benefit (compared with 15 percent in the general population). Forty-five percent were in a single-parent family with one adult (compared to 7 percent), 24 percent came from a family with four or more children (compared to 9 percent), and 28 percent suffered from overcrowding (compared with 7 percent). Nevertheless, the failure to make progress implies that the children have suffered from their earlier care experience. The worse performance of children who had been abused or neglected reinforces Rutter's argument that the reasons for separation are critical in influencing the child's future adjustment.

There do seem to be some lasting effects on social and emotional development. At 4 years 6 months, the three groups of institutional children tended to be either more emotionally detached, or more clinging and over-friendly, or more attention-seeking than the comparison group. At 8 years, mothers of the adopted and comparison children were more likely to say their children were more closely attached to them than were mothers of restored children and staff in the institution, and mothers of adopted children felt more attached to the children than mothers of restored children. Teachers' assessments confirmed that the restored group were the most vulnerable group in terms of behaviour in class, attention seeking, and relationships with other children. Indeed, there was a discrepancy between the assessments made by teachers and parents in that teachers identified more problems in all of the groups who had been in care in comparison with the control group (Tizard and Hodges, 1978). Colton and Heath (1994) also identified high levels of behaviour difficulties relative to national norms in both the ex-care group and the group experiencing problems but living at home.

The study followed the children into adolescence (Hodges and Tizard, 1989). By this time, the original design of the study could not be sustained. In addition to the problems faced by all longitudinal studies of keeping in contact with the participants and maintaining their cooperation – a particular problem when their early life experiences have been fraught with difficulties – the young people could no longer be allocated neatly to their original groups. Some of the children in institutional care became adopted, some of the adoption arrangements broke down, some restored children returned to the institution, or returned there and then went back to their family. The original comparison group was no longer adequate, largely because the family circumstances of the adopted group were now more favourable than those of the original group. At this age, the principal comparisons were between 23 adopted children and 11 restored children.

There remained some differences between these groups. Adopted children were more closely attached to their mother and were more likely to show affection, had fewer difficulties in their relationships with siblings, were more involved in family life, and had fewer arguments. There were also differences between these two groups of ex-institutional children taken together and their comparison groups. The over-friendliness and difficulties with friendships that had been evident at 8 years remained problems for ex-institutional children. In school, teachers rated them as more quarrelsome, more likely to bully others, and less popular than the comparison groups. They demonstrated more problem behaviours when rated by teachers on a behaviour problems checklist. The restored children had a higher total problems score and were more likely to be rated for antisocial behaviours; the adopted group evidenced fewer problems than the restored group, although more problems than their comparison group, and they were more likely to be rated as anxious and worried. The finding of much previous research, that antisocial behaviour is associated with early separation into care, is replicated in this study, with the important qualification that children who are separated and then adopted are no more likely than those who were never separated to evidence this behaviour.

Relationships within the family seemed to be more influenced by the differences in the *current* family conditions of the adopted and restored group than by the early life events. The close attachments reported by the adopted group are associated with more satisfactory relationships at home, although they do not inoculate the young person against difficulties in relationships outside the home. Although it was now some 12 years since they had left residential care, the young people, whether adopted or restored to their own home, still showed some long-term effects, particularly in their personal relationships outside the family and at school. Whether these difficulties persist into adulthood, or whether they become less apparent, perhaps because adolescence might present particular problems for young people who have had adverse experiences early in life, is a question that needs to be addressed by future research.

Evidence for long-term consequences of early care experience is provided by Cheung and Heath (1994), who analysed data from the National Child Development Study, a longitudinal survey of 17,000 children born in one week in 1958, to show that at the age of 23 years participants who had been in care as children had lower educational qualifications than those who had never been in care – 43 percent left school with no educational qualifications compared with 16 percent of the non-care sample. They were also likely to be in lower status occupations and to be at greater risk of unemployment.

The findings from Tizard's research imply that there is no inevitable connection between institutional care and later adjustment, and they also suggest some of the factors that might modify its influence upon development. How do people 'escape' from the influence of early adverse experience? This question has been addressed in longitudinal studies carried out by Quinton and Rutter (Rutter *et al.*, 1983; Quinton and Rutter, 1988). These were surveys of women who had been brought up in residential institutions for reasons to do with their parents' inability to cope with child rearing rather than because of any behaviour of their own. The main objective of the research was to examine the style of parenting of these women. One investigation traced a group of over 100 adults who had been studied when they had been children in residential care. This group had many problems compared with a group of women of similar age and social background who had not been in care. They were more likely to have psychiatric disorders, to have problems in their relationships with a partner, and to be a single parent. They were more likely to have serious difficulties in parenting, as assessed by interviews and evident in more objective indices; for instance, 18 percent of the sample had had a child in care or fostered, compared to zero percent among the comparison group. Overall, there was a tendency for the difficulties in one generation to be repeated in the next, but not all women followed this course. For example, women who had a spouse who was supportive and who had no problems of his own (such as psychiatric disorders, criminality, alcohol abuse, difficulties in forming relationships) were more likely to demonstrate good parenting than women who had no spouse or who had one who was non-supportive or 'deviant' in the sense of having his own problems. An effective partnership can offer many kinds of support, financial, practical and psychological. The effects can be cumulative: the availability of support can lead to a better relationship with the child – the parents are less stressed and tired and better able to cope with the demands of parenting – and this can result in a more settled and less difficult child, who makes fewer demands and produces less stress, and so on. Of course, there are factors that will make it more likely that a woman will enter a relationship with a deviant or non-supportive partner. For example, pressure to marry because of an early pregnancy or to escape from a violent or difficult home life increases the probability that she will enter an unsatisfactory relationship.

The links between the original breakdown in the women's own home life to their own parenting difficulties can be regarded as one particular route among a set of possible routes emanating from the experience of being in care. Other routes can lead to more satisfactory outcomes. Along these routes are 'turning points', and the direction that is taken at these points either increases or decreases the likelihood of a satisfactory end to the route. A woman returns from care to a home life that is harmonious or else to one filled with conflict; she can have successful or unsuccessful experiences at school; she can have a pregnancy at an early age or later; she can marry in haste or after careful consideration; she can have a supportive or deviant partner, and so on. There are probabilistic links between these turning points.

One route identified by Quinton and Rutter was where a positive school experience was significantly more likely to lead to more careful choice of marriage partner and to marriage through choice rather than because of pressure, and this, in turn, led to increased likelihood of marital support and good parenting. This trend can be contrasted with the experiences of girls who had also been in care but who had less successful school experience and who found the route to marital support and good parenting more difficult; however, the route was not closed off to them. Positive experience was defined in terms of examination success, a positive evaluation of school work and relationships and a positive attitude to various aspects of school life. Negative experience was defined in terms of persistent truancy, lack of a peer group in school, or unhappiness with schoolwork or with relationships there. Negative experiences were more prevalent among the ex-care group than among the comparison group. Positive school experiences in themselves were not sufficient to compensate for disadvantage, as many women with positive experiences went on to have poor outcomes, and this was much more likely to be the case in the ex-care sample than in the comparison group.

Nevertheless, school experience can contribute to breaking the chain that links poor parenting across generations. A school fulfils many functions in society and makes various contributions to the lives of its students. This research reminds us that school can provide opportunities for a child from a disadvantaged background to change the direction of his or her life. It can provide a source of stability in an otherwise unstable environment. It can provide skills and instil self-confidence that will prepare students for entry into fulfilling employment. All the more reason for the school to be sensitive to the needs of its students, including those who sometimes cause it the most problems, and to avoid the labelling and low expectations that can only serve to send those students along one of the more probable routes available to them, to the cost of the individuals involved and of society.

Bowlby revised his original position in response to criticisms and in order to accommodate new evidence, particularly the important research carried out by Ainsworth into patterns of attachment behaviour. Maternal deprivation theory was superseded by attachment theory (Bowlby, 1988). This placed less emphasis upon the necessity for continuous interaction between mother and infant but it maintained the importance of the establishment of emotional bonds between infant and care-giver. Observations of how a child reacted to the Ainsworth Strange Situation Test – which involves a child and mother being together in a room, the entry of a stranger into the room, and the departure and subsequent return of the mother – suggested that children could be classified as one of three types on the basis of their reactions to the situation. The 'securely attached' child plays confidently in the new situation, without necessarily staying close to the mother, and reacts positively to the stranger. The child shows signs of distress at separation and immediately seeks proximity to the mother on her return. The child quickly becomes calm and resumes play. The 'avoidant' child pays little attention to the mother in the first phase of the test and is little distressed by her departure, being easily comforted by the stranger. When the mother returns to the room, the child either ignores her or makes, at most, a tentative approach. The 'resistant' child is fussy and wary while the mother is still present and is reluctant to move away from her to explore the room. Upon her return to the room the child seems ambivalent, seeking but at the same time resisting contact with her, and finds it difficult to resume play. The classification seems to be a reliable measure, and a considerable body of research suggests that these three patterns of attachment are related to more enduring properties of the parent–child relationship. In particular, there is an association between secure attachment and parental sensitivity and acceptance.

The mother or mother-figure and her style of parenting was still assigned a crucial role in the child's development. The theory paid less attention to the mother's presence and more to the quality of the relationship, but she is still regarded as responsible for this, to a considerable extent, as the security of attachment is a reflection of the sensitivity and responsiveness she shows to the child. Research into the effects of day care has also reflected this shift in attention, from emphasising the effects of separation to emphasising the nature of the relationship, and the question whether separation has adverse effects upon the child has been displaced by the attempt to identify the characteristics of high-quality care, based on the assumption that the quality of provision was the important factor for development (Singer, 1992).

In attachment theory, the notions of fixed phases of development and of irreversibility were replaced by the concept of the 'developmental pathway'. A pattern of attachment tends to persist and to become self-perpetuating. It becomes internalised, so that while it begins as a property of the relationship between parent and child it becomes a property of the child him- or herself. The child constructs 'working models' of relationships based on his or her own experience and these operate as templates for interpreting subsequent relationships. There has always been a tension in Bowlby's thought between assigning importance to actual events, such as separation, and to the meaning that the child places upon those events. The ethological observations about critical periods for the establishment of bonds between mother and infant, which suggested to Bowlby a model for human bonding, emphasise the former; whereas psychoanalytic theory, in which he was trained, regards the latter as crucial. Bowlby's concept of working models has moved away from assigning significance to the event of separation itself as the determinant of subsequent life events towards regarding the child's interpretation of experience as a vital mediating factor.

Attachment theory still places an onus on the mother-figure, but it now also assigns a role to attributes of the child and reintroduces the notion of personality as having an influence upon events as well as being influenced by them. The concept of developmental pathway has been extended to include the child's temperament as a factor. For example, Rubin (1993) has proposed a developmental pathway from inhibition to later problems of adjustment. Inhibited children find it difficult to deal with novel situations and their parents, in turn, find the child difficult to soothe and placate. Parents might respond to their child with insensitivity or hostility or by attempting to control the child's behaviour, and the pattern of insecure attachment relationship that is set up may become internalised by the child to form his or her 'internal working model' that will contribute to later unsatisfactory relationships with peers and at school. 'Thus, one can predict a developmental sequence in which an inhibited, fearful, insecure child withdraws from the social world of peers, fails to develop those skills derived from peer interaction and, because of this, becomes increasingly anxious and isolated from the peer group' (p. 297). However, the path from inhibited infant to anxious, withdrawn child is not the only one. A relationship with parents that is more secure can lead the child along a different path to a more satisfactory social life.

An additional mediating factor is the support that other people can offer during times of stress. Tizard's study showed that adopted children had closer attachments to their parents than did the restored children, and they generally fared better on measures of adjustment. Quinton and Rutter's study identified the crucial role of the supportive spouse. Dubow *et al.* (1991: 587) defined social support as 'information indicating to the individual that he or she is valued and esteemed by others'. This information could be provided by parents, teachers and peers. A measure of the child's appraisal of social support predicted children's academic achievement two years later, and increases in social support over the two-year period were associated with improvements in achievement and reduction in behaviour problems.

CONCLUSION

Although much more evidence is needed to sustain the thesis that personality might be due to non-additive combinations of genes, it is clear that research is leading us away from ideas that genes determine behaviour in any straightforward way. Many psychologists now believe that genetic factors combine with the environment to produce personality; we have mentioned these interactions at different points in this chapter, and it might be useful to summarise here some of the different ways in which they can take place. First, genetic and environmental influences may be correlated. If we assume that intelligence is at least partly due to genetic factors then the children of intelligent parents inherit that intelligence and are also brought up in an environment that has been shaped by intelligent parents. Conversely, the offspring of parents with low intelligence inherit those genes and may be brought up in an environment that fails to provide the kind of stimulation that would develop their intelligence. If it were the case that shyness was inherited then children might not only inherit the genes for shyness but also might have few opportunities for social interaction because of the less sociable life style preferred by their shy parents.

Second, a particular environment might offer advantages to children with certain temperaments rather than others. For example, the experience of school as it tends to be organised may be more difficult for more restless children or for those with less aptitude for the activities that are favoured there. Or some children might be more robust than others in the face of adversity, like illness, bereavement, divorce, or even poor teaching. Third, children born with a particular temperament might tend to evoke particular reactions from their care-givers, their siblings, and all those who know them, and these reactions will influence their subsequent development. A child who is aggressive will be more likely to evoke hostile responses from others. A child who is good at school tasks will be more frequently praised. Finally, a child's temperament might lead him or her to seek out particular kinds of experiences, a tendency that might become more evident as the child becomes older and has more opportunity to make these choices.

These relationships can be illustrated by the case of gender. A child's sex is inherited, and children are born into a society that has different niches, roles and expectations for men and women. Parents respond differentially to boy and girl babies. Teachers have different expectations for them. Other children are quick to seize upon behaviour that in their eyes is not gender-appropriate. A child whose preferences challenge society's expectations will have a more difficult time than the child who complies with them. More fundamentally, children internalise these expectations and come to evaluate their own behaviour in terms that they believe to be 'natural'.

Life events can contribute to the development of personality, but in a complex way and in interaction with characteristics of the child and his or her relationships with others. There seem to be factors within the child that can make him or her more vulnerable to stressful life events. There can be factors within the environment that protect the child by offering support at times of stress. Simplistic cause and effect explanations have been replaced by notions of developmental pathways and chains of contingencies in development. This research also offers an explanation for the low correlations between measures of temperament in infancy and later personality that have often been reported. Temperament, attachment relationships, and life events interact in the development of personality.

A recurrent issue has been the role of the family in the development of personality. Being removed from the family into the care of strangers at an early age does have long-term consequences although, as we have seen, its effects can be modified. Divorce, too, is associated with elevated rates of behaviour problems. The problems that children experience, and cause, at school are often associated with more general difficulties that the child has with relationships and, as we see in our chapter on aggression, these difficulties can persist into adulthood. The nature of the family has changed and will continue to change, and this has many implications for society. The message from psychological research is that secure relationships between the parents and between parents and children serve to support children in periods of stress, and the impact of separation owes more to family discord and conflict than to separation in itself. The school can have a benign influence which may only become apparent when a child is under stress and lacks other sources of social support (Rutter, 1991: 8). These findings have many implications for the school and for society and will surely attract further research in the coming years.

Part II

Five personality traits

Chapter 3

Aggressiveness

Aggression is a generic term for a range of phenomena. Although it is usually associated with acts of physical violence, it should not be identified with these acts. What people say, or even what they don't say, or how they look at someone, can all be construed as aggressive acts in particular situations, and the matter of intent must also be considered. The distinction between aggression and violence, on the one hand, and offending on the other, must be maintained. Decisions about what constitutes offences are political and legal ones, and an Act of Parliament can change the legal status of any behaviour. This is an important point because many studies of aggression draw upon statistics about rates of offending. These statistics can give only an approximate guide to the determinants of aggressive behaviour, partly because many acts of aggression are never reported to, dealt with, or recorded by the legal system, and partly because the rates of offending within the population can be so very high, among certain age groups; if minor and unrecorded offences are included, up to 100 percent of adolescents have committed some offence! (Farrington, 1987).

Baron (1977: 7) defines aggression as 'any form of behavior directed toward the goal of harming or injuring another living being who is motivated to avoid such treatment'. This definition is prepared to admit any kind of behaviour provided it meets the conditions about the motivation of the perpetrator and the recipient. Even a definition as broad as this runs into problems. Does behaviour include states of mind, such as hostility or hatred? Is it aggression if there is intent to cause harm but the victim is willing to be harmed? Can aggression be directed against the self? These problems of definition are not confined to psychologists. The legal and educational systems have to make decisions about behaviour, and to take the individual's intentions and the consequences of his or her actions into account when doing so.

Aggression and conduct disorders

Much discussion of aggression within education has been in the context of maladjustment and conduct disorders. Classification of adjustment problems distinguishes, as we have seen, between two broad classes. One distinction is between intra-punitive or internalised behaviours and extra-punitive or externalised behaviours, the terminology reflecting the psychodynamic assertion that there are different ways of dealing with psychological conflict. Feelings of hostility can be directed towards the self or towards other people, and it is the latter group who are defined as having conduct disorders. Their behaviour can include fighting, bullying, disobedience, telling lies and stealing, and even more serious offences like arson and causing severe physical injury to others. The American Psychiatric Association's *Diagnostic and Statistical Manual* (1987) locates conduct disorders alongside two other disruptive behaviour disorders: oppositional defiant disorder and attention deficit hyperactivity disorder. We discuss the relationships among these in a later section.

Conduct disorders are typically first identified in the school and several teacher checklists have been developed to help assess the incidence and severity of problems; for example, the Bristol Social Adjustment Guides and the Rutter Child Behaviour Scale are most commonly used in Britain. Teachers respond to a number of items describing behaviours by indicating how frequently these are displayed by a particular individual. On the basis of population norms, cut-off scores can be set to indicate that there is a potential problem worthy of more thorough clinical investigation. Administration of these checklists to large samples of school children invariably show that there are gender, age and socio-economic differences in the incidence of behaviour problems. We consider the issues of gender and age in greater detail below.

The higher representation of pupils from less advantaged socio-economic groups presents difficulties for explanations in terms of personality factors, unless it is believed that personality is distributed unevenly across different social groups. Some argue that individual differences in intelligence are implicated in these trends, since IQ scores are also associated with socio-economic status, and suggest that impulsiveness, a low threshold for frustration, or reliance on physical aggression rather than on negotiation, are all symptomatic of lower intelligence. Of course, plausible alternative explanations are available. One is that there is a bias in teacher reports since, it is argued, teachers are mostly 'middle-class', at least by education and occupation if not by background, and therefore have different values and hold contrary perspectives on aggression to their 'working-class' pupils. A related point is that schools themselves are dominated by middle-class values of preference for negotiation to solve disputes whereas the communities where the more difficult pupils live place greater emphasis upon more direct methods of conflict resolution.

However, there seems no doubt that a small number of individuals account for a high proportion of serious aggressive incidents and present problems to schools and to society in general. Many longitudinal studies have shown that children can be difficult at an early age and their behaviour remains problematic throughout their school career; we summarise below an example of this research. Accordingly, the focus in the first part of this chapter is on explanations of individual differences in aggressive personality. We then turn to the question of bullying where aggression seems to be endemic to schools rather than the property of individual pupils.

THE AGGRESSIVE INDIVIDUAL

Given the range of behaviours that are covered by the term aggression, it is hardly surprising that there have been many psychological theories taking different perspectives. Some theories propose biological explanations and others emphasise socialisation practices. Some psychologists regard aggression as a learned class of behaviours that is evoked by particular conditions whereas other psychologists regard it as a trait that predicts how individuals behave across a range of different situations.

Biological accounts draw upon evidence from different species as well as from human research. They argue that fighting is universal across species and that it serves many functions, including killing for food, fighting off predators, taking and defending a territory, establishing patterns of dominance, winning the right to mate, controlling access to the mate, and protecting the young. Of course, they will admit, there are differences among species in fighting; non-human species don't kill members of their own species or invade the territories of other animals in quite the same way as our own species does, and their behaviour is not influenced by aggression-inducing drugs like alcohol. Nevertheless, it is argued, the similarities are too striking to ignore when trying to understand human aggression.

The issue of gender

Within the human species, biological arguments point to the marked gender difference in aggression and to the evidence of heritability of an aggressiveness trait. We now turn to consider this evidence.

Gender differences in aggressive behaviour are so well established that many important studies of antisocial behaviour (Farrington, 1991) and bullying (Olweus, 1978) concentrate only on boys. Men are much more likely than women to be convicted for violent crimes, a trend that is found across different cultures and in the history of our own society (Heidensohn, 1996). Women are responsible for less than 10 percent of convictions for violence against the person and sex offences in Britain (Home Office, 1994). A survey of crime in 31 countries established that men accounted for 87 percent of all arrests and 90 percent of arrests for homicide (Simon and Baxter, 1989; cited by Turner, 1994: 233). Men are the perpetrators of violent crimes in general, most domestic violence and acts of violence in public places. The sex difference in violent crime is maintained throughout the life span, in contrast to the trends in general crime, where the magnitude of the sex difference is large at age 10 years, increases to a peak at around 18 years, and then declines at a steady rate throughout adult life (Farrington, 1986).

There are also gender differences in questionnaire measures of aggression (Hyde, 1984). Surveys of the incidence of conduct disorders also show gender differences. Chazan *et al.* (1994) review several large-scale surveys of British pupils that show the incidence of 'emotional and behavioural difficulties' among boys is about twice as high as among girls and that the largest gender difference is in antisocial behaviour. These studies tend to rely upon teachers' nominations and hence may reflect to some extent beliefs about gender differences; alternatively, aggressive behaviour may take different forms in boys and girls and the male form is less acceptable; or perhaps the same kind of aggressive behaviour is less acceptable or more worrying to teachers when it is practised by boys. Whatever the reason, the trends are highly consistent from study to study.

Biological explanations

One explanation for these consistent sex differences is in terms of the hormone testosterone. The 'sex hormones' – testosterone, estrogen and progesterone – are all produced by the man's testes and the woman's ovaries. They function in the pre-natal period to produce sexual differentiation, and they function in puberty to produce the physical differences between men and women and to introduce hormonal changes in women related to the regulation of the reproduction system. There is a surge in the level of testosterone among males at puberty, and then levels decline progressively with age. Anabolic steroids that are taken, illegally, by adults to increase their sporting prowess raise the levels of testosterone in the body, encourage the synthesis of protein to make muscles stronger and quicker to recover from stress, and increase energy levels. These observations suggest that testosterone may be a factor in the greater aggression showed by males, particularly in adolescence.

Evidence comes from different kinds of studies, from animal research and studies of individual differences in testosterone levels among men (and women). Experiments with animals have shown that an increase in testosterone levels is correlated with the incidence of aggressive behaviour during the mating season. Castration reduces aggression and injections of testosterone administered to castrated animals increase aggression. However, these effects are not found among all species (Turner, 1994). The fact that males are more aggressive than females also requires qualification. In some species, for example, gerbils and hamsters, females are just as aggressive as males, and females across a range of species are aggressive when they are suckling their young. Aggression among animals is often seasonal and is linked to breeding patterns and to needs for territory, and hence presents a complex picture of the relationship between hormones and behaviour.

There is evidence among humans that high levels of testosterone are associated with aggressive behaviour. Olweus *et al.* (1987) applied the statistical technique of causal path analysis to examine correlations between testosterone levels (estimated from blood samples) and scores on aggression questionnaires. The data were collected from a large sample of adolescents on two separate occasions, when they were, on average, 13 and 16 years of age. The study also looked at the influence upon aggression of child rearing techniques and parental attitudes, as assessed by interviews with parents when the subjects were aged 13. Testosterone levels were correlated significantly with aggression scores ($r = 0.44$) and the highest correlations were with questionnaire items that referred to aggression as a response to provocation, rather than items referring to fighting in general or unprovoked aggression. The causal path analysis showed that testosterone had a direct causal effect on aggression as a response to provocation, and the strength of the relationship was not reduced when the child rearing measures were taken into account. The picture was rather different when predicting unprovoked aggression, for example when questionnaire items refer to the initiation of fights. Here, there was an indirect influence of high levels of testosterone on unprovoked aggression. Higher levels of testosterone produced a tendency towards increased irritability and lower tolerance of frustration and these, in turn, were associated with more aggression.

The relationship between testosterone levels after puberty and measures of aggression has been extensively replicated in research. Archer (1991) has reviewed a large number of studies that draw upon different kinds of evidence, including comparisons between groups who are high and low in aggressiveness, for example measuring the testosterone levels of convicted violent offenders, and comparing these with the levels among those convicted for non-violent crimes. The trend is for studies to show significantly higher levels among the violent offenders, with correlations ranging from 0.24 to 0.64 and a median coefficient of 0.56. Studies in the non-prison population show lower but still positive correlations between measures of testosterone levels and scores on personality questionnaires assessing aggression and hostility. Some studies report correlations that are rather higher but, as Archer concludes (p. 13), 'It is ... difficult to obtain an overall picture since the studies vary widely, not only in the measures of testosterone used but also in the type and age of the subjects, whether they were selected or unselected, the sample size, and in measures of aggressiveness.' Adopting a different approach, other studies have measured testosterone levels before, during and after sports competitions but, again, the findings can be difficult to interpret, since testosterone levels can be affected *by* competition, raising the question whether high levels are a consequence rather than a cause of aggression.

Some recent psycho-physiological research has sought a clue to aggressive behaviour in brain chemistry, looking in particular at the neuro-transmitters, the chemical substances that carry electrical stimulation across the synapses between nerve cells. There are three important monoamine neurotransmitters – dopamine, norepinephrine and epinephrine – that excite the generation of action potential in nerve cells, and one neuro-transmitter, serotonin, that acts to inhibit excitation of the neurons. Several studies have shown that low levels of serotonin are found among violent offenders. For example, Virkkunen (1991) summarised a longitudinal study over three years of 58 men who had been released from prison after serving sentences for serious crimes, including homicide and arson. Thirteen of the men were subsequently convicted for further crimes, all committed under the influence of alcohol. It was possible to predict those individuals who reoffended on the basis of monoamine measurements, specifically low levels of a metabolite of serotonin, 5-hydroxyindoleacetic acid (5-HIAA) in cerebrospinal fluid. Virkkunen and Linnoila (1993) reported that low levels of 5-HIAA were associated with impulsive aggression and early onset of alcoholism and antisocial personality disorder. The evidence suggests that low levels of serotonin are associated with impulsive acts of aggression, particularly under the influence of alcohol, rather than premeditated violence, for example in conjunction with other crimes or terrorist activities.

Brunner *et al.* (1993) have traced a genetic link between monoamine metabolism and aggression. They studied a family where one of the members had kept records about the prevalence of mental retardation across several generations, and where the researchers themselves assessed 24 individuals. Some male members of the family showed a pattern of behaviour that involved borderline mental retardation, evidenced by low IQ, lack of school success, and failure to gain and keep employment, and also violent behaviour, including rape and attempted rape, indecent assault, causing grievous bodily harm, and arson. Often aggressive behaviour was an angry outburst that was disproportionate to its cause and that produced episodes of violent behaviour lasting up to three days. Pedigree studies suggested that this was a disorder linked to the X chromosome. Females, including obligate carriers of the relevant genes, were unaffected.

Chemical analyses of urine samples of seven family members showed abnormalities in monoamine metabolism including reduced levels of monoamine oxidase A (MAOA) that is known to metabolise dopamine, noradrenaline and serotonin. Analysis of DNA from blood samples of 24 family members identified a genetic locus for the disorder on a gene at a location on the X chromosome, Xp11, that has been shown by other, independent research to be linked with abnormal MAOA activity.

These careful studies have suggested a neuro-chemical basis for at least some kinds of recurrent aggressive behaviour in at least some males, usually behaviour that is impulsive and apparently out of control. Ellis (1991) has argued that these differences are not restricted to individuals with specific disorders, but that within the general population, average levels of serotonin are significantly higher among females than among males. It is tempting to conclude that the greater impulsiveness of males may have its origins in the chemical balance of the human brain, although not all research finds a straightforward relationship between serotonin and aggression. For example, Castellanos *et al.* (1994) found *positive* correlations between these variables in a study of boys aged from 6 to 12 years, diagnosed for attention-deficit hyperactivity disorder.

Socialisation

Despite the indications of this line of research, there are competing explanations of gender differences that emphasise the influence of socialisation. Society holds different expectations of boys and girls and research has shown that the same behaviour is reinforced differently when performed by boys than when it is performed by girls; behaviour that might be labelled as aggressive may be more tolerated among boys than among girls. The peer groups that boys move among behave in different ways from the groups that girls inhabit and, for much of childhood, there is little mixing between the gender groups. Observations of activities in the playground reveal very clearly the different worlds of boys and girls. These patterns of behaviour do not arise *de novo* in each generation. Games, activities, 'dares', nicknames, and so on, are passed on across the generations. Adult men and women have different interests and roles to play, and these form the context for the child's development as, of course, do depictions of men and women in the media.

Several theorists have argued that acts of aggression are behaviours that are learnt like most other human behaviours, and Bandura (1973) has presented an influential account of the processes involved in terms of social learning theory. Children engage in aggressive or disruptive behaviour because it is reinforced, that is, it is under the control of particular environmental influences. The behaviours are learnt by direct processes where an action is instigated and then followed by some reinforcing event, or by indirect processes, where the individual observes the actions and their reinforcing consequences as they apply to other people, who serve as 'models' for the individual. Models can be provided by the family, the community, and the general culture.

One of the classic studies of social learning theory was the well-known 'Bobo doll' study (Bandura, 1973). Children who had observed an adult playing in an aggressive way with the large doll were more likely to show aggression towards the doll when they had an opportunity to play with it than children who had not observed the adult's behaviour. Children who watched the adult behave in a non-aggressive way towards the doll were less likely than the control group to behave aggressively themselves. There are many implications from these results.

Children can learn through observation, in that their own aggressive behaviour copies aspects of an adult's. Their already learned aggressive responses can be either facilitated or inhibited by the behaviour of the person they are watching. These results also imply that an act need not be directly reinforced for it to be repeated. A child might learn to be aggressive because he or she sees someone else behaving like that and apparently enjoying it or reaping some benefit, like increased power or respect. The teacher has to be aware that his or her behaviour towards the difficult pupil – for example, turning a blind eye or being inconsistent in response – may be serving as a model for other children, showing the kind of response that others might expect from the teacher.

This emphasis upon observational learning offers explanations of the correlation between socio-economic status and conduct disorders, and of the relationship between depictions of violence in the media and the incidence of aggression. There is evidence that people are more likely to be aggressive after watching a screen depiction of aggression and that this effect can be modified if another person who is present provides a commentary upon the action and places it in a moral context. The wider implications of this research for the media and their treatment of factual and fictional violence, and the issue of the balance between freedom of expression, on the one side, and public distaste for depictions of violence, on the other side, are highly controversial. Technological advances in cable, satellite and digital communications will make these issues even more pressing as there will be a proliferation of channels and programmes, more international broadcasting, greater competition for audiences, and less control over broadcasting standards.

These trends will also have an influence upon the relationships between teachers and pupils, as they will inevitably shape the cultural context of the school. The technology also has an enormous positive potential for education, although there are, as yet, few signs of the investment that would be needed to harness it for these ends. Psychologists have not been in a position to offer clear advice about the association between media and actual violence as there is no consensus in their interpretations of the empirical evidence, indeed, in many cases, there is fundamental disagreement about this.

Gender differences are also susceptible to the influence of socialisation. For example, there are regular claims that rates of violent offences are rising among women. Home Office statistics show that the number of women charged with violent offences increased by 70 percent over the past 10 years although the statistics for the numbers of men charged with similar offences remained stable over the same period (*The Observer*, 24 September 1995). A national attitude survey cited in the same article (Wilkinson and Mulgan, 1995) showed a substantial increase over the same period in the numbers of women prepared to endorse the view that they would be prepared to use violence to get something they wanted. These differences in attitudes presumably reflect cultural changes rather than biological factors.

However, these are small trends in the context of the magnitude of the gender differences in aggression that are universally found. The numbers of women involved in violent crime are very small and an increase of 70 percent may give a misleading impression of the magnitude of change. Small numbers are also more subject to fluctuation, influenced by changes in reporting or in police responses to crime (Heidensohn, 1996: 5).

Aggressive 'careers'

Heritability

A second strand of evidence on biological factors in aggression concerns the inheritance of aggressive tendencies. Rutter *et al.* (1990 a,b) reviewed the evidence for the heritability of criminal and antisocial behaviour. Studies of adults and children should be treated separately for clarity. Among adults, the concordance rates for criminality, that is, the frequency with which a pair of relatives both show evidence of criminal behaviour, range between 26 and 51 percent for MZ twins and between 13 and 22 percent for DZ twins. There is also a degree of concordance between the antisocial personality and criminal behaviour of parents and their children even when the children have been adopted into different families. This correlation is, however, stronger for recidivist petty crime than for violent offences. As Rutter *et al.* (1990b: 42) summarise their findings, 'having a criminal parent is a major risk factor for juvenile delinquency'.

Rushton *et al.* (1986) examined the scores of a large sample of 573 pairs of twins on a questionnaire measure of aggression. The ages of the twins ranged from 19 to over 60, with a mean age of 30. Aggression scores reflected endorsement of statements like 'Some people think I have a violent temper', and disagreement with statements like 'I try not to give people a hard time'. The correlation between the aggression scores of MZ twins was 0.40 and between DZ twins 0.04. This provides an estimate using the model we outlined in Chapter 2 of 72 percent due to genetic factors and 60 percent due to shared environmental factors. That these add up to more than 100 percent is a common problem with the application of this model when the DZ correlation is so low, as seems usually to be the case for personality measures. An alternative mathematical model provided estimates of 39 percent genetic factors, zero percent shared environment and 61 percent non-shared environment. These values are comparable to those generally found for personality factors which, as we have seen, imply strong contributions of genetic and non-shared environmental factors and a minimal role for shared environmental factors.

Concordance rates in data collected from children present a rather different picture, and the role of shared environment seems stronger, with a high concordance rate among DZ twins (Rutter *et al.*, 1990b: 42). It should be remembered that the majority of juvenile crime does not persist into adult life, and that the incidence of criminal behaviour reaches its peak about the age of 16, with a steady decline thereafter. It is not contradictory to find that the environment has a large effect upon this behaviour before the age of 16 and a minimal effect after that age. The behaviour of young people is influenced by their peers and the opportunities that are afforded by the environment that they experience. This environment is also shaped by their age group. This environment changes with entry into adulthood, and those who persist in the behavior are distinctive in some way from those whose behaviour reflects the norms and values of the adult world. Drug taking provides one example. Rave parties and similar kinds of events expose young people to drugs like Ecstasy and provide social incentives to try the drug. Its use might be so widespread among certain groups of young people that it would be difficult to identify any factors that would reliably predict who would use the drug and who wouldn't. However, this environment is the province of a particular age group, and as people grow out of that age group they no longer fit into it. The minority of people who persist in drug use or move from one drug to another might have distinctive psychological characteristics that can be more clearly identified. The persistence of antisocial behaviour among young people can only be established by longitudinal studies, and it is to these that we now turn.

Longitudinal studies

We illustrate such research by considering the Cambridge Study in Delinquent Development (see Farrington, 1991). This was a prospective study of 411 males, beginning with a sample of all the boys who were pupils at six state primary schools in a working-class district of London. These children were interviewed and tested in school when they were 8, 10 and

14, and interviews were also held with parents and teachers. When they had left school they were interviewed when they were 16, 18, 21, 25 and 32. At the ages of 10, 14, 18 and 32, separate scales for assessing antisocial behaviour were constructed on the basis of interview data and police records of offences like burglaries, thefts and taking away vehicles, but omitting minor offences.

The items assessing antisocial behaviour at age 10 make reference to 'being troublesome', 'showing conduct problems', 'being difficult to discipline', 'dishonest', 'has stolen', 'gets angry', 'is daring', 'lacks concentration', 'is impulsive', and 'plays truant'. Although these items refer to a range of different behaviours and are based on different sources of information, they form a statistically reliable measurement scale, and individual children can be assessed as scoring high or low on this scale. Similar scales can be constructed for each age group and, as one might expect, the items that measure antisocial behaviour at one age are not necessarily the same items that measure it at other ages. Thus, criminal convictions, regular smoking and having sex appear for the first time as items at age 14; heavy drinking, heavy gambling and drunk driving first appear at age 18; and divorce and poor relationship with wife appear at age 32 (drunk driving was so frequent in the sample of 32-year-olds that the item no longer correlated with the antisocial score). The items with the highest correlations with antisocial behaviour were being rated as 'troublesome' by teachers and peers at age 10, and records of having been convicted of an offence at the other three ages.

The particular question we consider here is whether the children who are assessed as antisocial at, say, 10 years are also the antisocial 32-year-olds. This question can be approached in two ways in a prospective study. What proportion of antisocial 10-year-olds is still antisocial when they are 32? What proportion of the antisocial 32-year-olds was antisocial when they were 10 years old? In order to answer these questions, a decision must be made about what particular score on the scale designates antisocial behaviour at a particular age.

One decision is to concentrate on the extreme scores at any age, by choosing, for example, the 25 percent of males with the highest antisocial scores at each age as the criterion for being antisocial. Thus, looking backwards, one could start by considering the worst 25 percent at age 32. Of those who meet this criterion, 57 percent were also antisocial when they were aged 18, 48 percent were antisocial at 14, and 35 percent were antisocial when they were 10. Looking forward, consider the worst 25 percent of 10-year-old boys; 37 percent of these were still antisocial when they were 32. Of course, this also means that 63 percent of these 10-year-olds were no longer in the most antisocial adult group, and one should also consider that 21 percent of the antisocial adults had not been in the antisocial group at 10.

In all, the study shows evidence of both continuities and discontinuities. There is a 'hard core' of children, albeit a minority, some 34 boys, or 8 percent of the original sample, who behave in an extremely antisocial way at age 10 and who are still causing problems to themselves and to others more than 20 years later, having acquired a criminal record and broken family relationships. On the other hand, the majority of children who behaved in an antisocial way at age 10 have not gone along this particular route. These findings are open to different interpretations, depending on thecut-off score that is adopted for classifying someone as antisocial. There is nevertheless a coherent pattern of statistically significant relationships and evidence of considerable long-term consistency in antisocial behaviour.

Attention deficit disorder

Definitions and incidence

Biological explanations of aggressive behaviour in children have received fresh impetus from the surge of interest among psychologists and educationalists following the definition of the diagnostic category attention deficit disorder (ADD) in the American Psychiatric Association's *Diagnostic and Statistical Manual* (DSM-III) in 1980. This proposed three sets of diagnostic criteria: items refer to inattention, impulsivity and hyperactivity.

The condition initially emphasised over-activity and this was explained in terms of 'minimal brain damage' although there was little evidence about the nature of any such damage and eventually the more neutral term 'dysfunction' was substituted for the term 'damage'. The American Psychiatric Association's DSM-II, published in 1968, described the condition as 'hyperkinetic reaction of childhood', with an emphasis upon over-activity. DSM-III, as we have seen, introduced the category of ADD, and also offered a further distinction: between ADD, where problems of attention were emphasised; and ADD-H where children show problems of both attention and over-activity (hyperactivity). The revision of the DSM-III, published in 1987, labelled the disorder attention-deficit hyperactivity disorder (ADHD) and proposed a single set of 14 diagnostic criteria, eight of which should be present to warrant the diagnosis. The criteria items present a picture of a child who has great difficulty in sitting still, who is easily distracted, and who tends to act on impulse without thinking.

The diagnosis also required that the behaviours are exhibited more frequently than would be expected for a child of that mental age, that they have persisted for at least six months, and that they have been evident from before the age of 7 years.

In the most recent edition of the *Manual* (DSM-IV), terminology has changed to attention-deficit/hyperactivity disorder (AD/HD), and three types are identified: two subtypes, depending whether there is a predominance of inattention or of hyperactivity-impulsivity; and a combined type where both types of symptoms are present. Rather than a single list of diagnostic criteria two alternative lists are provided, one listing problems in attending and the other describing both over-activity and impulsiveness. Thus, over the years, the definition of this syndrome has changed from an initial emphasis upon hyperactivity to focus on problems of attention and, most recently, to distinguish two kinds of problems, inattention and hyperactivity/impulsivity. As we discuss below, recent explanations of the syndrome have also maintained a distinction between attention problems, on the one hand, and impulsiveness and hyperactivity, on the other. The precise nature of the causal relationships between these types of problems remains an unresolved issue.

Since 1980 there has been an explosion of studies into ADD. Figure 3.1 shows the number of studies published each year from 1980 to 1995, based on citation counts in a large database of social science research, BIDS (Bath Information and Data Services). We cannot possibly do justice to this research in the space available to us, but we offer some points about the status of this disorder.

The incidence in the United States is estimated to be between 3 and 8 percent of the elementary school population. In the school population, the diagnostic criteria are met significantly more frequently by boys than girls, and boys are diagnosed with the disorder up to 10 times more frequently than girls. In Britain, the Secretary of State for Health replied to a parliamentary question on 12 December 1994: 'Recent findings have estimated a prevalence of 1.7 per cent in a population of primary school boys but there are gender differences and geographical variations in distribution' (Hansard, 1994). In a further written answer on 26 June 1995, he replied, 'Attention deficit hyperactivity disorder is one of several possible causes of behavioural problems, including aggression in schools. The number of pupils is not available centrally. Recent research suggests that severe hyperkinetic disorder, which is one form of attention deficit hyperactivity disorder, is found in about 1 in 200 children' (Hansard, 1995).

The disorder is associated in childhood with poor academic achievement, low self-esteem, and difficulties in social relationships, and it predicts a range of problems in adulthood, including alcohol abuse, poor social relationships and difficulties with finding and keeping employment. Patterns of temper tantrums and serious aggressive behaviour cause great difficulties for families as well as the school, and they also adversely affect the child's relationships with his or her peers. Aggressive behaviour is widely regarded as unacceptable and explanations in terms of a psychiatric disorder do not make it any more acceptable, and this can add further to the difficulties of the family. The commonly held belief that child rearing practices are responsible for children's behaviour also adds to the family's stress and self-blame.

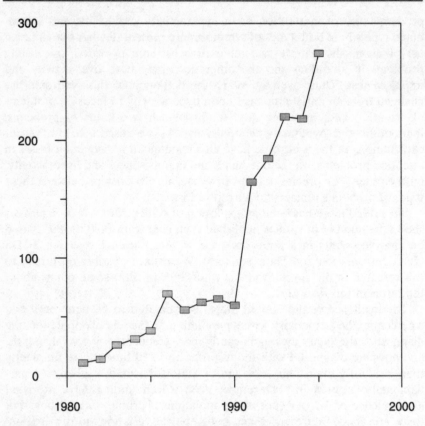

Figure 3.1 Annual citations of attention deficit disorder
Source: Based on information from Bath Information and Data Services.

Causal explanations

No consensus has emerged about the causes of the disorder. Explanations
have been framed in terms of diet but these have not received widespread
support. The role of serotonin metabolism has been advocated. It is
possible that AD/HD is not one condition but a constellation of problems –
the shifting terminology and the range of different symptoms suggest this
– and it may therefore have multiple causes rather than a single cause.
Barkley (1994) distinguishes between impulsivity and hyperactivity, on
the one hand, and problems of attention, on the other, and argues that
the former are the defining characteristics of the disorder. He proposes
that impulsivity and over-activity are both caused by the child's inability to
sustain a delay between stimulus and response. This results in a dominance
of behaviour by the immediate situation. The child's attention is captured
by the most recent event, resulting in impulsive behaviour, heightened
activity levels, and inability to sustain concentration.

Impulsivity is also emphasised in Quay's account (e.g. Daugherty and Quay, 1991). Quay draws upon Gray's (1982) distinction between two systems of arousal located in the septal-hippocampal system of the brain, the behavioural activation system (BAS) and the behavioral inhibition system (BIS). The BAS is sensitive to reward and serves to activate behaviour; the BIS is activated by signals of punishment or of absence of reward, and functions to inhibit behaviour and permit analysis of the signal. Quay argues that impulsive behaviour in conduct disorder is due to an over-active BAS, where the individual focuses excessively on potential rewards. The impulsivity in AD/HD is due to a poorly functioning BIS, and the individual is insufficiently constrained by threats of punishment. Daugherty and Quay (1991) tested this proposition by investigating the performance on tests of perseveration of children who had been diagnosed as having either conduct disorders or AD/HD. The child faced a task where his or her response was initially rewarded but, as the task continued, rewards became less and less frequent, until reaching a point where optimal performance demanded that the child stopped responding. Conduct disorder children were much slower to stop than either the AD/HD group or a control group. Schachar and Logan (1990) studied performance on a task where the child had to interrupt an ongoing task whenever a signal was given. No rewards or punishments were involved. Here, AD/HD boys were slower to interrupt their responding, compared with a conduct disorder group and a control group. Schachar and Logan interpreted this pattern of results as evidence that the problem in AD/HD is in the inhibition of behaviour. Problems with inhibition are only apparent among conduct disorder children when it is a matter of forgoing rewards; otherwise, they are able to inhibit behaviour appropriately.

Many critics of the disorder argue that it is an attempt to apply a medical label to problems that are essentially social in origin. Behaviour that is unacceptable to the school is regarded as a medical condition of the individual child rather than as an indication that there are problems within the school system. Meents (1989) has argued that AD/HD is primarily an educational problem and that the emphasis should be on the search for an educational solution rather than relying upon medication. Too much attention, she argues, has been paid to the individual's problems and not enough on asking what features of the school environment are contributing to the difficult behaviours. This position draws support from evidence that many more children are diagnosed from lower, relative to higher, socio-economic groups.

Perhaps the most controversial feature of the condition, at least in Britain, is its control by medication. Serotonin agonists are currently in pharmaceutical trials targeted at impulsiveness, aggression, self-destructive behaviours and anxiety (Stahl, 1992). The most common form of medication involves psychostimulant drugs like Ritalin (methylphenidate) and

Dexedrine (dextroamphetamine) which have been shown to reduce hyper-activity and are widely applied in treatment in the United States. Gadow (1986: 40) cites data from a survey in 1977 that show that between 1 and 2 percent of all elementary school children in USA received medication for ADD, and that 90 percent of these cases were treated with Ritalin. The average daily dose was from 20 to 30 mg although some children received as much as 140 mg. The duration of treatment was also highly variable, ranging from three months' medication to many years, with an average duration between two and three years.

Gadow's review of studies evaluating the effects of medication concludes that Ritalin leads to significant reductions in activity, improvements in sustained attention and in performance on short-term memory tasks. There is also evidence that children are significantly less aggressive and disruptive. Teachers' ratings of behaviour on checklists designed to show signs of AD/HD are more positive for children who are receiving Ritalin compared to children who are being treated with a placebo. However, there seems to be little evidence that the treatment has led to any significant improvements in academic performance.

Part of the unease about this treatment is due to the lack of a clear demarcation between the disorder and forms of over-active, impulsive or aggressive behaviour that are widely seen in children. There is some-thing deeply unsettling about the notion that these behaviours should be controlled by medication. Gadow (1986: 31) draws attention to the 'Accusations . . . that teachers and physicians conspire to enslave boister-ous school children in chemical straight jackets'. This uneasiness is, I think, a common reaction where medication is used for the treatment of psychiatric conditions.

The ethical problems are difficult. Children with AD/HD can be danger-ous to themselves and other people, and adults have a responsibility for the protection of the child and others. On the other hand, there is a danger that treatment that might well be useful for a limited number of cases who meet strict diagnostic criteria is regarded as a panacea and becomes widely applied. Psychological conditions are rarely as well defined as physical conditions, as the history of this particular diagnostic category illustrates.

It must be borne in mind that AD/HD is classed as a developmental disorder, that is, it appears early in childhood and is longlasting. There should be resistance to reliance upon teacher observations or ratings over the short term, as difficult behaviour can be symptomatic of many factors in a child's life and family circumstances, such as unemployment, bereavement and divorce, disputes in the family and neighbourhood, abuse in the home, bullying, academic problems, and so on. There must always be special caution when the core of the condition is behaviour that is problematic to figures in authority and also when those who receive the treatment are children who have little control over the decisions that affect them. A further issue is the availability of alternative forms of treatment. Behavioural methods have been successfully applied to the control and self-regulation of disruptive behaviour and these should be explored before alternatives are sought.

Part of the growing interest in this disorder has been that it offers an explanation of aggressive behaviour among children. There is considerable evidence that the disorder is associated with aggression. However, psychiatric classification systems distinguish this disorder from conduct disorders which are more directly defined in terms of antisocial and aggressive acts. Applications of factor analysis to ratings of behaviours relevant to these disorders have shown that these represent distinguishable, but correlated factors (Hinshaw, 1987). This raises the question whether the correlation between AD/HD and aggression is due to the association of both with conduct disorders. Fergusson *et al.* (1993) tested this hypothesis with a large sample of children as part of a longitudinal study in New Zealand. Separate but highly correlated factors of 'attention deficit' and 'conduct disorder' were identified. The correlation between attention deficit at 8 years and a measure of offending at 11 to 13 years was sizeable and statistically significant ($r = 0.61$) and was commensurate with previous research. However, this relationship was found to be negligible and non-significant when the influence of conduct disorder was controlled by statistical means.

BULLYING

> Twelve to one:
> What chance had Angus? They surrounded him,
> Pulled off his coat and trousers, socks and shoes
> And, wretched in his shirt, they hoisted him
> Into the huge waste-paper basket; then
> Poured ink and treacle on his head. With ropes
> They strung the basket up among the beams,
> And as he soared I only saw his eyes
> Look through the slats at us who watched below.
> > (from John Betjeman, 'Summoned by
> > Bells', in Betjeman, 1964)

Aggression has long been described as integral to school life, certainly the life of the English public boarding schools. The disorderly behaviour that was prevalent among boys in the public schools during the eighteenth century could develop into violent behaviour, and the militia had to be called in to suppress riots at schools including Winchester and Rugby. The aggression of one or more pupils towards another has long been called bullying, and this too has been frequently described in the recollections of many past pupils. The most famous literary descriptions are provided in

Thomas Hughes's *Tom Brown's Schooldays* (1857/1994) – which is set in Rugby School in the 1830s, at the time when Thomas Arnold was head-master.

Accounts of public school life in the early twentieth century still refer to the prevalence of bullying. The incident of bullying at Marlborough School in the 1920s recalled by Betjeman in his poem 'Summoned by Bells' is far from unique. The incident has elements of cruelty and of public humil-iation, and Betjeman recalls that the disgrace experienced in 'basketing' was very much more painful than the beatings that were routinely inflicted by teachers and senior boys. The pretext for bullying could be as mundane as distinctiveness of appearance or breaking a dress 'code', as Betjeman writes:

Why Angus . . . ? Never mind. The victim's found.
Perhaps he sported coloured socks too soon,
Perhaps he smarmed his hair with scented oil,
Perhaps he was 'immoral' or a thief.

The prevalence of this kind of behaviour can be understood in the context of the organisation of the public schools. Traditionally these had been run along laissez-faire lines where the boys were not closely supervised by teachers, and where the activities of the boys were under the control of the senior boys, the captains, prefects and the 'cock of the school'. These senior boys had the authority to beat the boys and to require the juniors to play subservient roles such as 'fags'. Whatever their individ-ual unhappiness, the pupils accepted these activities as the routine of school life and, of course, a boy was not a junior for ever and would grow up to take his turn among the 'ranks and privileges' of the captains.

The nineteenth century saw reforms to the public schools both in the curriculum and social behaviour. Thomas Arnold at Rugby sought to intro-duce discipline into his school, adopting measures to deal with disorderly behaviour. He took over the system of patronage exerted by the captains and prefects to make the senior boys more accountable to the headmaster. He encouraged sports like football in order to direct the boys' energies into more approved activities. Order was achieved by teachers taking control over practices that were already within the school, like the dominance of older boys over younger boys. Nevertheless, the accounts of contemporary school life show that bullying remained an integral part of school life, although it was officially frowned upon, and was to an extent hidden from the teachers. There are many pressures on pupils to keep quiet about such activities, even when they are its victims. Time seems to have cast a kind of glamour over these activities, when former pupils recall their own experiences and send their own children to their old schools. Indeed, these activities could be seen to have positive qualities, in forming a boy's character and developing 'manliness'.

The title of an article by Michael Prestage in the *Times Educational Supplement* (26 February 1993) – 'Skeleton is dragged out of the closet' – suggests that the schools, and indeed society in general, have been accomplices in failing to face up to the implications of bullying. An account of routine aggression in contemporary state schools is provided by Beynon (1988), who conducted an ethnographic study of an anonymous comprehensive school in south Wales. An ethnographic study is one where the investigator spends a great deal of time in the school, trying to remain inconspicuous as he or she observes and listens to its routine activities. Beynon (pp. 139–40) argued that acts of violence between teachers and pupils and between pupils themselves were accepted as routine features of school life:

> teachers generally were prepared to write off most pupil violence as normal, healthy, boyish exuberance, and horseplay . . . The need for and acceptability of macho posturing and violence was conveyed to boys (and by boys) in the form of what I term 'myths of aggression'.

These myths were accounts of particular confrontations which were much discussed, embellished and enjoyed within the school. Their discussion was not confined to the pupils and also contributed to staffroom conversation.

One problem with facing up to the issue of bullying, and with studying it, is the lack of any clear definition of what constitutes bullying or consensus whether particular incidents should be treated as instances of it. In the case of some actions, like the basketing described in Betjeman's poem, there might well be consensus that this is a case of bullying, and the inequality of power between the victim and his assailants, the use of force to ensure his participation, and the cruelty of his treatment would be factors influencing that consensus. However, many actions involve inequality of power and aggression – notably instances of teachers' behaviour towards pupils described by Beynon, and, of course, sports – without their being labelled bullying.

Many playground and out-of-school activities involve what is often called rough-and-tumble play, and this can lead, perhaps unintentionally, to children being injured. Boulton (1993) observed children in the playground and interviewed them about fighting. This was a common occurrence: between 60 and 75 percent of boys and approximately one in three girls claimed that they had been involved in a fight in the playground within the previous year, and observations showed that the rate of fighting ranged from an average 1.1 fights per hour (for 11-year-old girls) to 3.7 fights per hour (among 8-year-old boys). Fighting was more frequent among boys than among girls and among 8-year-olds compared to 11-year-olds. The most common causes for fighting were teasing, disputes over games, disputes over possessions, and being hit for no reason.

The testimonies of victims suggest that psychological forms can be the most painful, and these include teasing, name calling and ostracisation, unpleasant experiences that nevertheless can be commonly encountered without being labelled as bullying.

A further problem is that the communities and families of pupils attending individual schools can have different norms and values concerning aggression and its role in resolving conflict. This may underlie the attitude that although bullying is undesirable it is a fact of life inside and outside school; members of the wider community settle their differences in aggressive ways, and therefore children cannot be protected from this 'fact of life'. Fortunately, research does show that schools can have an influence upon bullying by taking and implementing a firm stance that it is unacceptable behaviour, and this is no doubt to the relief of their pupils.

Sharp and Smith (1994: 1) define bullying as 'a form of aggressive behaviour which is usually hurtful and deliberate; it is often persistent, sometimes continuing for weeks, months or even years and it is difficult for those being bullied to defend themselves. Underlying most bullying is an abuse of power and a desire to intimidate and dominate.' They propose three kinds of bullying: physical, verbal and indirect (rumour-mongering and social exclusion). Besag (1989) listed four features of bullying: it may be psychological as well as physical; it is characterised by inequality in power between bully and victim; it is a persistent activity that carries the threat of future bullying; it may take the form of behaviour that is socially acceptable but that is painful for the individual involved. These insidious psychological features are exemplified in the recollections of one woman:

> We made her life a complete misery. I don't really know what was different about her, what made her the class victim. She wasn't an unpleasant person but if she came near any of us or just brushed past, we'd immediately react and go, 'Oh, Sarah's germs' as if they were smeared on us. We did this all the time, every time she came near us. She must have felt like a leper.
>
> (reported by Sara Parker, *The Guardian*, 22 July 1992)

The nature and incidence of bullying

Although bullying has, therefore, been recognised for many years as an integral part of school life, there has recently been a surge in interest in the topic. In part, this is due to several tragic cases of suicide among the victims of bullying that received much attention from the mass media. In part, it also reflects the findings from the first surveys of the incidence of bullying that its frequency was much higher than had hitherto been realised. There is public consensus that bullying is an unacceptable part of school life that should be eradicated, although there may be differences among teachers in where they would draw a line between bullying and boisterousness or the 'rough and tumble' of children's life. Against this background, a large number of psychological studies have been published in recent years.

Pioneering empirical research was undertaken in Scandinavia by Olweus (1978). He devised a questionnaire that invited students to report anonymously on their experiences of bullying others and of being bullied. The guarantee of confidentiality would, it was hoped, encourage students to be frank, without the fear of themselves suffering further victimisation by bullies, or being punished by teachers for admitting to bullying or by their peers for 'grassing' or telling tales, breaking codes of silence about wrongdoing. This method has been taken up by psychologists throughout the world and has strongly influenced research into bullying. Alternative methods have evolved, including interviews and asking students to keep a diary on their regular activities. One method invites children, again anonymously, to nominate those of their fellow students whom they regard as victims or bullies. This is a useful approach for establishing the identities of these students for further examination, for example, to assess the self-esteem of victims of bullying (Boulton and Smith, 1994). These methods have yielded considerable insight into the incidence of bullying of different kinds and the psychological characteristics of students involved. We now offer a brief overview of some of the principal findings of this research.

The frequency of bullying

Whitney and Smith (1993) distributed an anonymous questionnaire to more than 4000 pupils attending junior, middle and secondary schools in Britain. Ten percent of junior and middle school pupils and 4 percent of secondary school pupils reported having been bullied at least once a week during that school term. Twenty-seven percent of junior and middle school pupils and 10 percent of secondary pupils had been bullied 'sometimes or more'. The self-reported frequency of bullying others was different for boys and girls. In junior and middle schools, 16 percent of boys and 7 percent of girls bullied others 'sometimes or more' whereas 6 percent of boys and 1 percent of girls bullied others at least once a week. In secondary schools, 8 percent of boys and 4 percent of girls bullied others 'sometimes or more'; the frequency of self-reported regular bullying was too small (1 percent of pupils) to establish any gender differences.

These figures are in line with those reported by several other studies. A recent survey conducted for *The Guardian* by ICM, an opinion survey organisation, interviewed a quota sample of 507 children aged from 11 to 15 years in 52 randomly selected parliamentary constituencies (*The Guardian*, 15 May 1996). Sixty-nine percent of boys and 67 percent of girls responded in the affirmative to the question, 'Is there bullying at your school?' Thirty-one percent of boys and 36 percent of girls claimed to have been bullied. Middle-class children were somewhat more likely to report that they had been bullied (40 percent) than children from skilled working-class families (27 percent) or unskilled working-class families (32 percent).

Forms of bullying

In the Whitney and Smith study, the form of bullying that was most frequently endorsed by pupils who had experienced bullying was being called names, nominated by 50 percent of junior and middle school pupils and 62 percent of secondary pupils. The next most common categories were being physically hurt (36 and 26 percent, respectively), being threatened (30 and 25 percent) and having rumours spread (26 and 24 percent). Other forms of bullying frequently endorsed were being called racist names, being ostracised, and having belongings taken. Physical violence, threats, and having belongings taken – the more physical forms of bullying – figure largest in the accounts of the pupils, but name-calling is the single most frequently mentioned behaviour.

Age and gender differences

The frequency of bullying seems to reach a peak in the later years of primary school and the early years of secondary school, and to fall off after the age of 14 or 15. This decline might be due to many factors. It may reflect a change in reporting, with older pupils being less willing to admit to being bullied, or be due to a change in respondents' interpretations of behaviour. Research has established that there is a surge in feelings of self-consciousness and a reduction in self-esteem among this age group, and these pupils may attribute their difficulties with peers to their own inadequacies rather than to the actions of their peers, and as a consequence tend not to label rejection or teasing as bullying or to report them to anyone. A more straightforward explanation is that children tend to be bullied by those who are larger and stronger than themselves, and there are fewer of these potential bullies available as one moves through the school. Particularly difficult individuals might also be more likely to have left the school, perhaps because they have been expelled or have moved to another school. For any particular child, potential bullies would, of course, be most numerous when he or she was in the first form of secondary school. However, there may be other processes at work. Research does show that, more generally, there are age changes in the incidence of aggression. There are also changes in the patterns of personal relationships. Finally, it might be that older children have developed social skills that enable them to cope with bullying or that make bullying a less effective means of exerting control over others.

Boys do seem to bully others more often than do girls, although each gender is equally likely to be a victim. These statistics regularly emerge in surveys of bullying. They are also apparent in an analysis of calls made by children to the telephone helpline Childline concerning bullying (La Fontaine, 1990). Boys and girls were identified by callers as bullies in almost equal numbers. However, further analysis revealed that callers reported that the majority of instances of bullying that involved physical aggression were carried out by boys whereas the majority of incidents involving teasing, name-calling and social isolation were carried out by girls.

The stereotype of physical aggression among boys and verbal or psychological aggression among girls is not altogether supported by survey data. The pattern of bullying certainly differs according to gender, particularly in secondary school, where girls are more likely to report being ostracised, name-calling and rumour-spreading whereas boys are more likely to report being physically hurt. However, this gender difference is a matter of degree, in that psychological forms are also prevalent among boys, and girls frequently perpetrate and suffer from physical aggression. This pattern was also reported by Keise (1992) in an analysis of single-sex schools. Verbal abuse, hitting, and taking money were the most prevalent forms of bullying in the boys' school; 'bitchiness' was the most prevalent form in the girls' school, but there was evidence there too of physical aggression. The gender differences in types of bullying are also much less marked in junior and middle schools, implying that it is the relationship between age and gender that is important, rather than gender *per se*.

One factor might be gender differences in the pattern of friendships. It is suggested that boys form more diffuse relationships with a large number of boys, perhaps coming together for particular activities like football, and participating more in large group activities, whereas girls' friendships involve smaller numbers of girls and are more intense. This might lead to a greater concern among boys with establishing dominance relationships within the groups and a greater concern among girls with affiliation and acceptance. Accordingly, boys would be more vulnerable to fighting whereas girls would be more vulnerable to rejection and isolation. Competition, too, would take different forms, with boys competing for dominance and girls competing for attention. Thorne (1993) has demonstrated some of these differences in personal relationships. Boys tend to form larger organisations like 'gangs' and there is much rough-and-tumble play. Girls are more likely to form networks of smaller groups, friendship pairs and trios which are formed, develop and divide. Girls' talk is often about 'best friends', and who is friendly or unkind to whom. Contrast the recollection of bullying in John Betjeman's poem with the following extracts from an account of a girl being bullied in Margaret Atwood's novel, *Cat's Eye* (1989: 116–7).

On the window-ledge beside mine, Cordelia and Grace and Carol are sitting, jammed in together, whispering and giggling. I have to sit on a window-ledge by myself because they aren't speaking to me. It's something I said wrong, but I don't know what it is because they won't tell me. Cordelia says it will be better for me to think back over everything I've said today and try to pick out the wrong thing. That way I will learn not to say such a thing again. When I've guessed the right answer, then they will speak to me again. All of this is for my own good, because they are my best friends, and they want to help me improve . . . I worry about what I've said today, the expression on my face, how I walk, what I wear, because all these things need improvement. I am not normal, I am not like other girls. Cordelia tells me so, but she will help me. Grace and Carol will help me too . . . They are my friends, my girlfriends, my best friends. I have never had any before and I'm terrified of losing them. I want to please.

The author goes on to describe the fear and eventual self-mutilation that this experience caused for this child and also the escalation into more dangerous forms of bullying. There are intense pressures towards conformity within the small group and the child's fear is that of rejection. Further observations made by Atwood that have been confirmed in research are that the interactions among the girls were hidden from other members of their class, and that although other girls within the group could be cast in the role of victim, one girl, Cordelia, acted as leader, initiating much of the bullying but never being the victim herself. Some girls made less satisfactory victims than the regular target: 'Carol cries too easily and noisily, she gets carried away with her own crying. She draws attention, she can't be depended on not to tell. There's a recklessness in her, she can be pushed just so far, she has a weak sense of honour, she's reliable only as an informer' (p. 121).

Characteristics of bullies and victims

Does research support the stereotype of the habitually aggressive macho bully and the shy, timid, weak victim? There is evidence that a minority of children are persistently involved in bullying. Yates and Smith (1989) reported that 8 percent of boys and 2 percent of girls in two secondary schools bullied once a week or more, figures somewhat larger than those reported in the much larger sample studied by Whitney and Smith (1993), although not outside the range of figures from different schools reported there.

In one of the earliest empirical investigations into bullying, Olweus (1978) established some personality differences among boys who were bullies, victims or not involved in bullying. His findings were based upon boys' self-descriptions and descriptions by their mothers and their peers. The bullies' self-reports and the reports at home indicated that they were more irritable and bad tempered, showed more intense and less controlled aggression, and had a more positive attitude to violence. They were more likely to endorse items such as 'I get angry with other people easily'; 'I often think it is fun to make trouble'; 'If I get angry I often don't show it'. They were less likely to agree with statements like 'I think fighting is silly'. Olweus also found that both bullies and victims had, on average, lower self-esteem than the control group.

Boulton and Smith (1994) compared middle school children who had been nominated by their peers as bullies, victims, or not involved on the Self-Perception Profile for Children (Harter, 1985), which comprises six sub-scales: 'scholastic competence', 'social acceptance', 'athletic competence', 'physical appearance', 'behavioural conduct', and 'self-worth'. They found that victims had lower self-perceived competence on the athletic competence, social acceptance, and global self-worth sub-scales. Only male bullies were studied, and these differed on only the athletic competence sub-scale. These differences may reflect a tendency for children to nominate physically stronger boys as bullies and physically weaker children as victims, and it would be useful to examine the self-concepts of children who perceive themselves as bullies or victims. Findings are complicated by the fact that some children consider themselves to be both bullies and victims. Bowers *et al.* (1994) reported that children nominated as bully/victims made more self-referential statements overall on the Bene-Anthony Family Relations Test than did bullies, victims or non-involved children, and also made more negative self-referential responses than the other three groups. They interpreted this in terms of the greater ambivalence about themselves within this group, and they suggested that these children were the group most at risk for future adjustment.

What can be done about bullying?

There are many reasons why schools might hesitate over taking steps to counter bullying. Government legislation that has encouraged competition among schools may discourage them from drawing parents' attention to their more negative features. Schools might also fear the implications of unwanted publicity for the processes of inspection. Individual institutions might also simply underestimate the incidence of bullying in their school. Schools may lack confidence that they are in a position to take effective action because they recognise that much bullying is hidden. Pupils have norms about what should and should not be disclosed to teachers and victims are often reluctant to draw their predicament to the teacher's attention for fear of reprisals.

Nevertheless, research has suggested that schools have an important role in controlling bullying, and that one of the most effective means for achieving this is the development of an explicit policy for bullying, setting out clearly the standards for acceptable behaviour. Policy statements define bullying, affirm that it is unacceptable, explain the consequences for bullies, and state explicitly the steps that should be taken to report it.

Of course, no statement by itself constitutes a policy, and the school must take concerted action where those involved at all levels of the organisation have a part to play in order to eradicate bullying. The school has to define procedures to deal with bullying and it must be consistent in the application of these procedures. The policy must be developed on the basis of consultation with all involved. Sharp and Thompson (1994: 35–7) list a number of questions that should be addressed in the process of developing a policy: What are its aims? How is bullying to be defined? What strategies can be used to prevent it? What procedures can be developed for reporting it? Who should respond to it, and how? What are the roles and responsibilities of teachers, non-teaching staff, parents and governors in implementing the policy? How should the policy be evaluated and monitored?

In the absence of a clear policy teachers can be inconsistent in their approach. Flanagan (1992) found evidence of this in a study of teachers' reactions to bullying. A sample of 53 teachers and seven headteachers was presented with two descriptions of hypothetical incidents and asked what steps should be taken. All of the respondents regarded both incidents as extremely serious but there was little consensus how to tackle them, whom to involve and what procedures should be followed. For example, one incident was reported to have taken place on the way home from school; this created considerable uncertainty among teachers as to the extent of their responsibilities, and they suggested that they were less likely to take action against the bullies and more likely to involve the parents and police in this case.

The recent attention paid to bullying has resulted in a number of recommendations for effective action and many schools have taken positive steps to reduce the incidence of bullying. Determining the effectiveness of these approaches demands carefully designed research studies. The first systematic attempt to design and evaluate a programme to counter bullying was undertaken in Norway by Olweus (1993). Information packs about bullying were provided for schools and parents, and the schools' efforts were supported by the researchers through frequent school visits and the provision of in-service training for teachers. Olweus claimed that this programme produced a substantial reduction in the incidence of bullying in the schools that participated.

In Britain a large-scale intervention study was carried out between 1991 and 1993 in 16 primary and seven secondary schools in Sheffield by Smith and his associates with the financial support of the Department for Education (Whitney *et al.*, 1994).

Their intervention took four approaches: the development of whole-school policies; discussing bullying within the curriculum; improving playground supervision arrangements; working directly with individual pupils and groups who were involved in bullying. The incidence of bullying had already been assessed in the participating schools and this provided a baseline measure with which the effects of the intervention could be compared. A range of approaches was presented to the schools and they were able to choose those they felt most appropriate; although this would create difficulties when analysing the effects of intervention across the sample of schools, the full cooperation of schools was necessary and this meant that they should be involved in the choice of approach for their school. After two years the incidence of bullying in the schools was again assessed, and a number of additional measures were taken (see Whitney *et al.*, 1994, for further details of these).

There was particular interest in assessing the changes that the schools had implemented to see which of these, if any, had significant effects on the incidence of bullying. Most schools succeeded in reducing the incidence of bullying, although there was evidence of variation among schools. The amount of change was greater in primary than in secondary schools. There was, taking the average across primary schools, a reduction of 15 percent in the likelihood of having been bullied during the previous term and a 12 percent reduction in the frequency of bullying others; across secondary schools the equivalent averages were slightly over 2 percent and 12 percent, respectively.

There were individual schools that reported much larger changes than the average. Schools that were rated by the research team as having put more effort into the programme and as having greater staff involvement in the programme were significantly more successful in reducing the incidence of bullying and were more often perceived by their pupils as having taken action. Again, these effects were larger at primary than secondary level. These correlations between features of the programme and measures of the rates of bullying are important for highlighting the more effective aspects of intervention; they also suggest that it is not the fact of intervention in itself that produces change and that the changes are not simply because the programme has drawn attention to bullying. Schools that did introduce a programme but did not develop it as fully as other schools were less successful in reducing the incidence of bullying.

This study assessed bullying at the level of the school. Teachers have also to try to deal with individual cases in an effective way. Public sympathy naturally lies with the victim and much research has been directed towards the effects of bullying and on how to help the victim. Sharp *et al.* (1994: 79) list five recommendations for an effective response.

1 Be clear, honest, and direct, avoiding the use of humiliation, sarcasm, aggression, threat or manipulation

2 Be immediate, with possible follow-up in the longer term
3 Record what has happened, who was involved and what action was taken
4 Involve the family at each stage
5 Provide opportunities for the pupils to discuss with one another ways of resolving the problem.

Research has tended either to ignore the bully or to treat him or her unsympathetically, as someone to be punished. In the study by Flanagan (1992) each participant's written protocol was analysed to see whether it included mention of either a punitive or a non-punitive response to the bully. The hypothesis that there were more punitive than non-punitive responses was clearly supported. Overall, 50 percent of responses involved punishing the bully without any non-punitive response; 10 percent involved both a punishing and a non-punitive response; 16 percent involved only a non-punitive response to the bully; the remaining 24 percent of responses made no reference to any action directed at the bully. There was considerable variation in the kinds of punishments proposed by teachers. For example, eight participants recommended public exposure of the bully, as an example of unacceptable behaviour or to make an issue of the incident. Some teachers thought this could be a learning experience for the bully:

> I would confront Sandra [the bully] and reprimand her. Then later in a drama lesson, I would put her in the middle of a circle and tell the class that she was fat or something pejorative. Then each person would have to point at her and say something horrible to her, sneering as they said it. Then, with the class, I would ask Sandra how she felt.
>
> (Flanagan, 1992: 50)

However, other teachers saw dangers in this approach. For example,

> What I would definitely NOT do is punish Sandra by making her look inferior in front of the whole school, i.e. making her the subject of an assembly, because I believe, the feelings that this would generate in somebody can only lead to worse.
>
> (p. 57; emphasis in original)

Yet there are many reasons for looking more closely at the perpetrator, and for considering alternatives to punishment. Bullying is a relationship, requiring both bullies and victims in interaction – indeed one of its defining characteristics is that it involves the same people over a period of time – and the eradication of bullying must take that into account. Dealing with one of the actors in isolation is unlikely to be successful.

Some recent research suggests the potential effectiveness of approaches that try to uncover alternative ways of resolving conflicts in cases of aggression. Lane (1989) argues that it is important to assess the factors that give rise to bullying and to have available a range of intervention approaches including psychotherapy and effective liaison between the school and support services in the community. Foster and Thompson (1991) recommend discussion between all the children concerned to draw up a contract for the behaviour of bully and victim, a contract to be monitored by all the children. Maines and Robinson (1991) assert the potential of mediation techniques that bring together the different participants in aggressive incidents to discuss the situation and suggest ways of resolving the problem.

CONCLUSION

There seems to be evidence that there is a considerable degree of continuity between conduct disorders during the school years and antisocial behaviour in adulthood. Some young people set out early on a career of disruptive and difficult activities. Many of these pupils are recognised early by the school, but little progress has been made in diverting these careers along less destructive paths. This remains an important challenge for society. Rates of offending among young men are high, and this seems always to have been the case. Social factors like discordant family life, unemployment or easy access to alcohol have significant contributions to make to these rates. Nevertheless, further research into the factors that influence the persistence of antisocial behaviour among a minority of young people could have real practical benefits.

The extent to which these individuals contribute to the incidence of aggression within schools is not yet clear; recent research has established that bullying is widespread and involves large numbers of pupils. Nevertheless, in parallel with trends in offending, boys bully more often than girls, and the rate declines with age. Bullying tends to take different forms among boys and girls, although the extent of this difference can be exaggerated.

Recent research has taken two directions, emphasising either individual or school factors. There has been interest in identifying a biological or temperamental basis for aggression. Genetic studies of the possible role of serotonin and experimental research into perseveration have emphasised impulsiveness as a factor in aggression. Barkley has argued that many of the difficult behaviours exhibited by children with attention deficit disorder can be explained in terms of the dominance of their attention by the 'here and now' and an inability to delay before responding. Other accounts have placed greater emphasis on inappropriate sensitivity to rewards and punishments.

Despite this converging evidence of the importance of impulsiveness, there remains the possibility that this is a result of difficulties in adjustment rather than their cause. Young people with high levels of energy might be expected to be impulsive and inattentive if they cannot cope with schoolwork. For example, Fergusson et al. (1993) found that much of the correlation between attention deficits and poor performance on tests of academic competence could be explained by their mutual association with low IQ. This ambiguity over what is cause and what is effect has also characterised interpretations of the relationship between aggression and levels of testosterone.

Within schools, intervention programmes that have attempted to reduce the incidence of bullying have been promising, and some schools have been successful in developing procedures to counter bullying. The important steps seem to have been in taking aggression seriously, with the whole school being explicit that it is unacceptable, and in developing effective procedures to help victims. These might seem common sense. However, Beynon's research showed the pervasiveness of positive attitudes towards aggression among both teachers and pupils. Does making pupils who have forgotten their games kit do 'press-ups' in the mud constitute bullying? Pupils perceive being humiliated by other pupils as bullying; does classroom control by humiliation constitute bullying? Schools that address these questions can create an environment where less aggression takes place. This is surely a significant finding. Schools can be forgiven for feeling helpless to change behaviour, being so often the scapegoat of government's inability to find solutions, and perceiving themselves to have little influence over trends in society at large. Yet schools, it seems, can make a difference.

Chapter 4

Anxiety

APPROACHES TO ANXIETY

The nature of anxiety

A child's life at school differs in many ways from his or her life at home or among friends. Jackson (1968) discussed three sources of these differences: the child is part of a crowd; evaluation of the child relative to his or her peers is salient; inequalities of power become conspicuous. The life of a school is governed by a myriad of formal and informal rules and norms. Other children, particularly those who are older, larger, or more aggressive, can be threatening. The work that has to be undertaken can be remote from the child's everyday concerns. The school or college can be preoccupied with assessment and examinations, and success and failure can be conspicuous. It is hardly surprising that the experience of school can give rise to anxiety, which sometimes becomes so intense that the child is frightened of going to school. We have already seen in Chapter 1 that the association between trait measures of anxiety and low academic attainment is one of the most consistent findings in personality research. However, this correlation leaves many issues unresolved. Is anxiety a cause of failure or is it a consequence of it? If anxiety is a cause, how does it have its effects on academic performance? How can we understand the frequent observation that anxiety can enhance performance, for example in preparation for examinations, in acting or public speaking, or in sports events?

We address these questions in this chapter. First, we consider the definition of anxiety, and the distinction between trait and state anxiety. Since anxiety is a term in everyday use as well as a theoretical construct in psychology, it is informative to begin with a dictionary definition. The Concise Oxford Dictionary gives four meanings: 'state of being anxious – troubled, uneasy in mind; concern about the future; earnest desire (as in anxious to please or to succeed); morbid state of excessive uneasiness'. The *Penguin Dictionary of Psychology* gives the following definition: 'a vague, unpleasant emotional state with qualities of apprehension, dread, distress and uneasiness' (Reber, 1985: 43). Clearly, anxiety is an emotional state of an unpleasant kind characterised by a particular kind of state of mind, described in both definitions as uneasiness. It is uneasiness that perhaps serves to distinguish anxiety from fear, which seems more focused on a particular target, but this distinction is not always easy to draw, and different theories take different positions on this. Anxiety is a core concept in many psychological theories, including psychoanalysis, humanistic psychology, behaviourist learning theory, and cognitive psychology.

Personality theorists distinguish state and trait anxiety. Many situations, like examinations, public speaking, interviews, and going to the dentist are likely to evoke a state of anxiety in most people. The trait position proposes that some people are more prone to anxiety than others, in that they react to more situations with anxiety or react to particular situations with more intense emotion. This distinction is captured by one of the most widely used questionnaire measures, the State–Trait Anxiety Inventory (Spielberger *et al.*, 1970). This assesses both anxiety that is experienced in particular situations and a predisposition to feeling anxious. Anxiety or neuroticism is regarded as a basic personality trait by all the major classification systems, including the theories of Cattell and Eysenck and the Big Five system.

Eysenck proposed that the trait has its origins in inherited differences in the reactivity of the sympathetic nervous system which results in a greater tendency to form conditioned associations between stimuli and emotional responses. Although there is considerable evidence that those who obtain high scores on questionnaire measures of the trait report more bodily symptoms than low scorers, there is little evidence of any differences between the groups when physiological measures are taken (Fahrenberg, 1987). It might be the case that highly anxious individuals are more sensitive to their psychophysiological state or perhaps monitor it more closely; alternatively, improvements in methods of physiological measurement might show significant differences in the future. In any case, the regularity with which the trait appears in statistical analyses of personality questionnaires and the predictions about behaviour, particularly in test situations, that can be made, mean that trait anxiety will remain the centre of much research attention.

Anxiety and motivation

According to learning theory, anxiety is a learned response to a stimulus that warns the person that an unpleasant event is going to happen. This theory attributes motivational properties to anxiety, which it regards as functioning as a conditioned drive that motivates the individual to avoid the event. It is regarded as a conditioned, or learned, drive in the sense that a stimulus evokes the state of anxiety; this motivates the individual to take some action to avoid the state; the anxiety is reduced; and this reduction reinforces the action that was taken and makes that action more likely to be initiated again when anxiety is high.

Although this account offered an explanation of some of the phenomena associated with anxiety, and showed how it has an adaptive function for the individual, in enabling him or her to anticipate and avoid unpleasant or dangerous events, it did not have much to say on the relationship between anxiety and performance. This issue was addressed by an account that emphasised the links between anxiety and the concepts of drive and of arousal. This account was proposed by two American learning theorists, Hull in 1943 and Spence in 1958, and has become known as the Hull–Spence theory (Teigen, 1994, provides a valuable historical survey of these concepts).

Their account drew upon several core concepts from learning theory, which conceptualised learning as a matter of conditioning links between a stimulus and a response. A stimulus could be, say, a mathematics question that required a particular answer, or a foreign language text that needed translation. The theory proposed that an individual would have built up links between these stimuli and responses, and that these links could vary in habit strength. That is, some responses were well established and readily available, other responses were less well established. When presented with a mathematics problem one student will have available a practiced repertoire of procedures for answering the question, whereas another student would not be clear how to set about it. Drive was another key motivational concept in the theory, serving to energise behaviour; it could take on different levels from low to high drive, from inaction to highly charged behaviour. A student faced with an approaching examination may put more effort into his or her studies, spend more time on them, and be preoccupied with them.

Hull proposed that the likelihood that a conditioned stimulus would elicit a conditioned response was dependent on two factors: the habit strength associated with the response, and the overall drive level of the individual when the stimulus occurs. The theory proposed that drive and habit strength combine in a multiplicative relationship to determine the likelihood of a particular response. When habit strength was high, where the task was familiar and the response well established, then high levels of drive would facilitate the response. In a complex or novel task, where the response was less well prepared, high levels of drive will interfere with performance, by facilitating other less relevant learned responses. At low levels of drive, responses are, in general, less likely, but well-established habits are more likely than less well-established responses.

According to the theory, anxiety acts like a drive, and persons who are highly anxious have a high level of drive. Drives act in an additive fashion (for example, sources of anxiety might be inherent in the situation, an examination, and in the individual, who has a propensity towards anxiety) and these sources combine to produce a high level of drive state. The prediction is that the anxious individual will perform the same task more poorly in an examination than in the classroom if the task is of low habit strength, that is, is unfamiliar or the skill is less well established. Well-learned tasks, those with high habit strength, would be less affected by anxiety.

Anxiety can either help or hinder performance, depending on factors like the level of anxiety, the nature of the task, and the individual's past learning. This relationship between drive and performance is reminiscent of the inverted-U relationship between arousal and performance that we introduced in Chapter 1, where there is an optimal level of arousal for performance, and levels of arousal either lower or higher than the optimal are associated with deterioration in performance.

Predictions about the pattern of the relationship between anxiety and performance have found support in very many studies. Taylor (1953; see Phares, 1984: 460) drew upon the Hull–Spence theory to produce a self-report questionnaire measure of anxiety, the Manifest Anxiety Scale (MAS), which contains items like 'I find it hard to keep my mind on a task'; 'I worry over money and business'. Spielberger and Smith (1966; see Phares, 1984: 462) found that people with high anxiety scores on the MAS performed better than those low in anxiety on simple verbal learning tasks, but more poorly on more difficult tasks, particularly when these tasks were first presented.

Sarason (1978; see Sarason, 1984) introduced a different version of this questionnaire which concentrated on anxiety about tests, the Test Anxiety Scale (TAS). This contained items like, 'If I were to take an intelligence test, I would worry a great deal before taking it'; 'During tests, I find myself thinking of the consequences of failing'. A substantial body of research, carried out in both actual examination and simulated test conditions, has shown that students with high anxiety scores on the TAS tend to perform less well on tests than do students with lower scores. Their performance is particularly poor when the evaluative nature of the test is emphasised. For example, Deffenbacher (1978) manipulated students' perceptions of the evaluative nature of the same task by assigning them to one of two groups, each of which received a different introduction to the test. One group received 'ego-involving' information, and was told that the test about to be taken was an intelligence test and that poor performance was indicative of low intelligence. The second, 'reassurance', group was led to believe that the test was a very difficult one and failure would not reflect on the students' abilities. Participants then undertook an anagram solution task. Overall, there was no difference in performance between participants who had high and low TAS anxiety scores, but the manipulation of the information did have a marked effect. In the ego-involving condition, highly anxious students performed much better in the reassurance condition than in the ego-involving condition (obtaining an average of 5.65 items correct compared with 3.29 correct), whereas low anxious students performed better in the ego-involving condition (average 5.29 correct) than in the reassurance condition (4.53 correct).

It is apparent that the stress on the evaluative nature of the task had a much greater impact upon the performance of highly anxious students. It is also clear that this pattern of results is compatible with the inverted-U function relating anxiety to task performance, if one assumes that trait test anxiety and ego-involving information are both sources of anxiety that are additive. The best performance is found when the level of anxiety is at the moderate level in this study – low anxious students who are in the evaluative, ego-involving condition, and highly anxious students in the reassurance condition have comparable levels of performance.

Anxiety and attention

Although the findings have been robust, the explanation that proposes arousal and habit strength as the factors that mediate between anxiety and performance has been challenged. This challenge has coincided with the more general trend in psychology away from behaviourist explanations towards accounts in terms of cognitive processes. This trend in anxiety research can best be illustrated by developments in research into test anxiety. The first development was Wine's (1971) theory that performance deficiencies were a product of attentional processes. This drew upon earlier research by Easterbrook (1959; see also Wine, 1971) that made two proposals: that high levels of arousal reduce the range of cues to which the person attends when performing a task; that cues that are irrelevant to the task are omitted before cues that are relevant. This predicts that increasing levels of arousal would initially facilitate performance by enabling the person to concentrate on relevant information, but that higher levels of arousal would result in attention that was too narrowly focused, with relevant cues being omitted to the detriment of performance.

Wine argued that test anxious persons were more likely to direct their attention to cues that were irrelevant to the task, more specifically to direct their attention towards themselves, to become preoccupied with their inability to perform well in tests. This attention would be at the expense of attention that ought to be paid to task cues. On the other hand, the person with low test anxiety directs attention outwards towards task-relevant cues. One prediction that can be drawn from this conceptualisation is that the text anxious person attends to fewer cues in the task than do persons low in test anxiety.

Wine's explanation is compatible with the arousal conception of anxiety, but she concentrated on attentional processes rather than learned habits in accounting for poor test performance, and this has given rise to a large body of research, to which we turn in a later section of this chapter. The second development was noted in Wine's paper, and has shifted the emphasis in research from the arousal component of anxiety to its cognitive component, worry.

WORRY

Worry and test anxiety

Researchers into test anxiety make a distinction between worry and emotionality as separable components of anxiety. For example, the study by Deffenbacher summarised above incorporated further questionnaire measures, a 'worry' scale whose items referred to negative self-evaluation and concern about the performance of self and others; an 'emotionality' scale, with items referring to upset stomach, racing heart and perspiration; and a 'task interference' scale, with items referring to thinking about aspects of the task that were not relevant to solving the particular items. Test anxious students had high scores on all three scales, but there was a tendency for worry and task-irrelevant thinking to contribute more to poor performance than emotionality. Deffenbacher (1986) replicated these findings in a study of students' performance on their actual university examinations. The TAS was significantly, negatively correlated with examination marks, and the worry scale had higher correlations with marks than did the emotionality and task interference scales. Indeed, the worry scale had a higher correlation with marks than did the TAS scale.

Sarason (1984) produced a new test anxiety questionnaire, the Reaction to Tests Scale (RTT). The 91 items that were written in the development phase of this test were submitted to factor analysis, and four factors were extracted. One factor was labelled 'worry', and related to items like 'Before taking a test, I worry about failure'; 'During tests, I wonder how the other people are doing'. Another factor was labelled 'tension': 'I feel distressed and uneasy before tests'; 'I feel jittery before tests'. A third factor was labelled 'test-irrelevant thinking', as its most salient items included 'During tests, I think about recent past events'; 'Irrelevant bits of information pop into my head during a test'. The fourth factor was labelled 'bodily reactions', the items with highest loadings referring to 'I get a headache during an important test'; 'My stomach gets upset before tests'.

The final version of the questionnaire comprises 10 items for each of these four components. The total score for the 40-item questionnaire correlated significantly and negatively with performance on an intelligence test, but only the worry and test-irrelevant thinking scales were related to performance. The bodily reactions and tension scales were not related to test scores.

The consensus in test anxiety research is that it is worry and self-absorption rather than emotionality that is associated with poor test performance, a view reflected in Sarason's (1984: 933) proposal that test anxiety should be conceptualised in terms of 'worrisome, self-preoccupying thoughts that interfere with task performance'. Research offers support for the hypothesis that this interference is due to attentional mechanisms of the kind hypothesised by Wine. For example, Sarason developed a measure called the Cognitive Interference Questionnaire (CIQ). This is not intended to measure a trait, but is presented to students immediately after a test to ask them about the frequency and kinds of task-irrelevant thinking that they experienced during the test. Typical items are: 'I thought about how poorly I was doing'; 'I thought about how much time I had left'.

High test anxious students are more likely to respond that they have more task-irrelevant thoughts, particularly thoughts of a self-deprecatory kind and concerns over how other students are doing and what the examiner will think of them and their performance. Total scores on the RTT are significantly correlated with scores on the CIQ, and the worry sub-scale has the highest correlation with CIQ scores (Sarason, 1984).

There have been several attempts to assess worry during tests. Arnkoff *et al.* (1992) developed a checklist of 36 adjectives that candidates completed before and shortly after their PhD viva (oral) examination. Twelve items referred to positive thoughts ('I feel ready for this'), 12 items to neutral thoughts ('I'm rehearsing what I'm going to say'), and 12 to negative thoughts ('I'm really nervous about this'). The candidates also rated the impact of these thoughts upon their examination performance. The number of negative thoughts checked by the students correlated with their ratings of their own anxiety and also with the examiners' ratings of the candidate's anxiety.

Blankstein *et al.* (1989) asked participants to list as many thoughts and feelings as they could immediately after a test. Participants were asked, 'Please list as many thoughts and feelings as you can recall having during this test. Every thought and feeling that went through your mind during that time is important (i.e., thoughts and feelings about yourself, the situation, or unrelated to the experiment. Be spontaneous' (p. 273). Their responses were sorted by the researchers into three categories: thoughts that were self-referential, task-referential, and unrelated to self or task. Items within each category were then categorised as either positive, neutral or negative thoughts. In this study too, the frequency of self-referential negative thoughts was correlated with poor task performance, whereas the frequency of positive task-referential thoughts was correlated with good task performance. This conceptualisation of test anxiety has stimulated research into two questions: what is the nature of worry, and how can students be helped to overcome their anxiety.

The nature of worry

'If worry was dollar bills, I'd buy the world and have money to spare.' The words of this traditional blues song allude to the pervasiveness of worrying. This has been defined by psychologists as the cognitive component of anxiety. Borkovec *et al.* (1983: 10) offer a more detailed definition:

> Worry is a chain of thoughts and images, negatively affect-laden and relatively uncontrollable. The worry process represents an attempt to engage in mental problem-solving on an issue whose outcome is uncertain but contains the possibility of one or more negative outcomes. Consequently, worry relates closely to the fear process.

This definition is intended to capture some of the distinctive characteristics of worry. It is persistent and pervasive, in that it is longlasting and can be intrusive, making it difficult for the worried person to think about, or concentrate on, any other topic. O'Neill (1985) has disputed the utility of this definition, particularly its emphasis on problem-solving, arguing that it is rarely true of worrying that it produces a solution to a problem, and pointing out that a person can worry about events that are outside the realm of problem-solving. For example, someone might have taken an examination or attended an interview, and he or she worries about the outcome, even though it is now beyond their control.

Much worrying seems to involve the mental rehearsal of eventualities, specifically the potential negative outcomes of events. 'Worst case' scenarios figure largely, and Pruzinsky and Borkovec (1990) have coined a dramatic phrase to describe this, 'cognitive catastrophisation'. The contents of worry scales and adjective checklists developed in test anxiety research imply that much worrying is self-deprecatory and self-blaming, and is not directed at the search for effective coping strategies. Worrying may also serve as a protective strategy, akin to magical thinking; if I worry about the event or if I concentrate on the worst outcome, then that outcome will be less likely to happen. This belief might be deduced from the premise that undesirable outcomes are unexpected, which is, of course, often the case in life, for example in terms of difficulties with personal relationships, illness, and accidents. (Experienced viewers of television soaps like *Neighbours* just know that an overtly happy character is simply a catastrophe waiting to happen.) The reasoning seems to be: if undesired events are unexpected, then events that are anticipated must be less likely to happen.

Worry seems to be a thought process rather than, say, mental imagery. Borkovec and Inz (1990) asked highly anxious patients and a control group to report on their thoughts and images during a relaxation period and also when they were worrying. They were asked at intervals during each period to decide whether the contents of their mind were thoughts, images, both of these, or if they were not sure. They also rated whether these contents were pleasant or unpleasant. During the relaxation period the non-anxious subjects reported mostly imagery and very little thought, whereas the anxious group reported equal amounts of thought and imagery. During the worrying period, the amount of thought reported by the control group increased considerably and the amount of imagery reported by the anxious group decreased significantly. This pattern of results implies that worrying is associated with thought, and analysis of the pleasantness of these thoughts showed that they were rated more unpleasant during the worrying period, and this was true of both groups. There is also evidence that there are few differences on physiological measures between worriers and non-worriers. Borkovec has argued that one of the functions of worry might be to inhibit the physiological component of fear and this could help the individual to cope with his or her anxiety, although there is little direct evidence to support this hypothesis.

The fact of individual differences in worrying implies that worrying involves a bias in the perception or interpretation of events. There are many things that can be brought to mind about examinations or public speaking, but worriers dwell on the things that could go wrong. Is this because they believe that these outcomes are more likely to occur, possibly because they feel they lack the skills to avoid them? Or are worriers more sensitive to possible signs of threat in any given situation? Perhaps they take a realistic view of events whereas it is non-worriers who are subject to bias, avoiding warnings of danger or prone to believe that bad things can't happen to them?

Silverman et al. (1995) addressed some of these issues when they asked children to estimate how often the events they worried about actually happened. Events that children recognised to be unlikely to happen could nevertheless be a source of worry, for example, the single most worrying event was being attacked, yet the children predicted that this was not likely to happen. In general, the children did not worry most about the most likely things that could happen; I calculate the correlation between the intensity of worry and the judged frequency of events to be –0.44, across the 14 kinds of events included in their study.

Other research (Mathews, 1990) has compared the estimates of the likelihood of the same events made by worriers and non-worriers to find that worriers estimate the likelihood of threatening events as higher than non-worriers. They are also more prone to interpret an ambiguous event as a threatening one. For example, subjects might be asked to listen to a series of words and to write them down. Some words are homophones (die/dye; pain/pane) and it is found that anxious subjects are more likely to write down the more threatening version of the pair (die, pain). In another form of the task, subjects are presented with a sentence that is open to interpretation ('The two men watched as the chest was opened') and subsequently are tested for recognition memory of sentences. Anxious subjects are more likely to choose a threatening interpretation ('The two men watched as the patient's chest was cut open') than a non-threatening sentence ('The two men watched as the treasure chest was opened').

Worriers seem more 'vigilant' towards information that is relevant to their worries (Mathews, 1990). One way of studying this involves the Stroop effect. Subjects are presented with either a threatening or non-threatening word printed in a particular colour, and their task is to name the colour as quickly as they can while ignoring the word's content. For example, subjects who have a phobia about spiders might be presented with a set of words printed in different colours and one of the stimulus words would be 'spider'. Anxious subjects take longer to name the colour when the word is threatening than when it is non-threatening, implying that they have allocated more mental resources to processing its meaning. People take longer to name the colours when the stimulus word is relevant to their particular worries, for example, subjects with social worries would take longer to respond when the word was related to criticism than someone with, say, worries about their physical health. Patients with generalised anxiety disorder show longer latencies to naming colours in the presence of threatening words than do control group subjects. Patients who have received therapy subsequently report less worry and also show less word interference on the Stroop task (Mogg et al., 1995).

There is some evidence that this effect may be due to pre-conscious processes, that is, to an attentional bias before the information has resulted in conscious awareness. The effect can still be obtained among anxious subjects when the words are presented subliminally on a computer screen and patients who have recovered from generalised anxiety disorder no longer show an interference effect under these subliminal presentation conditions.

Arntz et al. (1995) describe a further bias where anxiety is maintained simply because the very fact that anxiety is experienced in itself provides evidence for the belief that there is something to be anxious about! Subjects were presented with scripted descriptions of hypothetical events, and variations in the scripts served to manipulate information about danger or safety in the situation and about anxious and non-anxious responses. Subjects rated each script on the extent to which each situation was dangerous. The ratings of non-anxious subjects were influenced by objective danger but not by the putative anxiety of the described response. However, four groups of subjects who were receiving treatment for spider phobia, social phobia, panic attacks, and generalised anxiety disorder were influenced both by danger information and by scripted information about their anxiety response.

The contents of worry

What do children worry about? A study by Pintner and Lev (1940) provided American 11- and 12-year-old children with a list of 53 things that could be worried about and asked the children how often they worried about them. The 10 most common worries expressed by boys were, in descending order: failing a test; mother working too hard; mother getting sick; being blamed for something you did not do; father working too hard; having a poor report card; being scolded; spoiling your good clothes; people telling lies about you. The most common worries were similar among girls: failing a test; mother working too hard; mother getting sick; being late for school; getting sick; father working too hard; being scolded; being blamed for something you did not do; doing wrong; father getting sick. When the items were grouped by the researchers on the basis of their judgement of how similar they were, the most common worries were to do with the family, school, and social adequacy (largely concern with being scolded or punished). The paper was submitted for publication in 1938, which might explain why none of the items made reference to the Second World War, which the USA entered in 1941.

Silverman *et al.* (1995) interviewed a sample of children aged from 8 to 12 years about their worries. The most frequently mentioned worries were about personal harm from others, school performance, hurricanes, dying or getting killed, social things (e.g. worry about others' feelings), sports performance, parents might break up, not enough money for necessities, and being picked on by classmates. The single most frequent worry, personal harm, referred to being attacked by other people, for example, by being mugged, stabbed or shot. When their worries were arranged in categories, the most *frequently mentioned* categories of worries concerned health, school, and personal harm, and the categories that elicited the most *intense* worry were war, money, disasters, family and personal harm.

School remains a topic of worry for children across the 55 years separating these two studies, but the contemporary child is more worried about personal harm, war and disasters. Perhaps the experience of children is different today, for example, in patterns of play outside the home and in parental warnings of the dangers posed by strangers; alternatively, television and the other contemporary mass media might make children more conscious of crime, war, sexual abuse, and all the harms that could befall them.

There have been several analyses of the worries of adults. Eysenck and Van Berkum (1992) identified 10 clusters within a worry questionnaire: physical health; panic and loss of control; the health of close ones; social evaluative; personal relationships; physical appearance; financial; personal fulfilment; international and nuclear issues; society and the environment. Factor analysis revealed two factors. The first had highest loadings on personal fulfilment, social evaluation, finance, personal relationships and physical appearance, and was labelled Social Evaluative Worries. The second factor accounted for a smaller proportion of variance, and was labelled Physical Threat because of its highest loadings on health of close ones, society and environment, international and nuclear issues, and physical health.

Who worries? Not surprisingly, children and adults who score highly on tests of trait anxiety worry more than low scorers on these tests (Silverman *et al.*, 1995; Meyer *et al.*, 1990), as do adults who have low self-esteem, who are self-conscious and who are socially anxious (Pruzinsky and Borkovec, 1990). According to the *Diagnostic and Statistical Manual of Mental Disorders* (DSM-IV; American Psychiatric Association, 1994: 435), 'excessive anxiety and worry (apprehensive expectation) occurring more days than not for at least 6 months, about a number of events or activities (such as work or school performance)' is the principal diagnostic criterion for generalised anxiety disorder. Several studies have confirmed that worry is characteristic of patients with generalised anxiety disorder (e.g. Borkovec and Inz, 1990).

Anxiety, worry, and test performance

We argued above that anxiety can either help or hinder performance, depending on factors like the level of anxiety, the nature of the task, and the individual's past learning. We indicated too that there was a shift from explaining the relationship between task difficulty and anxiety in terms of habit towards an emphasis upon attention processes. However, the concept of 'task difficulty' is rather vague. Alternative explanations of performance deficits have been framed in terms of cognitive processes other than attention and we turn to consider these accounts.

Leon (1989) tested the hypothesis that the range of cues that is used narrows with increased anxiety by examining the use of relevant and irrelevant cues in performance on analogical reasoning tasks varying in the amount of information included. She was particularly interested in two kinds of errors, errors of inclusion, where subjects introduced material that was irrelevant to the problem, and of exclusion, where subjects omitted necessary information. Attentional explanations of anxiety have emphasised exclusion errors due to narrowing of the focus of attention. When the task involves little information, anxious subjects should make fewer inclusion errors because they attend to less information. When the task is rich in information, anxious subjects should make more errors of exclusion, due to their narrow focus of attention. However, she found little support for the attentional hypothesis in that anxious subjects tended to make more inclusion errors than non-anxious subjects, whatever the amount of information in the problem. They tended to make more exclusion errors than non-anxious subjects when the problem involved little information, and they made more inclusion than exclusion errors when the problem was information-rich. She argued that a more parsimonious explanation was that the anxious subjects processed the information more slowly, either because their anxiety captured available attentional resources or it reduced working memory capacity.

Darke (1988: 501) measured speed of performance on different kinds of inference tasks. Subjects were presented with pairs of sentences like 'A trumpet was being played. The musical instrument was very quiet'. After some filler sentences, the subjects would receive the probe question, 'True or false? – The trumpet was quiet'. These sentences were categorised by Darke as requiring a *necessary* inference, in the sense that the reader has to match the trumpet with the musical instrument as he or she is reading in order to understand the sentences. An unnecessary inference is where the sentence can be understood without making the inference: 'The man pounded the nail. He was very tired. True or false? – The man used a hammer'. Darke argued that necessary inferences were made unconsciously and made little demand upon information capacity, whereas unnecessary inferences were conscious and involved processing capacity, specifically the use of working memory. There were no differences between anxious and less anxious subjects in speed of responding to sentences involving necessary inferences, but anxious subjects were significantly slower on the unnecessary inference sentences than low anxious subjects.

Both studies refer to the concept of 'working memory' in explaining deficits in performance. Eysenck (1992; Eysenck and Calvo, 1992) has elaborated 'Processing Efficiency Theory' in order to account for the effects of anxiety and worry upon performance. This assigns a central role to working memory. Baddeley and Hitch (1974; see also Eysenck, 1992) presented a model of working memory that had three components: an articulatory loop used to rehearse verbal material; a visuo-spatial sketch pad, used for non-verbal material; and a central executive. As the term 'working' implies, the theory is an attempt to understand the role that memory plays in processing information and it recognises that in many tasks, like reading, or following a conversation, information has to be held in the cognitive system long enough for it to be processed, related to information that has just been received or is stored elsewhere in the system, and so on. Management of this role is the task of the central executive. If, for example, the task is to hold a list of names in memory, then the central executive will initiate a rehearsal strategy to meet the demands of this task. Where tasks have been learned so that they have become routine, then the central executive is not needed, but if difficulties are encountered, then processing resources have to be allocated to the task.

It can be seen that the theory offers a way of conceptualising task difficulty, in that an easy task is one that makes few demands on working
memory. Processing efficiency theory asserts that 'worry pre-empts some
of the processing and storage resources of working memory' (Eysenck and
Calvo, 1992: 415). However, it would be misleading to regard anxiety in a
straightforward way as a drain on resources. Anxiety can have many effects
on behaviour. The first response to threat of failure might be to devote
additional attention and effort to preparation for an examination; alternatively, the person might be motivated to avoid thinking about it and put
off any preparation. In order to understand these, it is useful to postulate
a control or self-regulatory function within the working memory system
that comes into operation when the person encounters difficulties with
an ongoing task. This control system has an overview of the task and can
evaluate current performance relative to task goals, and can draw upon the
resources of working memory in pursuit of these goals. It might be the case,
then, that performance might not suffer from anxiety; however, the claim
is that this level of performance has only been achieved with a cost, the
additional cognitive resources that have had to be used. It would be more
accurate to say, as in the name of the theory, that anxiety affects *efficiency*
of processing. By analogy, a factory might produce the same number of
goods despite the absence of key workers or material in one department,
because the organisation mobilises extra resources to compensate for this.
The output remains the same, but the costs are higher and the enterprise
has been less efficient.

The theory proposes that anxiety will not adversely affect performance
on tasks that do not require the central executive or the articulatory loop,
and support for this prediction comes from the study by Darke (1988)
summarised above. It is also compatible with the findings of Leon's study,
as it asserts that processing time is an index of processing efficiency. The
notion that the anxious person uses more of his or her available working
memory system than the less anxious person can be tested by examining
the effects of introducing an additional task to a task where anxious and
non-anxious persons have comparable levels of achievement (see Eysenck,
1992: 142). The prediction is that the anxious person will do less well on
this additional task because he or she has committed more resources to the
initial task.

These problems become salient for students who are preparing
for examinations. Exams typically come in sets, like GCSE, A-levels,
Baccalaureate, or university finals papers, rather than individually,
and the student has to plan a revision schedule that allows for this. A
survey by Sloboda (1990) found that university students expressed most
worries about their overall workload and about not having enough time
for revision, and the most anxious students had most worries of these
kinds.

OVERCOMING ANXIETY

How can students be helped to overcome their anxiety? The situations that produce most anxiety in education are examinations. Students express considerable anxiety about these, and the examination period in the school year coincides with a rise in the number of students seeking help from doctors or counsellors. Sloboda (1990) reported findings about final examinations in one British university, where 28 percent of respondents to a questionnaire reported frequent anxiety and depression in the revision period before finals, and 38 percent experienced general anxiety during the examination period. The university medical officer estimated that 10 percent of all finalists consulted the doctor with problems related to their examinations.

Many characteristics of the traditional form of examination contribute to this anxiety. First, there is the personal significance of the outcomes of assessment. The outcome means a great deal to students in terms of their aspirations, there is considerable stigma associated with failure, and there is often the fear of disappointing family, friends and teachers. Assessments are 'ego-involving'. The most common public examinations are 'unseen' and the candidate will only know the questions to be answered when he or she reads the question paper in the examination hall. Clearly, this can produce intense anxiety immediately before the examination itself, but it can also affect the process of revision beforehand, as a student can never be sure how much preparation to do, or what to learn. There is also the stress that coincides with any performance that demands effort. The form of the examination makes considerable demands on memory, and candidates can worry whether they will be able to recall material under examination conditions. However, forms of assessment like coursework and writing essays also create anxiety, particularly if, as is typically the case, a number of assignments have to be completed within a short space of time.

The research that we have summarised suggests some methods for coping with the anxiety that is associated with examinations and also helps explain why some methods that are often recommended to students might be successful. Researchers into test anxiety have carried out intervention studies to try to change anxiety levels and performance. Sarason has shown that instructions that emphasise the evaluative nature of the test have an adverse effect upon performance. In one study, a confederate of the researcher drew the examiner's attention in the middle of a test to say that she couldn't cope with the problems, and the examiner responded in a supportive manner by explaining that many others shared that experience and showing how the student could cope; this intervention produced better performance by other students present relative to a group where no such incident took place. Social support prior to a test, in the sense that candidates participated in discussion groups and shared their anxieties about the examination also had a beneficial effect upon the subsequent performance of highly anxious students; it made little difference to that of less anxious students. The effectiveness of these two approaches seems to lie in diverting candidates' attention from self-deprecation and in giving guidance on coping strategies.

Good preparation is an aid to good examination performance and at least part of this relationship is due to its implications for anxiety. Sloboda (1990) found that self-reported anxiety during the revision period was associated with poorer examination marks and had more impact upon performance than anxiety during the examination itself. Well-prepared material is least disrupted by anxiety, and research has shown that under test conditions anxious students perform more poorly on tasks that are novel or difficult. Preparation makes tasks more familiar and less complex. Effective preparation, in the sense of organised revision that is clearly planned, increases self-confidence whereas inadequate preparation adds to anxiety.

A further advantage of organised revision is that it leads to task-oriented thinking and allows less scope for ego-oriented or self-deprecatory thinking. The best way to counter worry is to direct energies towards planning rather than spending time in rumination or in denial. Teachers can help reduce anxiety by encouraging students to plan their revision and by explaining in detail the form the examination will take, including providing past relevant papers and working through these with the students to model how answers can be planned and tackled. Working through is essential and it is unhelpful simply to provide the students with the material. When students have not yet completed their revision, the questions on the sample paper may seem unfamiliar and complex and simply exposing them to the questions may only undermine their confidence. Modelling also increases their confidence by reducing the unknown element in the examination, and by presenting them with a series of steps that they can follow immediately on entering the examination itself. This can provide a protection against the debilitating effects of anxiety.

Sarason et al. (1990) report a study comparing the performance of students scoring either high or low on the worry scale of the RTT under one of three different sets of instructions. One group was simply reassured and advised not to worry. A second group was given guidance on how to attend to the problems and engage in task-relevant thinking; the third group acted as a control group. The reassurance and attention-directing instructions had beneficial effects on the performance of the high-worry students. After the test, participants completed the CIQ, and it was found that high-worry students reported fewer intrusive negative thoughts following attention-directing instructions. (Low-worried students did more poorly following reassurance, implying that a moderate level of anxiety aids performance).

Modelling, in the sense of demonstrating approaches to problem-solving by 'thinking aloud', helps performance by providing examples of coping strategies and by influencing students' expectancies. Parents can support preparation by providing physical space in which to work and over which the student has control. They should be prepared to listen to the anxieties that are expressed and not minimise these.

Effective preparation means planning work sessions so that they are spaced at intervals rather than long, unbroken sessions. There is considerable evidence to support the 'spacing effect' in learning. The equivalent amount of time in learning is much more productive if the time is divided into shorter, spaced sessions.

Taking breaks, spending time on other activities, physical exercise also contribute to coping with anxiety, sustaining motivation and avoiding fatigue. Revision that is left to the last minute seems particularly ineffective and prone to elicit high levels of anxiety. Sloboda (1990) found that an inability to 'switch off' and relax was correlated with stress levels during examinations.

There are benefits from sharing experiences with others. The recognition that others are faced with the same demands and experience them in similar ways helps to minimise ego-involvement and avoid self-deprecation. We have seen evidence for this in Sarason's studies of the beneficial effects of social support. Students should try not to exaggerate the importance of examinations. Performance is particularly poor when the evaluative nature of the test is emphasised, as we saw in Deffenbacher's study of the adverse effects of ego-involving instructions.

It is important to recognise that strategies that are successful in coping with anxiety may not in themselves lead to good examination performance. For example, Houston (1977) interviewed candidates after an examination about their thoughts and feelings and inferred from their responses the ways in which they had tried to manage their anxiety. Their anxiety levels were assessed several weeks before and also immediately before the examination and, finally, their marks were known. Students were classified into 10 groups on the basis of their coping strategies as inferred from the interviews. High anxiety levels were associated with worrying, the failure to develop a coping strategy, and comparing oneself with how other students would perform. Less anxiety was associated with 'intellectualization' (taking an objective, analytical approach towards the examination), avoidant thinking, and 'resignation'. Good examination performance was associated with intellectualization and poor performance with avoidant thinking, worry, resignation, lack of strategy, and social comparison. Avoiding thinking about the examination and being passive and resigned are successful in reducing anxiety but produce poor performance, presumably by interfering with adequate preparation. The findings confirm the association between levels of anxiety and performance and worry and self-deprecatory comparison of the self with others.

Other strategies can be successful in making productive use of anxiety. Norem and Cantor (1986) describe a strategy of defensive pessimism. A tendency to adopt this was assessed by a questionnaire including items like, 'I go into academic situations expecting the worst, even though I know I will probably do OK'. Students who are anxious about the outcome of a test set themselves low expectations of success but use the anxiety raised by these to motivate themselves to prepare well for the test. Norem and Cantor found that this strategy was vulnerable to reassurance; pessimistic students who were encouraged to believe that they would find no difficulty with the test performed less well than those who were given no reassurance. These findings demonstrate the complex relationships that can obtain between anxiety, performance, and students' perceptions of themselves and tests.

CONCLUSION

Thinking about the relationships between anxiety and performance has been influenced by two perspectives. The first emphasises the organising function of anxiety, where mental and physical resources are mobilised to focus attention on the source of the threat and to find an escape. The second emphasises disorganisation, and is, perhaps, epitomised by Corporal Jones, the character in the classic BBC television comedy series *Dad's Army* who responds to every problem by rushing around in a flap, urging everyone, 'Don't panic! Don't panic!', while producing confusion and impeding all the group's efforts to solve the problem. Psychological theories have tried to embrace both perspectives, and this raises the question of how to specify the conditions under which anxiety helps or hinders performance.

There have been two recurrent notions. The first is that arousal or excitation that enhances performance can develop into agitation that gets in the way of effective action. The second is that easy or well-learned tasks are less susceptible to the disabling influence of anxiety, whereas complex or novel tasks are more readily disrupted. This explanation was originally couched in behaviourist terms, but more recent approaches have emphasised cognitive processes. Worry has been identified as a factor in poor performance. Explanations have been framed in terms of the role of the executive control and working memory components of the information-processing system. This approach has had the advantage of suggesting in greater detail, and using a less circular form of argument, how task difficulty might be related to anxiety.

It has also accompanied a shift from a mechanistic view of anxiety towards the notion of strategies that can be adopted by individuals to cope with the threats that they face. Studies of test anxiety have identified several of these strategies and have suggested which might be more effective in academic settings. Methods of academic assessment have traditionally been stressful, and the reliance upon unseen examinations has encouraged approaches to studying that themselves foster stress: reliance upon rote memory, a risky strategy of anticipating questions, and peak performance within a short period of time. Individuals who have high scores on measures of anxiety and test anxiety tend to do less well on these assessments. While they can be helped to cope with their anxiety, it would be desirable to include a range of assessment methods in any course, to allow students with different personality profiles to reveal their academic abilities.

Chapter 5

Motivation

'Must try harder!' School reports typically comment on a pupil's effort and seem to regard it as being as important as achievement in summarising his or her performance over the term. Teachers often have little sympathy with children who are lazy, and the able child who puts little effort into lessons attracts much greater censure than the child who has achieved less but who has put in more effort. From a different perspective, children who are disaffected with school frequently attribute this to the fact that school is boring and that it is simply not worth trying. The majority of young truants interviewed by Carlen *et al.* (1992) claimed that they were bored both in school and out of school. Interest and boredom were also recurrent themes in interviews conducted by Hesketh (1987) in an attempt to understand young people's dissatisfaction with school. Mark, a student at sixth form college, reflected on what makes a good teacher:

> I don't like work sheets or loads of questions on the board. I think a good teacher talks and discusses the topic with the class and then gives them notes at the end of the discussion. Worksheets are really boring. If you just sit all lesson doing that, you end up chatting with your friends and they are the sort of lesson where the teacher doesn't even learn everyone's name. If you get involved in the subject it's much more interesting. At sixth form college at the moment, biology is discussed and you can argue with the teacher. But in chemistry the atmosphere is really boring. We just copy off the board. (p. 33)

MOTIVATION AS A TRAIT

Is it useful to characterise students as either motivated or lazy, that is, to regard these predispositions as stable, personal attributes rather than perceiving them as descriptions of how students behave in particular situations? Why do many students seem to put little effort into their studies? This chapter addresses these questions. We begin by briefly reviewing evidence that suggests that there may be some value in thinking of motivation as a personality trait. We then consider some recent theoretical positions in research into motivation that regard the question of effort as more complex than can be explained simply by reference to a personality trait. These positions emphasise the processes that lead to more or less effort being expended in particular situations and, in particular, they assign importance to the meanings those situations have for students.

A number of psychological approaches suggest that effort is a stable characteristic of individuals. One approach has been to identify the distinctive personality characteristics of those people who are the most eminent in different walks of life. Cox (1926; see also Simonton, 1987) examined documentary material on one hundred 'geniuses' to investigate which personality traits predicted their exceptional achievement, and she emphasised the role of motivation, concluding that 'high but not the highest intelligence, combined with the greatest degree of persistence, will achieve greater eminence than the highest degree of intelligence with somewhat less persistence' (p. 187, cited by Simonton, 1987: 138).

Similar findings were obtained in a series of investigations of highly creative individuals carried out at the Institute for Personality Assessment and Research at the University of California by McKinnon and his associates in the 1950s. The research strategy here was first to identify those individuals who were regarded as the outstanding creative leaders in their field, drawing upon nominations by their peers and published indicators of their standing in their field. These creative individuals were then invited to the Institute for a period of several days where they were interviewed at length and where they also completed standardised tests of personality and intelligence. Motivation emerged as an important theme in all their studies.

For example, McKinnon (1962/1970) compared the most creative architects with two groups of less eminent architects. A consistent pattern of results emerged. Interviewers rated the most creative group as distinctive on a number of traits, and judged them to be responsible, ambitious, industrious, conscientious, determined, energetic and persevering. The four statements on a Q-sort test that were chosen by interviewers as most descriptive of this group were: 'enjoys aesthetic impressions'; 'has high aspiration level for self'; 'values own independence and autonomy'; 'is productive/gets things done'. Findings from standardised psychological tests confirmed these impressions. In conclusion, McKinnon (p. 310) emphasised the creative individual's 'independence in thought and action, his high level of energy, his unquestioning commitment to creative endeavor and his unceasing striving for creative solutions to the ever more difficult architectural problems which he constantly sets for himself'.

More recently, the Creativity in Later Life project conducted by Csikszentmihalyi and his associates at the University of Chicago obtained similar findings when they conducted a series of in-depth interviews with men and women over the age of 60 who have made highly significant contributions to natural science, the social sciences, the arts and humanities, and business, media and politics (see Mockros and Csikszentmihalyi, 1996). Their study reveals that these individuals are characterised by high levels of motivation, discipline, perseverance, autonomy and self-confidence. Thus, individuals who achieve eminence are characterised by high levels of motivation that are evident throughout their lives, motivation that enables them to achieve mastery over the knowledge and skills of their area of specialisation, to produce original ideas and exert leadership in their field, and to persist in the face of obstacles and, frequently, hostility or rejection by their peers. Their high levels of motivation seem to distinguish them from other very able and talented people who do not achieve the same degree of eminence.

Rathunde and Csikszentmihalyi (1993) measured 'undivided interest' among a sample of talented high school students. This was defined as spontaneous and directed involvement in a task. The students carried electronic pagers for one week and reported their activities at frequent intervals during that period. The pager prompted them to record what they were doing at the time and they completed self-report forms on whether they were excited, bored, involved, and so on. Those who reported greater undivided interest in, say, music, had greater engagement in, and achievements in music when these were tested on their graduation, three years later. Similar results held for talent in art, science and mathematics.

A second strand of evidence comes from research into trait measures. For many years, research was dominated by the construct of achievement motivation. This has its origins in Murray's concept of 'need for achievement' and was originally assessed in projective tests by content analysis of responses to ambiguous pictures. Subsequently, questionnaire measures were developed (McClelland, 1987) and scores on these tests were found to be correlated with academic attainment. Motivation is a core trait in the Big Five factor model of personality (see Chapter 1). Individuals who score high on the 'conscientious' factor are organised, hard-working, self-disciplined, ambitious and persevering, whereas those who obtain low scores are aimless, lazy, careless, lax, negligent, weak-willed and hedonistic. Unsurprisingly, as we reported in Chapter 1, conscientiousness is significantly correlated with academic achievement.

Despite the evidence that motivation is a stable characteristic of individuals, this aspect has attracted much less attention in recent years. One reason for this is the impact of arguments that behaviour in a given situation is influenced more by characteristics of the situation than it is by the individual's personality, and that an individual's behaviour differs markedly in different situations. Mischel's points struck a chord with researchers into motivation. It is apparent that people who are prepared to invest a great deal of effort in one situation lack interest elsewhere. A child who is bored and restless at school might be very keen in playing or following sport, or in playing computer games, and he or she might demonstrate in pursuit of these activities the very qualities that their teachers have looked for in vain in school.

It is often the case, too, that expressions of boredom can reflect complex relationships between the individual and the school. The persistent truants who participated in the study by Carlen *et al.* (1992) had rejected school and claimed to find it boring. However, when asked about the reasons why anyone should attend school, truants and non-truants alike nominated the most important reasons as helping to get a job, meeting friends and socialising, learning something useful, enjoying lessons, and obtaining qualifications. Truancy did not seem linked to lack of motivation, if this is defined in terms of their perceptions of the benefits that could be obtained from attending school. Rather, it seemed that these young people judged that school had little to offer them as individuals. These judgements were associated in the majority of cases with adverse economic and family circumstances (20 of the 40 truants had been in residential care, family discord was common, and there were histories of unemployment, divorce, and abuse in their families). Interviews suggested that many of the routine features of school life, such as wearing a uniform or doing homework, were perceived by the young people as signs that school was 'not for them'. Once a career of truancy had been embarked upon, the responses of schools and local education authorities and the influence of other truants often served only to alienate them even further from school. When one examines more closely students' expressions of boredom at school one can find themes of alienation and personal discontent that cannot simply be reduced to a trait of conscientiousness.

A second and somewhat different example of an apparent lack of motivation can be found more generally in the behaviour of many adolescents. A common pattern of inactivity that is familiar to many parents is exhibited by young people who spend a lot of time alone in their room, listening to music or lying in bed, who are difficult to get up in the morning, who seem exhausted at even the faintest suggestion of doing homework or helping with the household chores, and who seem to reject the shared activities of the home that they embraced only a short time previously. During this time, watching television with the family decreases and solitary viewing increases. Solitary music listening becomes the predominant pastime. 'Laziness' often seems the most apt description of this behaviour and it can be a source of considerable friction within the family. How is it to be explained?

Some recent approaches have emphasised processes of identity formation. Adolescence has long been regarded by psychologists as a crucial period in personality development, particularly by Erikson (1968), who suggested that it provided a *moratorium*, a time in which the young person has an opportunity to form his or her personal identity. Research has shown that adolescence is associated with lower self-esteem, more intense self-consciousness and more unhappiness, and surveys show elevated rates of depression, eating disorders, and suicide among this age group. Larson (1995: 547) argues that young people use this solitary time and its activities for self-exploration and for coping with the negative emotions character-istic of this period. Writing of listening to music, he says,

> Adolescents use music listening ... to directly engage with issues of identity. Solitary music listening, I have argued, is a fantasy ground for exploring possible selves. Sometimes this involves pumping oneself up with images of power and conquest; other times, it may involve fantasies of merger and rescue by an idealized lover; yet other times, it may involve intense worry about personal shortcomings and their significance for one's future. The images and emotions of popular music allow one to feel a range of internal states and try on alternate identities, both desired and feared.

Although the adolescent often appears indolent and aimless to an observer, he or she can be actively engaged in intense psychological 'work'.

Both these examples show that persistent patterns of behaviour that are characterised as laziness or lack of motivation can be better understood in terms of a complex of personal and situational factors rather than in terms of stable personality traits. Our examples illustrate two of the themes of recent research into motivation: the individual's evaluation of the relevance of any given situation to their goals, and the involvement of the self. A third theme needs little exemplification: education involves experiences of success and failure. Sometimes these are inherent in the nature of learning, since mastering skills of any degree of complexity inevitably involves setbacks. Success and failure are a consequence of mass education systems, where limitations of resources mean that there are restrictions on the time and individual attention available for teaching and learning, and selection or streaming for different kinds of educational experiences on the basis of students' achievements is one of the methods of coping with scarce resources.

Categorising students on the basis of their achievements, even if this is done with the best intentions, inevitably produces feelings of failure among those in lower streams or special classes. This is evident in the cases brought against educational authorities in America by civil rights groups, who argued successfully that the higher proportion of minority children receiving special education was caused by bias in the assessment of children. Their perception was that these children were unfairly treated, and stigmatised, although these special classes are ostensibly set up with the interests of children in mind.

Finally, success and failure also reflect the contradiction between the standardised and uniform curricula of the educational system and individual differences in learning, whether these are differences in prior experiences, abilities, aptitudes, learning styles or interests. We begin our exploration of these themes with attribution theory, which has had a huge influence on contemporary thinking about effort.

ATTRIBUTION THEORY

Explanations of success and failure

This approach to understanding behaviour emphasises the causal explanations that people frame for their success and failure experiences. It drew upon Heider's (1958; see also Weiner, 1979: 6) interest in the psychology of 'common sense' and his argument that psychologists should study the ways in which people interpret their everyday environment. An individual's interpretation will depend on how he or she conceives the causes of events, and attribution theory distinguishes whether an event is caused by the individual, factors that are external to the individual, or some combination of the two. If someone believes that he or she has caused an event to happen then their understanding of that event and its implications will be different than if they thought that some other factor caused the event. Weiner (1979) set out an influential application of this approach to motivation in education. His account proposed three dimensions of causality, whether the cause was internal or external, whether it was stable or unstable, and whether it was controllable or uncontrollable. Everyday explanations of success and failure experiences could be located along each of these dimensions.

A student can account for success in terms of her ability, that is, she succeeds because she is clever or is good at the task. In terms of the causal dimensions, ability is internal (it is a characteristic of the person), it is stable (cleverness shows some consistency over time) and it is uncontrollable (there's nothing much one can do about one's ability or lack of it). A second factor influencing achievement outcomes is effort: one succeeds because one has worked hard or fails because one didn't try. In terms of the causal dimensions, effort is internal, unstable and controllable. Although it is each individual's responsibility how much effort they exert and this is something that is internal and under their control, this varies over time and across situations, and hence is unstable. A third influence upon achievement is the difficulty of the task, and this is seen as external to, and beyond the control of the individual, and also as a stable attribute of the task. The final influence is luck, which is external, unstable and, of course, uncontrollable. Luck does not figure as prominently in explanations of educational success and failure as in other areas of life, although it does appear, for example, in students' accounts of their performance in examinations – one can be lucky in the choice of questions that one revised or in guessing the answer to a question – and a student can also be lucky to be in the class of a good teacher or in having a sympathetic examiner.

The theory stresses the personal nature of these attributions, and it might be that an individual's judgements about the internality, stability, or uncontrollability of ability, effort, task difficulty or luck is idiosyncratic. We have provided a classification of these factors on the causal dimensions, but interpretations that diverge from those of attribution theory are also tenable. It is arguable that ability can be controllable, in that one can choose whether or not to apply it in any given task. Effort can surely be either stable or unstable, and it can also be perceived as controllable or beyond one's control. The perception of how difficult a task is can fluctuate over time. Attributions to task difficulty can be external, in the sense that a particular task would be difficult for anyone, or internal and related to ability: this is a difficult task for me even though other people can do it. Some psychologists have raised doubts whether controllability is in fact a separate dimension from the other two. Additional dimensions have been proposed, for example, globality, the extent to which a cause is specific to one situation or is applicable to a range of situations (Abramson *et al.*, 1978). The influence of other people, such as parents or teachers, is also a relevant dimension. Despite these reservations and modifications, the theory has been very influential in shaping current understanding of motivation, and we now look at some of the reasons for this.

It articulates a process that relates motivation to educational outcomes. One entrenched view of this process has been that success leads to continued involvement with a task whereas failure leads to giving up. This view has a long history within educational psychology and it can be traced back to Thorndike's Law of Effect, which proposed that actions that lead to a satisfying outcome would be repeated whereas those that produce an unsatisfactory outcome would not. Behaviourist theories, more generally, propose predictable relationships between the probability of behaviour and the rewards or reinforcements contingent upon that behaviour. Behaviour that is reinforced is more likely to be repeated in an equivalent situation in the future. Behaviour that is not reinforced will tend not to be repeated.

In opposition to this view, attribution theory proposes that it is the individual's interpretation of an outcome that is crucial in influencing future actions. It suggests the following sequence of events mediating between outcome and future behaviour. When the individual perceives the outcome of an action, he or she tries to interpret the causes for this outcome in terms of the causal dimensions of ability, effort, task difficulty and luck. Depending upon the attribution made, the person experiences an emotional reaction to the outcome, for example, feelings of pride or shame, each of which is more likely following internal rather than external attributions of outcomes. These interpretations also influence the expectations that the individual holds about the likelihood of future success and failure. Finally, these expectations and emotions together influence future performance on the task. For example, failure at a task that is perceived as easy (in the sense that other students succeed), and where one has tried hard, produces feelings of shame and lowers expectations that one will succeed in the future. Thus, the theory makes explicit predictions about relationships between outcomes, emotional reactions, interpretations of events, expectations of future outcomes, and future behaviour.

Empirical studies

The theory leads to empirical investigations of people's explanations of their success and failure experiences and the relationship of these explanations to motivation. One derivation from the theory that has been extensively investigated is that students with high achievement motivation attribute their success to internal and stable causes and their failures to external and unstable causes. This tendency has also been labelled as 'self-serving bias' or 'egotism': the individual takes credit for his or her success but denies responsibility for failure – a pattern perhaps most familiar in the political arena! It is argued that students high in achievement motivation show this bias whereas those who are low in achievement motivation do not share this bias.

Several approaches have been taken to the problem of measuring causal attributions in order to test these hypotheses. Elig and Frieze (1979) categorise these approaches into unstructured and structured techniques. The former employ open-ended questions, for example, interviews where students are given an opportunity to reply in their own words to a question such as why they thought they had failed on a test. Their responses are coded into different categories of causal attribution and the researcher can count the number of references to ability, effort, and so on. Structured methods have tended to rely upon rating scales, where participants rate on a numerical scale the extent to which different factors contributed to their success or failure. These scales have been the most widely used method but they have the disadvantage that they prescribe the terms that participants use for their self-descriptions, and these terms might not be the ones that are salient in their common sense explanations.

Elig and Frieze (1979) compared both kinds of measures in an experiment where success and failure outcomes were induced among students by manipulating the difficulty of anagram problems. The students were then asked, in different ways, for explanations of these outcomes. The structured tests had sounder psychometric properties in that they showed greater convergent and discriminative validity than the open-ended measures. That is, there was greater consistency in attributions between different versions of the structured tests than between the open-ended and structured tests.

Individual differences in causal attributions

A review of research into the causal attributions made by children aged between 6 and 13 years found consistent evidence of self-serving bias. Whitley and Frieze (1985) applied the statistical technique of meta-analysis to the findings of 25 published studies that varied in the measurement technique they adopted and that investigated attributions in real-life educational settings as well as in controlled laboratory tasks where success and failure is manipulated. Meta-analysis enables the investigator to make comparisons among studies even when they differ in their experimental designs and in their sample sizes and it also provides an indication of how large any difference is between groups or conditions. Across the studies as a whole, ability and effort were perceived as causes of success rather than of failure, whereas failure was attributed to task difficulty. Meta-analysis showed that these effects were significantly larger in classroom tests and examinations than in the experimental tasks.

This bias in attributions has been explained in terms of its value for protecting self-esteem. It is a painful experience to take responsibility for one's failures and there seems to be a strong tendency to avoid this. For example, interviews with disaffected school pupils carried out by Hesketh (1987) elicited attributions in terms of external factors. Their difficulties were attributed to the school's lack of interest in less successful pupils, to the school rules, to the school picking on pupils ('Anything done in school was blamed on a few people; me and four others', Jason, aged 15; quoted by Hesketh, 1987: 36) and, above all, to teachers: 'There are some [teachers] who like everyone else and they take it out on me. Well, everyone will be talking in class and if I am talking then they'll take it out on me and no one else ... they get on to me and no one else' (pupil quoted by Chaplain, 1996: 107).

However, there are individual differences in this pattern of attributions and these are linked to low self-esteem and vulnerability. Phillips (1984) studied a sample of 11-year-old pupils who were among the highest achievers in their school and were in the top 25 percent on a test of academic achievement. These pupils were divided into three groups, high, average and low, on the basis of their scores on a test of self-esteem, Harter's Perceived Competence Scale. They then completed a number of measures of their expectancies of success and motivation, including ratings of the influence upon their achievement of ability, stable and unstable effort, attention and concentration, task difficulty, luck, interest, and help by others (teachers and parents). The groups showed different patterns of attributions to ability and unstable effort. Students high in perceived self-competence rated ability as more influential than effort in determining their success, whereas the low self-competence group ascribed more importance to effort than to ability. In their explanations of failure, students high in perceived self-competence attributed their failure to task difficulty and played down the role of effort and ability, but those with low self-competence beliefs attributed failure primarily to lack of effort and, to a lesser extent, lack of ability.

These findings are significant, for several reasons. These children were high achievers and all had a consistent record of success. This was not sufficient, however, to produce feelings of competence among all the students, and this reinforces the core assertion of attribution theory that objective success is not a sufficient condition for expectancies of future success. Students who do not gain confidence from their success do not show the expected self-serving bias; rather, they attribute failure to internal factors rather than to external ones and they attribute success to unstable factors rather than to stable, internal ones. It is apparent that effort is the pivot to their explanations, to the extent that it is emphasised as a factor in both success and failure, in contrast to high self-esteem students who emphasise it as a factor only in success. This implies that these students fail to derive any sense that past success will lead to future success, since they do not attribute their achievements to their ability; only by working hard, can they ensure success. This belief is reinforced by the belief that failure is due to lack of effort, and this leads to students being continually driven to ever greater efforts, to a treadmill of work. One is only as good as one's last assignment and there is no confidence that one will be successful in the future. Furthermore, one cannot take pride in or draw emotional satisfaction from success, since it is so uncertain and has to be struggled for. On the other hand, one can feel shame and blame oneself for failure since this is caused by lack of effort, rather than by the difficulty of the task or other external factors.

Phillips studied the pattern of attributions among very successful children. Licht et al. (1985) investigated the causal attributions for failure outcomes made by a sample of children with learning difficulties who had been referred by an educational psychologist to special classes. These children were less likely than a control group, matched for age, sex, and IQ (both groups had mean IQs close to the population average of 100) to attribute failure to lack of effort, but their attributions to ability and external factors were strongly influenced by gender. Among girls, those with learning difficulties were more likely than the control group to attribute failure to lack of ability; among boys, the opposite pattern was found, and boys with learning difficulties were more likely than their peers to attribute failure to external factors. Thus, boys with learning difficulties tended towards the self-serving bias, whereas girls were more likely to show the more vulnerable pattern of blaming themselves for failure. This study did not include a condition where pupils provided explanations for their success, which is disappointing, not only in terms of providing a complete picture of their causal attributions but also in the fact that the design of the study itself tends to reinforce the pupils' experiences and, perhaps, expectations of school failure. Nevertheless, its findings provide further support for the thesis that outcomes in themselves do not determine psychological responses.

Learned helplessness

Another way of construing individual differences has been in terms of learned helplessness. This concept emerged in studies of animal behaviour that were carried out by Seligman and his colleagues at the University of Pennsylvania in order to explain a pattern of behaviour where animals unable to escape punishment eventually ceased to try to avoid it, even when the means for doing so became available. Dogs who had experienced electric shocks from which they could not escape showed a characteristic pattern of reactions when they were placed in a situation where a simple response could avoid the shock. They made few attempts to escape, they showed little emotional reaction to their predicament, and they did not repeat responses even when these led to safety.

Learned helplessness is typically defined in terms of lack of persistence at a task following failure because failure is regarded as insurmountable and subsequent developments of the concept linked it with concepts from attribution theory: failure is attributed to stable, uncontrollable internal factors like lack of ability. Abramson *et al.* (1978) interpreted learned helplessness in terms of individual differences in attributional styles. A 'healthy' attributional style involves attributing success to stable, internal, global factors and failure to unstable, external, and specific factors. A 'depressogenic' style involves the opposite pattern of attributions, where failure is ascribed to internal, stable, global causes and success to unstable, external, specific factors. A questionnaire measure, the Attributional Style Questionnaire, has been developed (Peterson *et al.*, 1982) where respondents rate their explanations of the causes of hypothetical negative events on the dimensions stable–unstable, internal–external, and global–specific. As the label suggests, this theory has been applied to explanations of depression, and it predicts that individuals who tend to explain failure outcomes in terms of stable, internal and global attributions are more likely to experience depression in the face of adverse life events.

There is considerable evidence of the relevance of the concept of learned helplessness to motivation and achievement in education. In the study of children with learning difficulties by Licht *et al.* (1985) children who attributed their typical failures to lack of ability were less likely to persist at a subsequent reading exercise, whereas there was no such trend among children who attributed their failures to lack of effort. In the study of high achieving children undertaken by Phillips (1984) teachers rated the group who were lowest in self-perceived competence as less persistent in class than those pupils who had high competence beliefs.

Diener and Dweck (1978) studied a sample of children who tended to attribute failure to lack of ability, and examined their reactions to failure experiences that followed success experiences. They found that, compared with a group who did not display that attributional style, children characterised by learned helplessness made more spontaneous self-deprecatory statements, referring to their lack of ability and personal inadequacies, and made more task-irrelevant comments and fewer problem-oriented remarks. They were pessimistic about their performance despite their earlier success on the task, began to complain of being bored and anxious, and showed deterioration in performance.

Some of the most consistent findings have come from Dweck's research into gender differences in learned helplessness. The findings of gender differences among children with learning difficulties that we summarised above seem to have considerable generality. Girls are more likely than boys to attribute their failure to lack of ability, they are less likely to persevere at a task, and they show greater deterioration in performance following a failure experience. These tendencies are not due to actual differences in ability and they are found on those tasks where girls are at least as proficient as boys. Dweck pointed to the paradoxical nature of these findings, given that girls tend to perform much better than boys on academic tasks and achieve, on average, consistently higher grades in school. They also tend to receive more positive feedback from their teachers. Success and praise do not seem sufficient to produce a self-confident attributional style among girls.

Dweck *et al.* (1978) hypothesised that these differences in attributions were due to differences in the *kinds* of feedback that were provided by teachers, and undertook a classroom observation study to test this hypothesis. Observations of fourth and fifth grade students and their teachers were carried out over a five-week period, and the feedback given by teachers to boys and girls was recorded and categorised. Feedback was categorised as positive or negative and as contingent or non-contingent upon behaviour, and contingent feedback was further classified as either work- or conduct-related. Finally, work-related feedback was classified as contingent upon either the intellectual quality of work or non-intellectual aspects, such as its neatness.

There was no gender difference in the overall frequency of teachers' feedback about the quality of students' work and no differences in the tendency to give either praise or criticism. However, 94 percent of the total positive feedback received by boys was related to the intellectual quality of their work compared to 79 percent of the total positive feedback received by girls. Where negative feedback was concerned, only 32 percent of the criticisms of boys referred to the quality of their work compared with 70 percent of the criticisms addressed to girls. Also, when feedback specifically about work rather than conduct was examined, girls were more likely than boys to be praised for non-intellectual aspects of their performance such as the neatness of their work, whereas boys were more likely to be praised for their competence or the correctness of their work. Only 54 percent of the criticism of boys' work referred to their competence or correctness, whereas 89 percent of criticisms of girls were framed in terms of these.

In general, girls receive less adverse criticism overall, but the criticisms they do receive emphasise their lack of ability. Boys receive more criticism but this tends to be as likely to be about non-intellectual aspects of performance as about its correctness. Thus, different messages are communicated to girls and boys, and these may influence their attributional styles, in that girls may be more likely to make ability attributions for failure whereas boys make effort attributions for failure. Support for this implication for attributional style was obtained in a second, experimental study also reported by Dweck et al. (1978) where a researcher provided children with feedback while they were attempting to find solutions for anagrams. Some of the problems were insoluble, thus guaranteeing failure on the task. Two kinds of feedback were given for failure, in an attempt to match the kinds of feedback observed in the classroom. Feedback either concentrated on the incorrectness of the solution (as did the criticism routinely received by girls) or was equally directed at incorrectness and non-intellectual aspects like neatness (like the criticisms routinely received by boys). The participants in the study were then presented with another puzzle task and were asked to provide an explanation for their performance on this task in terms of effort (not trying hard enough), the attitude of the tester (he was 'too fussy'), or ability (not very good at the puzzle). Children of either sex who only received feedback about the correctness of their performance were more likely to make attributions to lack of ability whereas those who received feedback directed at both correctness and neatness were more likely to make attributions in terms of lack of effort.

A number of perspectives on individual differences in motivation emphasise the student's interpretation of the implications of success and failure experiences. A recurrent theme is that these experiences have implications for the self, and there has been considerable rapprochement between research into motivation and studies of the self. Dweck and her associates (Dweck and Leggett, 1988) have argued that students have different intuitive conceptions of ability and these influence the goals that they set themselves and the approaches that they take to tasks. Other theorists have argued that the over-riding goal is to defend the self against challenges to self-esteem and that the kind of approach that students take to tasks is influenced by their evaluation of the implications of success and failure outcomes for their self-concept. We examine each of these approaches in turn.

Dweck argued that helpless students – those who regarded their difficulties as insurmountable and as evidence of their lack of ability – tend to hold one view of ability, that it is fixed, whereas other students who persist at difficult tasks and regard the obstacles as challenges are more likely to believe that ability can be changed and is incremental. Corresponding to these two views of ability or intelligence are two kinds of goals that are pursued. Those who believe intelligence is fixed have the 'performance' goal of attracting positive evaluations and avoiding negative evaluations from other people. If these students also believe that they have low ability then they will tend to avoid challenging tasks and lack persistence at them because these will reveal their lack of ability to others. It is pointless to try to improve performance if one believes that this cannot be achieved. On the other hand, those who believe that ability can be improved will welcome challenging tasks and will persist at tasks even if they are daunting because they believe that these tasks provide opportunities to learn; they set themselves learning goals.

There was empirical support for these relationships in experiments where goals were manipulated through instructions accompanying learning tasks and where different views of ability were encouraged by manipulating success and failure outcomes. Evidence for the causal role of views of intelligence is provided by research in which students are encouraged to hold one or other of these views by exposing them to written descriptions of famous people which illustrate either the fixed or incremental nature of intelligence, and then asking them to state their preferences among different kinds of tasks. Those who were exposed to the incremental account were more likely to choose tasks with learning goals and those who had been exposed to an account of fixed intelligence were more likely to choose performance goals. There is also evidence of individual differences in predispositions to hold these two notions of intelligence. A questionnaire was constructed, where the items referred to smartness being something that could or could not be changed. Children who endorsed statements supporting a fixed notion of intelligence were more likely to set performance goals in laboratory tasks and to endorse statements of preference about classroom activities that were indicative of performance goals, that is, that referred to a preference for easy problems so that they would be successful.

SELF-REGULATION

Students can be motivated by past events, current circumstances, or the anticipation of future outcomes, and all three need to be taken into account for explaining their behaviour. There is consensus in psychological theories that the student's approach to a given task will be influenced by past experience with that kind of task. However, people are also motivated by future events. Many of the goals that can be achieved in education are distant ones. A student might take two or three years to prepare for an examination; part-time students might have to attend classes in chilly rooms on winter evenings for several years before they gain the qualifications they seek, meeting the financial costs of their education as they go along. The intending musician has to commit himself or herself to perhaps thousands of hours of practice before the quality of their own performance is self-rewarding. Present effort is motivated by future outcomes.

Bandura (1986) conceptualises this in terms of two processes: goal setting and the comparison of goal attainment with standards. Setting goals has the effect of bringing the future to bear upon the present and provides a direction for behaviour. It also provides standards for evaluation, since the individual can compare the standards achieved with those of the goals. The attainment of goals provides self-rewards of feelings of pride and accomplishment. Awareness of a discrepancy between standards and goals results in feelings of dissatisfaction that can serve as a spur to further efforts. Whether this happens depends on the magnitude of the discrepancy, since standards that fall well short of goals may give rise to the belief that they are not attainable and should be abandoned. Self-efficacy beliefs also play a part in the individual's choice of goals and in whether he or she persists at a task in the face of difficulties. If the person believes that he or she can bring about the goal then effort will be renewed; on the other hand, a person with low self-efficacy beliefs is more likely to be discouraged by failure.

An individual might set him- or herself clear goals but fail to accomplish them. A personal example may illustrate this gap between intention and action. At the end of my first year in secondary school, the Latin teacher set an assignment to be carried out over the long vacation and submitted at the beginning of the next academic year – pupils had to read a book called *Everyday Life in Rome* and write an essay based on this. Although I was a diligent student and everyone in the class was intimidated by this particular teacher, I never completed the assignment, and I vividly recall my dread at entering the class at which the work had to be submitted. Why had I not completed it? I certainly intended to, and I didn't have any excuses like shortage of time or a foreign holiday. Nor did I overlook this obligation and I often promised myself that I would spend the following day on the assignment. Somehow, things always got in the way, including simply doing nothing, and I kept putting off the task. Growing awareness that the end of the vacation was approaching increased my anxiety but did not produce the work.

Kuhl (1994) has provided an analysis of this kind of failure to accomplish a goal in terms of the concept of self-regulation. Several stages intervene between recognising a goal and attaining it. The individual must initiate the task, plan the steps to be taken, and implement these even though there may be a delay before they reach fruition. He or she must persist at the task and resist any temptation to do other things instead, and devote sufficient attention to the relevant task information. It is also necessary to monitor the action plan and to change it if the current goal is unattainable or if the context for the task changes and produces new goals. These processes of self-regulation and self-initiated control are necessary to initiate a task and to maintain it.

In my example, one source of my prevarication was in maintaining self-regulation over an extended period of time, some two months, and in the absence of control by the teacher. In most teaching situations, the period would be much shorter, but just about every exercise that the teacher sets the class involves the need for the pupils to take a series of steps and to sustain attention over a period of time. Often the teacher will have to divide tasks into smaller, more manageable steps and to provide prompts and hints until the pupil is able to regulate his or her own behaviour. The teacher may have to exercise considerable control over the pupil's activities and leave him or her little room for autonomy or initiative. It may take considerable time until a child can carry out unaided the sequence of steps in, say, a long division problem in arithmetic. It may take several years of education before the teacher feels confident about giving the pupil the freedom to plan his or her own activities and to work without supervision.

Classroom life is crammed with instructions and exhortations from the teacher that require that the child knows what to do next. However, there can be gaps between instruction and completion, and Kuhl (1994) interprets these in terms of a distinction between action and state orientation. Action orientation is the ability to fulfil intentions by activating what Kuhl terms a motivational maintenance or supervisory control system that involves forming an action plan and sustaining it in the face of competing demands upon attention: he stresses 'the mediating role of self-reflective processes that support the maintenance of deliberate, self-initiated intentions, particularly when their enactment is jeopardized by strong emotional or habitual competing action tendencies' (p. 12). In state orientation, the individual becomes preoccupied with intrusive thoughts about past successes and failures, about possible future outcomes and about alternative courses of action. This thinking becomes 'excessive and compulsive . . . [and] makes it difficult for state-oriented individuals to deliberately initiate new, non-automatized actions' (Kuhl and Goschke, 1994: 129). This kind of thinking is an impediment to action, rather than a tool to sustain it, and it is important not to confuse it with reflection that is goal-directed; the distinction is not between action and reflection, but between planning and inflexible thinking or between decision-making and prevarication. Kuhl describes this kind of thinking as being de-coupled or disassociated from action.

This concept has much in common with other theoretical constructs such as worry (Borkovec *et al.*, 1983) and anxious self-preoccupation (Sarason, 1984). Previous research has also emphasised processes of executive control, planning and self-regulation, and metacognition. Kuhl has attempted an integration of these concepts and has offered a comprehensive account of their causes and consequences. In particular, he has looked at individual differences in predispositions to either action or state orientations, and has developed a self-report questionnaire, the Action Control Scale, to assess these differences. Factor analysis of the items of this questionnaire suggests three bi-polar factors: (1) action orientation subsequent to failure versus preoccupation (AOF); (2) prospective and decision-related action orientation versus hesitation (AOD); (3) action orientation during performance of activities versus volatility (AOP). Table 5.1 provides sample items for these three factors.

These items are informative about the nature of state orientation and its components, preoccupation, volatility, and hesitation. In a preoccupied state the person can't get task-irrelevant thoughts out of his or her mind, goes over them again and again and can't concentrate on the next thing to be done. Whenever they try to concentrate, these thoughts continually intrude. These thoughts occupy space in working memory and impede successful task performance. Volatility is similar to preoccupation in that it is associated with difficulties in realising intentions and in sustaining attention to the task, although in this case attention is directed at other tasks rather than at oneself. Even when the task is being carried out successfully, the individual finds it difficult to concentrate on it at the expense of other activities. In a state of hesitation, the ability to take a decision is impaired as

Table 5.1 Sample items from Action Control Scale

Factor	Sample item
AOF	When I am told that my work has been completely unsatisfactory:
Disengagement	I don't let it bother me for too long
Preoccupation	I feel paralyzed
AOD	When I know I must finish soon:
Initiative	I find it easy to get it done and over with
Hesitation	I have to push myself to get started
AOP	When I'm working on something that's important to me:
Persistence	I get into it so much that I can work on it for a long time
Volatility	I still like to do other things in between working on it

Source: Kuhl (1994: 57–9).

the person mentally rehearses possible outcomes of the decision, including remote or improbable outcomes, cannot set aside less relevant information, and creates for him- or herself an over-complex representation of the situation. Despite, or perhaps because of all this evaluation of information, the person cannot bring him- or herself to act, to commit him- or herself to one course of action. As soon as a decision is formulated to adopt one particular course of action the disadvantages of this action along with the advantages of alternative actions become salient and are the objects of rumination.

A number of studies have been carried out to test these predictions, either by selecting individuals with different tendencies towards action or state orientation on the basis of their scores on the Action Control Scale (ACS), or by attempting to induce state orientation, for example by arranging task conditions so that unrealistic intentions are activated or the degree of control that a subject has over his or her attainment is manipulated, or by raising motivation to very high levels . These manipulations do influence achievement as well as theoretically relevant variables such as helplessness, procrastination, the perseveration of task-irrelevant rumination, activity levels, and the amount of attention devoted to the task. We have noted that the concepts of this theory are similar to others in the fields of personality and motivation, and tendencies towards state orientation on the ACS have moderate correlations with other trait measures including introversion, self-consciousness, and test anxiety.

However, the theory does have explanatory power in that a number of different predictions can be derived from its postulates and it does aim for comprehensiveness. Thus it aims to explain various aspects of, say, anxiety, and the relationships among these aspects, rather than to make piecemeal predictions about specific aspects of anxiety, such as heightened arousal or worry or self-focused attention. It also aims to explore the relationships among beneficial and detrimental aspects of self-regulation rather than to talk simply in terms of failures of self-regulation – preoccupation and hesitation can be useful, just as it is sometimes effective to act on impulse.

The theory of action control emphasises the individual's initiation and control of his or her own activities and contrasts this with control that is exerted by external factors. However, the school curriculum is determined by a range of external agencies – the National Curriculum, the school, the faculty or department, the individual teacher – and tasks are set for the student.Within these constraints, academic success demands that the student develops into an autonomous 'self-motivated' learner, capable of independent study.

Boekaerts (1995: 3) reviews evidence suggesting that self-regulatory skills mediate between attributions, self-efficacy, and interest, on the one hand, and academic achievement and performance, on the other. Students who are more highly motivated have more developed self-regulatory skills and these permit higher achievement. Carr *et al.* (1991) argue that the influence of attributions and self-esteem upon achievement is mediated by metacognitive processes. They studied the relationships among measures of these constructs in predicting achievement in reading. Metacognition about reading refers to the student's awareness of the importance of planning and changing strategy according to the nature of the reading task. It was assessed by means of a questionnaire and, in addition, students' performance was analysed for evidence of the use of strategies. A measure of ability proved to be the best predictor of reading performance. However, there was also a cluster of related variables – self-esteem, attributions for success to effort, reading-awareness scores – that formed a further, indirect link between ability and performance. The researchers suggested that 'Inappropriate attributional beliefs impede the acquisition of strategic and metacognitive knowledge because children with external attributional orientations have little reason to learn or to use strategies that they feel will not help them to achieve' (p. 115).

SCHOOL INFLUENCES ON MOTIVATION

Half of pupils 'lacking in motivation'
Professor Michael Barber, of Keele University's education department . . . said there was a general lack of motivation among 40 to 50 percent of pupils. 'In addition to the disappeared and the disruptive, there are the disappointed and the disinterested. Seventy percent of pupils say they count the minutes to the end of lessons. Thirty percent believe that work is boring and 30 to 40 percent would rather not go to school.'
(*The Guardian*, 23 August 1994)

This newspaper headline and report on a study of the attitudes of 10,000 pupils carried out by Barber reflects public concern about educational standards in general and expresses alarm at the large proportion of pupils who seem to gain little benefit from their attendance at school. The findings from this report cast doubt on providing explanations of motivation that focus on characteristics of individual students. If so many students are disappointed and uninterested then this must tell us more about the school and its curriculum and organisation than about individuals. This point has always been made by sociologists of education, who have also emphasised the relationships between educational experience and structural factors in society like levels of unemployment and social mobility. Studies of students' beliefs about motivation consistently find that gaining qualifications and a good job are among the most important reasons for working hard in school (e.g. Carlen *et al.*, 1992; Kershner, 1996) and it is not surprising that high levels of youth unemployment and the demise of apprenticeship schemes can undermine motivation.

We can ask whether psychological theories of motivation that we have summarised can offer insights into the widespread dissatisfaction with school uncovered by Barber's research. We can ask, too, whether these insights offer suggestions about changes that can realistically be expected of schools, which have, of course, no direct control over societal factors affecting their students, but which might moderate some of the effects of these factors and also offer their students some positive experiences. These theories also have the advantage that they explicitly refer to individual differences and do not assume that all people, or even all people in comparable social or economic circumstances, respond in the same way to environmental pressures.

We suggest four implications: competition and the impact of failure on the self-concept; lack of 'fit' between school tasks and the individual student's knowledge and interest; the failure of lessons to capture imagination and interest; the lack of control by students over their learning.

Competition

The junior school sports day provides both an example and a metaphor for competition in school. The events consist largely of races, of short and long distance, for individuals or teams. Most of the events in each year group are invariably dominated by a small number of pupils, most children win nothing and are disappointed or else have come to expect very little, and a small number are distressed and embarrassed by the public exposure of their lack of coordination or fitness. It seems inevitable that the sports should be arranged in this way. Yet every student would have the potential to win prizes, points or praise if these were awarded for increasing mastery. Whatever their ability or skill, anyone can improve and take pride in surpassing their previous best. The research we have discussed has established the close relationship between high levels of motivation and mastery goals. However, school life pays much less attention to mastery and is organised in such a way as to emphasise students' success in attaining common standards.

The question of 'fit'

The second recommendation from psychological research is that learning activities should be designed so that their requirements are within the grasp of students but not so close to what they can do that they set no challenge. This idea has a long history in psychology. Piaget regarded motivation as inherent in learning and proposed the concept of equilibration, to refer to the process by which children respond to the challenges provided by their environment. This involves a balance between processes of assimilation and accommodation, between what the child understands and what the task demands. If the discrepancy between these is too great then the impulse to learn will be frustrated. A similar point was made by Hunt (1961) when he wrote about the 'problem of the match', arguing that motivation is greatest when there is a match, or an optimal amount of incongruity, between the task and the learner's competence. If the level of incongruity is too great, children become daunted; if it is too small, the task is unstimulating and there is no incentive to learn.

Two implications are drawn from this position. The first is that formal educational institutions actually set up conditions that interfere with the natural course of learning. Faced with the lack of motivation in their students they set up programmes of rewards and punishments that encourage compliance and convey the impression that learning is taking place. Of course, this position has a long history in education, particularly in the criticisms of educational practice made by writers from Rousseau to Carl Rogers. The same point is made by a character in B. F. Skinner's novel *Walden Two* who is advocating a behaviourist approach to the arguments of a traditional educationalist:

> The motives in education . . . are the motives in all human behavior. Education should be only life itself. We don't need to create motives. We avoid the spurious academic needs you've just listed so frankly, and also the escape from threat so widely used in our civil institutions. We appeal to the curiosity which is characteristic of the unrestrained child, as well as the alert and inquiring adult. We appeal to that drive to control the environment which makes a baby continue to crumple a piece of noisy paper and the scientist continue to press forward with his predictive analyses of nature. We don't need to motivate anyone by creating spurious needs.
>
> (1948/1976: 114–5)

A second implication is that tasks have to be designed to meet the needs of individual students. The match depends on the individual since no two learners will bring the same experience and competence to a task, and no activity could be presented to all of the members of a class with confidence that it would be equally stimulating to all. Skinner argued that this educational problem could only be solved by the careful analysis of the demands of learning exercises and by individual programmes of learning but, despite the rapid developments in information technology that have taken place since his first publications on this topic, these remain the exception rather than the rule.

Interesting lessons

In her interviews with pupils who had been identified by their teachers as 'hard workers' Kershner (1996) identified themes of both extrinsic and intrinsic motivation. Children worked hard to gain qualifications and to get a good job, but they also worked at lessons that interested them and which they found enjoyable. Interest and enjoyment are inevitably related to the difficulty of the task and to the 'match', as no one enjoys tasks that are either trivial or impossible. We saw in Chapter 1 that intrinsic motivation was associated with more effective learning strategies.

There are also differences between students in what they find interesting or enjoyable. Krapp *et al.* (1992) distinguish between individual or topic interest and situational interest. Topic interest is a stable attitude towards particular topics whereas situational interest is related to specific lessons. Thus, computer games might have interest to one child but not another; any particular game might be more or less engrossing. Interest involves both feelings of involvement and stimulation and a sense that the task is personally significant. There is evidence that topic interest is associated with adoption of a deep processing strategy to reading academic texts (Schiefele, 1996). It is also associated with the quality of experience during lessons and with attainment (Schiefele and Csikszentmihalyi, 1995).

Lessons that are of equivalent difficulty can be presented in ways that are lively and stimulating or in ways that are pedestrian and dull. Teaching materials can be designed to incorporate a variety of different activities rather than be repetitive in content or presentation. Novelty, surprise, incongruity, fantasy and humour can all be recruited to add to the enjoyment of teaching materials. Tasks should be challenging. They should provide opportunities for students to exercise creativity and to make decisions.

Many of these qualities are shown by some computer games. Although they have been heavily criticised by many educationalists for taking up so much of their students' time, there is no doubt that young people find them engrossing. Certainly they are heavily marketed and large amounts of money are invested in their production, but they do attract and maintain the active attention of young people in ways that would be the envy of the designers of many educational materials. Inspection of these games suggests that they have drawn upon many of the recommendations for motivation made by psychological research. They set challenges and each time the player successfully meets a challenge this is reinforced and followed by a further challenge. Colour, graphic design and sound are all used to enhance the novelty, incongruity and humour of the game. The games require skills of hand–eye coordination but many of them also need planning and the execution of strategies.

Control over learning

Deci and Ryan (1985) argue that there are two basic human needs, the need for competence and the need for self-determination. The latter is defined in terms of having choice or, in the terminology of locus of control theory, experiencing internal perceived locus of causality. According to their theory, motivation is undermined when students perceive that they lack autonomy and when they believe that their actions are controlled by others. Beliefs about autonomy and control are influenced by many factors in the classroom, teaching style and the teacher's relationships with students including the feedback they provide for performance. Teachers' responses can be classified as providing either 'informational' or 'controlling' feedback. That is, praise can let a student know if he or she is on the right lines in solving a problem, but it can also undermine the learner's autonomy by reinforcing him or her for adopting the teacher's way of approaching the problem.

The teacher can encourage self-determination by helping the student understand the reasons for undertaking a particular task and by placing it in the context of other activities. He or she can praise attempts at taking responsibility for learning and not restrict praise to successful outcomes. Careful management of tasks can minimise failure, but where it occurs, students should be encouraged to interpret this as an aspect of the task and not as evidence that they 'can't do it'.

The teacher can provide a 'scaffold' in the sense of helping students over the difficult parts of the task in order that they may experience the satisfaction of completing it. There is a difficult judgement to make here. The teacher wishes to promote self-regulation and this may demand imposing a structure that is incompatible with self-directed learning. The objectives of the teacher are crucial. In some recent approaches to teaching, he or she 'models' the processes of regulation in the sense of making these explicit and observable. They demonstrate processes of planning, monitoring, and self-reflection. Feuerstein (1980) describes the teacher in this role as a mediator, and mediated learning is an important step in the route towards self-regulation.

CONCLUSION

The highly motivated student sets high standards for him- or herself, works hard to attain these, and persists at tasks even when they are difficult. Lack of motivation takes several forms, including withdrawal or rejection of tasks as 'boring'. Some students seem to give up in the face of difficult tasks, and this is often associated with a particular pattern of explanations of their behaviour. They attribute their successes to their effort or to the easiness of the task and their failures to lack of ability. These beliefs can be stable characteristics of students but there is also evidence that effort can be fostered by the school. Teachers who strive to capture the interest of their students and who encourage self-directed learning can foster intrinsic motivation that produces more effective learning. An emphasis on competition or regarding success and failure as signs of the students' capacity to learn can undermine motivation and foster the belief that expending effort is not worthwhile.

Attribution approaches to motivation have suggested that metacognitive and self-regulatory processes moderate the relationship between attributions to effort and performance. Under-achievers tend to believe that they have little control over their ability to succeed and this is associated with an under-use of learning strategies that, in turn, makes success less likely. This pattern is also associated with low self-esteem.

Recent approaches to the explanation of motivation emphasise the association between students' beliefs about effort and their views of themselves. A lack of self-confidence and little expectation of success accompany failure and lead to the adoption of strategies that attempt to protect the self-image from the psychological consequences of failure. Motivation and self-confidence are inextricably linked and we address this relationship in the following chapter.

Chapter 6

Self-confidence

Sylvia Plath, the distinguished poet, was an outstanding scholar during her high school and college years in Massachusetts. She obtained straight A-grades throughout her time at high school and in successive years won the award for being an outstanding student. She received numerous scholarships and her poems and essays were accepted for publication. Her IQ was assessed at 160, which would place her as one of the most able students of her generation. Yet these successes never came easily for her and every assignment resulted in a pattern of hours of work accompanied by feelings of anxiety, low self-confidence and physical illness.

Certainly, she was highly motivated to achieve. Her mother had very high expectations of her, expectations which she internalised, and she set herself very high standards. Grades which were high but not the highest would have been a cause for celebration among other students but would be disappointing to her. Her relatively poor economic circumstances after the death of her father meant that the scholarships were a necessity if she was to continue her studies. These pressures to succeed must have contributed greatly to her anxiety.

Nevertheless, she was an exceptional student and the prizes, consistently high grades, and high opinions of her teachers and fellow students might have been thought sufficient to encourage her to believe that she could succeed without the stress and illness that she experienced. In her biography of the poet, Wagner-Martin (1990) draws upon Plath's letters and journals to present a picture of a student lacking in self-confidence. Her family circumstances meant that she felt out of place among the wealthy students at the prestigious university to which her family and friends aspired. Her academic success never encouraged her to believe that she was good enough to be at the university; as we have seen, to be good enough meant she had to be the best.

Plath's academic career suggests that academic success does not necessarily produce self-confidence. In many other cases, lack of confidence is linked to failure. Any teacher will recognise this relationship: some tasks, like doing statistics or working on a computer, elicit widespread anxiety and a belief that the task is impossible, and many students seem to go to pieces when they are faced with the task; there are also many individuals who seem to lack any confidence at all in themselves. Alternatively, there are students who seem prepared to tackle any problem, who are not daunted by failure or its anticipation. This chapter examines two approaches to understanding self-confidence: self-efficacy and self-esteem.

SELF-EFFICACY

The concept of self-efficacy was introduced by Bandura within the framework of social learning theory. This theory was an attempt to incorporate cognitive processes into the behaviourist approach which placed sole emphasis on the environment in the explanation of behaviour. The notion of vicarious reinforcement, of observing the consequences of the actions of others and modifying one's own behaviour in the light of those consequences, assigns a much more important role to processes within the individual. Bandura extended the notion of self-reinforcement to accommodate self-regulatory processes and self-efficacy beliefs. Within the person, he argued, there must be processes for perceiving and interpreting behaviour, for initiating action and for regulating behaviour in the light of its perceived consequences. In particular, people develop expectations about themselves and the environment, about what is likely or unlikely to happen, about what they can or cannot do. These expectations are based on four kinds of information.

The first is direct experience: we come to know what kinds of consequences follow from our actions. The teacher knows which lessons will work and which won't because he or she has taught them; the aggressive child knows what he or she can get away with, because of what has happened on past occasions. The second source of information is vicarious experience: the consequences of other people's actions can be just as informative as our own actions. The third source of information is the social world we inhabit: we learn from what other people tell us and from what we read, see on television, and so on. Many events are remote from our daily life, but we can learn about them and learn from them. For example, learning about morality – about right and wrong and truth – concerns abstract issues that might not necessarily be readily related to our own experience. Finally, we learn by applying our reasoning processes to what we observe and are told: we deduce new implications from what we know, and can reflect upon our own knowledge and beliefs. A child might develop aspirations for a particular career, or decide that other careers are not for him or her, not necessarily by experience or observing people occupying that role, nor by being told about it, but by inference from their knowledge of their own interests and aptitudes.

Bandura (1986: 391) defined self-efficacy as 'people's judgements of their capabilities to organise and execute courses of action required to attain designated types of performances. It is concerned not with the skills one has but with the judgements of what one can do with whatever skills one possesses'. Self-efficacy plays an important role in motivation, in influencing the kinds of activities that people will engage in, and their persistence at these.

Consider two hypothetical students who are equally good at mathematics; one has positive beliefs about her ability to perform well on a test, the other has less positive beliefs. The prediction is that the student with more positive self-efficacy beliefs will perform better on the test than the other student, even though their ability is comparable and even though both believe it is important to do well on the test. A large body of research has found support for this kind of prediction.

Bandura further distinguished efficacy expectancies from outcome expectancies, which are judgements of the likelihood that a particular action will produce a particular outcome. People can have strong outcome expectancies, believing, say, that a particular diet will bring about weight loss, but lack efficacy expectancies, and not be confident that they can stick to the diet. Alternatively, they might believe that they could stick to the diet, but doubt its ability to produce weight loss. A teacher's beliefs about whether it is worthwhile to introduce an innovative teaching method will be influenced by outcome expectancies, their confidence that the method can be effective in promoting student learning, and by efficacy expectancies, their belief that they could implement the scheme.

Measurement

Efficacy beliefs can be measured by assessing the willingness of teachers to endorse items like:

'If I try really hard, I can get through to even the most difficult or un-motivated students.'

'When it comes right down to it, a teacher really can't do much because most of a student's motivation and performance depends on his or her home environment.'

(Berman *et al.*, 1977; cited by Ashton, 1984: 28)

A teacher who agreed with the first item and also disagreed with the second item could be regarded as having positive self-efficacy expectancies about teaching. However, the wording of the items implies that the first is more concerned with what the individual teacher can do and the second with what teachers in general can do; that is, the first reflects self-efficacy and the second is, perhaps, closer to outcome expectancy – what the teaching activity can or cannot bring about. Gibson and Dembo (1984) found this distinction in a set of teacher efficacy items that they submitted to factor analysis. One factor was related to items like: 'When I really try, I can get through to the most difficult students'; 'If a student masters a new math concept quickly, this might be because I knew the necessary steps in teaching that concept'. The second factor was associated with items including: 'A teacher is very limited in what he/she can achieve because a student's home environment is a large influence on his/her achievement'; 'If students aren't disciplined at home, they aren't likely to accept any discipline'.

Bandura also proposed that self-efficacy expectancies varied in their magnitude, strength, and generality and these dimensions are reflected in attempts to measure self-efficacy. Measurement is often made relative to particular tasks; for example, one might want to assess students' expectancies of success on a mathematics test, by asking them to estimate whether they can perform at a given standard on the test and how confident they are that they can attain that standard. For example, they would be given a range of levels of attainment, from low to high, and they were to indicate which levels they could succeed at. Did they think they would get 40 percent correct, 50 percent, . . . 100 percent? How confident were they that they would attain 40 percent, etc., say, on a 10-point rating scale ranging from 0 (not at all confident) to 10 (highly confident)? Magnitude refers to students' expectancies about the level of the task they believe they can attain, measured, for example, by counting the number of levels they endorsed. Strength of expectancy refers to their confidence that they can attain a particular level, and this can be measured by taking the average confidence rating of the levels they felt they could attain. Measures of self-efficacy strength and magnitude are correlated with achievement in many endeavours including examination performance in social sciences (Lee and Bobko, 1994), tests of writing skills (Pajares and Johnson, 1994) and of mathematics (Pajares and Miller, 1995).

These measures of self-efficacy are linked to performance at particular tasks, but it is also possible to develop more general scales, for example the questionnaire measure of teacher efficacy described above, or a measure of mathematics self-efficacy like the Mathematics Self-Efficacy Scale (MSES), devised by Betz and Hackett in 1983 (see Pajares and Miller, 1995). This questionnaire includes items relating to students' judgements about confidence in solving maths problems, the grades that they expected to achieve, and their ability to use maths in everyday life. Scores on the questionnaire are correlated with outcome measures such as success in solving maths problems or the likelihood that students go on to specialise in maths. Pajares and Miller, however, found that predictions were much improved when the measure of self-efficacy specific to the outcome that was to be predicted was used, instead of more generalised measures. Bandura (1986) cautioned against the use of generalised measures, arguing that self-efficacy expectancies are expectancies about specific tasks.

Some educational implications

The finding that people's beliefs about their future performance are more accurate at predicting their performance than are measures of their ability has important educational implications. It is essential that teachers not only develop their students' skills and understanding but that they foster positive self-efficacy beliefs. This raises the question of the sources of these beliefs. As we have seen, Bandura emphasises direct personal experiences, vicarious experiences, social processes, and inference processes as sources of beliefs about the self. When estimating the likelihood that we will succeed at a task we draw upon our own past experiences of how we have performed those or similar tasks in the past. A history of failure produces low self-efficacy beliefs, which are not altered by the occasional success. We also observe how others perform at these tasks – 'If he can do it so can I'; 'If she can't do it, then I have no chance'. What people tell us is also a factor. If teachers have no belief in us, they can undermine our belief in ourselves – 'There's no point asking him to do it' becomes 'There's no point me trying to do that'. We can appropriate the labels that are applied to us.

Finally, we can infer our expectancies from our knowledge about ourselves – 'I have never worked with a computer before, but it reminds me of maths which I was never able to do, so it is unlikely that I will be able to work with it'. Bandura also proposed that we could base our judgements on our physiological reactions. Through past learning, cues in situations like examinations or public speaking can become stimuli that immediately elicit signs of tension or fear, like butterflies in the stomach or perspiring, and we may take these as signs that we are not going to do well.

As we have seen in our account of attribution theory, these judgements are influenced by the meanings that events have for the individual. Whether tasks are perceived as important or trivial, whether individuals accept responsibility for success and failure, whether they regard the outcome as within or beyond their control, all have an impact upon the self-efficacy implications of events. According to Bandura, the emotional self-reactions associated with experiences of success and failure, the self-rewards of pride and satisfaction, and the self-punishments of shame and disappointment, are the key motivational concepts: 'Contingent self-reward improves performance not because it strengthens preceding responses. When people make self-satisfaction or tangible gratifications conditional upon certain accomplishments, they motivate themselves to expend the effort needed to attain the desired performances' (Bandura, 1978: 349–50).

Bandura is here distancing himself from the traditional behaviourist conception of reinforcement as an event that strengthens the behaviour that precedes it. Rather, reinforcement serves to modify the student's view of him- or herself, and this self-perception has a significant role to play in the regulation of behaviour. A considerable amount of research has confirmed the claim of behaviourist theory that positive reinforcement is a much more effective means of changing behaviour than either negative reinforcement or punishment. This has led to the introduction of schemes of positive teaching with their emphasis on setting rules and targets for achievement and good behaviour combined with praise for good work and good behaviour (e.g. Wheldall and Glynn, 1989).

These schemes do seem to be effective, but many teachers and psychologists have reservations about the underlying philosophy, believing it to be mechanistic and controlling. Bandura offers an alternative explanation for the effectiveness of these schemes, which replaces the notion that students are *controlled* by the reinforcing consequences of their behaviour with the idea that students are evolving a model of themselves and of the classroom. Students can see themselves as agents in control of their actions. The emphasis is upon self-regulation within the constraints of the environment rather than regulation of behaviour by those contingencies.

Some of the qualities associated with high self-efficacy can be exemplified by considering the investigation of teacher efficacy undertaken by Ashton (1984). Teachers participated in the Thematic Apperception Test, a projective test which explored their attitudes towards themselves and their students. High self-efficacy teachers placed a positive value upon themselves and upon their teaching and felt that they had a significant role to play in their students' education; they believed that they and their students shared common goals; they had high expectations of their students; they took personal responsibility for the students' learning; they believed that they had developed effective teaching strategies; they preferred to involve students in reaching decisions about objectives and methods.

Gibson and Dembo (1984) observed the classroom lessons of eight teachers who were either high or low in self-efficacy. Although the numbers involved were very small, there did seem to be differences in teaching style. Teachers high in self-efficacy spent a significantly greater proportion of their time in whole-class activity and a smaller proportion of their time working with small groups. Yet whenever they did work with small groups, they seemed to manage the group more effectively and appeared more confident and less flustered when coping with interruptions.

SELF-ESTEEM

Self-esteem has attracted more research in education than any other psychological trait. One of the most influential studies was carried out by Coopersmith (1967). He defined self-esteem as (pp. 4–5):

the evaluation which the person makes and customarily maintains with regard to himself: it expresses an attitude of approval or disapproval, and indicates the extent to which the individual believes himself to be capable, significant, successful, and worthy. In short, self-esteem is a personal judgment of worthiness that is expressed in the attitudes the individual holds towards himself.

Coopersmith devised a questionnaire, the Self-Esteem Inventory, to assess children's self-esteem, rewording items that had originally been produced for use with adults. Typical items are: 'I'm pretty sure of myself'; 'I'm easy to like'; 'I never worry about anything'; 'I often wish I were someone else'; 'I spend a lot of time daydreaming'. Items referred to different areas of life including school and relationships with peers and within the family. Coopersmith administered the questionnaire to a large sample of children aged 10 to 12 years and selected children with high, medium and low self-esteem on the basis of their responses. He then collected further data on these children, using a range of techniques including interviews with them, their mothers and teachers, standardised psychological tests, observations of their activities, and measures of school attainments. He reported correlations of 0.28 between self-esteem and academic achievement and 0.30 between self-esteem and intelligence. Coopersmith identified four dimensions of self-esteem: competence (e.g. academic ability), virtue (adherence to moral standards), power (the ability to influence others), and social acceptance (the capacity to be accepted and receive affection from others).

This early research yielded many findings of interest (we refer later to data on familial influences on self-esteem); it provided the impetus for a very large number of studies of self-esteem and led to the development of several different questionnaire measures. However, this research has been severely criticised on the grounds that there was no clear definition of self-esteem and that many of the measures had poor psychometric properties. Problems of definition persist to the present time; for example, there does not seem to be consistency in the use of the terms self-concept and self-esteem. These are sometimes used as if they were interchangeable. The self-concept presumably includes factual knowledge about the self, such as gender, age, group affiliations, nationality, and so on. Coopersmith restricted the term self-esteem to refer to an attitude or a judgement of evaluation.

Problems of measurement are illustrated by the very different values obtained for the correlation between self-esteem and academic achievement. Coopersmith identified a coefficient of 0.28, and this is close to the average coefficient of 0.26 reported by Byrne (1984) on the basis of a review of 14 studies. Yet the *range* of correlations in these studies was from –0.01 to 0.52, and it is difficult to understand why studies should find such different coefficients unless, perhaps, the various self-esteem questionnaires are not measuring the same underlying construct.

Despite these criticisms, research into self-concept and self-esteem has flourished. There are several reasons for this. First, these notions strike a chord with many teachers' and students' experiences of learning. Second, the research has produced findings of interest, and studies have consistently shown that self-esteem is a personality trait that can predict educational outcomes. There might be problems in measuring the construct but it seems meaningful and has educational relevance. Third, the past 20 years have seen a surge of interest in the self. After a long period of neglect there has been renewed interest in earlier writings on the self by William James and by the symbolic interactionist theorists, Mead and Cooley. Social psychologists have become interested in the work of the American sociologist Goffman on identity and the presentation of the self.

Within a very short period of time psychologists have gathered a great deal of evidence about the development of the self and about the role of the self in social interaction. This has led to a richer conceptualisation of self-esteem and has helped overcome many of the problems of definition. Self-esteem has been embedded in more comprehensive theories of the self. For example, an important review article by Harter (1983) that itself contributed to these trends refers in its title to the 'self-system', and her review of self-esteem research is placed in the context of a lengthy account of the development of the self from infancy to adulthood. These trends have also influenced a shift in the focus of attention away from self-esteem as a fixed trait towards the study of psychological processes that maintain and enhance the self.

Dimensions of self-esteem

This research has clarified many issues concerning the measurement of self-esteem, and we turn first to this issue. We have already noted that early researchers preferred the notion of 'overall' or global self-esteem and questionnaires yielded a single score that indicated an individual's position on this single dimension. Coopersmith, and others, had been aware that self-esteem was relevant to different areas of a person's life but they did not pursue this issue, nor did they ensure that the items in their question-naires sampled in any systematic way different domains of the self.

James had introduced some order into the study of the self, first by distinguishing between the 'I', that part of the self that is the knower, and the 'me', the part that is known; and second by proposing a further distinction between different aspects of the 'me', specifically, the social self, the spiritual self and the material self. An individual's sense of self-esteem or, as he described it, 'a certain average tone of self-feeling', was a function of that person's self-esteem about all of these different aspects of the self. Specifically, self-esteem was defined as the ratio of one's success to one's pretensions. One interpretation of this is that self-esteem is more influenced by successes and failures in areas of life that are important to one than it is about less important areas. Thus, poor performance as a dancer has little impact on self-esteem if dancing is not taken very seriously but it would be wounding for someone who wanted to join friends in a dancing class and devastating for someone who had aspirations to be a professional dancer. A further implication is that one can discount judge-ments of one's performance made by someone who had little knowledge of dancing but self-esteem would be threatened by the adverse judgement of someone whom one regarded as an expert. Rosenberg (1965) took a similar position, arguing that some domains are more central than others to the sense of self.

Taking a lead from James, some have argued that concentration on the unidimensional self obscures evaluations that an individual might make about different aspects of the self; one might have high self-esteem where one's social self was concerned, but low self-esteem about, say, one's bodily self. Harter (1989) attempted to isolate the different dimensions of the self at different ages. Children from 4 to 7 years distinguished four dimensions: cognitive competence, physical competence, social acceptance, and behav-ioural conduct. When children respond to questionnaire items that assess these dimensions, there are moderate inter-correlations between scores on the four scales; factor analysis suggests two underlying factors, one with loadings on cognitive and physical competence items and a second with loadings on items from the other two dimensions.

Between the ages of 8 and 12 years children can discriminate five domains of the self: scholastic competence, athletic competence, social acceptance by peers, behavioural conduct, and physical appearance. In addition, by this age, children respond meaningfully to items that refer to their overall sense of self-worth, that is, items that refer generally to the self without being tied to specific domains. Harter has preferred to treat global self-worth separately from domain-specific self-esteem rather than, for example, taking it as the average of the separate self-evaluations, as is implicit in Coopersmith's approach or the weighted average, as suggested by James. Further differentiation of the self-concept, in the sense that different domains of self-esteem can be identified, occurs at adolescence and in adulthood. Harter has produced a set of self-report questionnaires, the Perceived Self-Competence Scales, that assess self-esteem at these different ages.

One implication of this approach is that children can have different profiles of scores on the dimensions. Children who are similar to each other in global self-esteem might have quite different profiles. One child might believe she is good at schoolwork but has few friends; another might believe the reverse. Alternatively, two children might have similar profiles, both, say, thinking they are good at sports but poor at schoolwork, yet one child might have high self-esteem and the other low self-esteem. These patterns can readily be explained by a model that proposes that self-esteem reflects self-evaluations in the various domains weighted by the relative importance the individual attaches to each domain. Harter has found support for this model. She obtained subjects' ratings of the importance of domains and computed a discrepancy score for each domain, reflecting the discrepancy between self-perceived competence and judged importance. The larger the discrepancy, the lower was global self-worth. She has also shown that some domains are more central to global self-esteem than others, in the sense that there are differences in the significance of the discrepancy between self-evaluation within a given domain and the importance attached to that domain. Among younger children, disappointment with one's physical appearance and social acceptance had more impact upon self-esteem than disappointment with cognitive or athletic competence or behavioural conduct.

However, other studies have failed to support the hypothesis that global self-esteem is a reflection of self-esteem in domains that are important to the individual. Marsh (1986) compared several approaches to predicting global self-esteem on the basis of measures of the importance of domains, including weighting self-evaluations by their importance ratings and importance/self-esteem discrepancy scores, and found that none of these models was superior to treating global self-esteem as a simple average of self-evaluations across the different domains.

Pelham and Swann (1989) also argued that there is little support for the 'importance hypothesis', as it is usually stated, but that there would be more support if importance was measured in an ideographic way. That is, importance should be treated as the relative importance to an individual of one domain compared to another domain, rather than the importance one person attaches to a particular domain compared to another person. In other words, the impact of proficiency at dancing on someone's self-esteem is a matter of how important dancing is to that person compared to how important, say, aptitude at mathematics is; not how important dancing is to them compared with the importance other people attach to dancing. They found qualified support for this version of the importance hypothesis. Specifically, it held only for those subjects who had negative views of themselves across many domains; for these people, attaching importance to the things they were good at contributed positively to their overall self-esteem. For subjects with positive self-views across many domains, it did not make much difference to their self-esteem whether any of these domains were rated more important than others.

To return to our example: if you are good at dancing and mathematics then high self-esteem does not require that you assign more importance to one than to another. However, if you are good at dancing but poor at maths then you will have high self-esteem only if you attach more importance to dancing. This raises the question whether you can influence your level of self-esteem by the meaning you attach to the different domains, for example, by exaggerating the importance of things you are good at and discounting the things you are poor at. This introduces a more dynamic conception of the self, and we return to this in a later section of the chapter.

A further implication is that self-esteem within specific domains is more closely associated with performance in those domains than global self-esteem, and considerable evidence supports this. For example, Byrne's review of research into the relationship between self-esteem and academic achievement found an average correlation of 0.38 between measures of academic self-concept and achievement. Not only is this correlation substantially higher than the coefficient of 0.26 found for global measures of self-esteem, the range of correlations obtained shows less fluctuation. Furthermore, if measurements are taken at the next level down in the hierarchy, the correlations are higher again. For example, Marsh (1992) reported an average correlation of 0.57 between self-concepts for specific academic subjects and achievement in those subjects.

Shavelson *et al.* (1976) argued that, in addition to being organised and multidimensional, as Harter proposes, the self-concept is hierarchical. General self-concept is at the apex of the hierarchy, and the self becomes increasingly differentiated through the different levels of the structure. At the second level there is a distinction between academic and non-academic self-concept. Academic self-concept is further differentiated into different academic subjects. Further studies have suggested a need to distinguish two academic factors at this level of the hierarchy – 'mathematics/academic self-concept', with loadings on maths, science and computer studies self-concepts; and 'verbal/academic' self-concept, with loadings on English language and literature (Marsh, 1990a). The non-academic self-concept is comprised of social self, emotional self and physical self, and at the next level these are further differentiated, for example, the social self into peers and significant others. Finally, self-evaluations of behaviour in specific situations are at the base level of the hierarchical structure.

This kind of model is found in other areas of the psychology of traits, for example, theories of the structure of intelligence or Eysenck's theory of personality, and has been influenced by hierarchical techniques of factor analysis. This approach to self-esteem has several implications. First, self-esteem is a highly differentiated construct, since the model allows for very many potential combinations of self-esteem.

Second, predictions about how an individual behaves in a specific situation, for example, a particular classroom exercise, can be made with greater confidence on the basis of measures taken at lower levels in the hierarchy. Conversely, measures of global self-esteem can only be expected to have moderate correlations, at best, with specific measures of performance. A corollary of this is that behaviour in specific situations is sensitive to its context and the self-concept might be quite mutable at that level. Experience of success at a particular arithmetic task might increase self-confidence at that task. However, as one ascends the hierarchy, self-concept reflects increasing numbers of experiences, and hence might be more resistant to change in the light of specific experiences. Thus, academic self-concept might be little affected by that isolated mathematics success.

Third, care has to be taken in the construction and interpretation of measures of self-esteem to ensure that there is no confusion about the level that is being assessed. This issue might be one source of the diversity of correlation coefficients between self-esteem and academic achievement that has been reported by different studies.

Fourth, it offers an interpretation of general or global self-concept in terms of something that is common to or is shared by self-evaluations at the other levels, that is, measures of different domains of the self have some common factor that can be labelled 'general self-concept'. This is a different conception from Harter's notion of a global self-concept that is 'content free' and separate from self-evaluations in particular domains. General self-concept, in this model, is a hypothetical variable rather than something that can be directly measured in the way that Harter does. It is, however, possible to construct a measure of general self-concept on an empirical basis by producing a set of items, correlating and factor analysing the items and selecting those with high loadings on a common factor. Marsh and O'Neill (1984) produced the Self-Description Questionnaire III, based on the hierarchical model, which included self-ratings on 12 dimensions and on one general self-esteem scale.

These investigations have contributed to resolving some of the issues of definition and measurement that have hindered earlier research. They also address some of the challenges to trait theory that arose during the person–situation debate and encourage a view of self-esteem that takes into account both stability and change. We now turn to the question of how individuals arrive at their particular level of self-esteem in given domains.

Antecedents of self-esteem

Research finds that academic self-concept is positively correlated with academic success, and this association may reflect either of two processes. Success provides the evidence for the individual's evaluation of him- or herself; alternatively, high self-esteem makes success more probable by giving students the confidence to tackle challenging tasks, to persevere in the face of difficulty, and to minimise anxiety. However, the evidence from Plath's college career suggests that there is no necessary connection between success and self-confidence. Indeed, given the consistency of her successes and the objective and public recognition of her achievements in competition with other very able students, it is difficult to avoid the conclusion that there are psychological processes that actively discount all this evidence.

Explanations of such processes have been framed in terms of the individual's beliefs about success and failure and their implications for the self-concept. For example, if one sets perfect scores as the minimum standard for achievement, one will inevitably fall below this standard. One account, attribution theory, was discussed at greater length in Chapter 5. Suffice to say at this point, the theory proposes that students with high self-esteem attribute their success to their own abilities but attribute their failures to external factors such as the difficulty of the task. Students with low self-esteem draw little credit from their successes, believing them to be due largely to their effort rather than their abilities, whereas they blame themselves for their failure and attribute this to lack of ability. Thus, Plath could never believe that her ability brought about her success and she thought that this could only be achieved by driving herself harder and harder. Past successes could never provide sufficient grounds for believing that the next task would be successfully completed.

Early family experience

If it is the case that self-esteem is not completely determined by prior accomplishments, what experiences give rise to high or low self-esteem? Harter's research suggests that individual differences in self-perceived competence can be detected at an early age, and the resistance of self-esteem to disconfirmatory evidence also suggests that self-esteem has been established early in life. Sroufe (1978) argued for the significance of early attachment (see Chapter 2), proposing that securely attached children have higher self-esteem.

Some of the classic studies of the antecedents of self-esteem have identified parental attitudes and behaviour as crucial influences. Coopersmith (1967) reported correlations between self-esteem and four indices of child rearing practice. Children of high self-esteem were more likely to have parents who were more accepting, loving and were more closely attached. Their parents exercised firm discipline, rather than being either permissive or punitive; they set firm and clear limits, and were prepared to listen to the child's point of view concerning these limits and their relaxation. Their parents set high standards for themselves and for their children; they encouraged independence in their children.

Rosenberg (1965) found that adolescents of high self-esteem reported that their parents took more interest in them and were more knowledgeable about their friendships and activities. Those with low self-esteem perceived their parents as indifferent towards them, rather than negative or punitive.

Despite the limitations of the reliance of these studies on retrospective reports of early experience, there are suggestions that the foundations for self-esteem might be laid early in life. Pelham and Swann (1989) propose that this early undifferentiated sense of self-esteem is complemented by more specific self-conceptions and that these influence self-esteem in terms of the meanings that children attribute to them. Children evaluate themselves in specific domains and these evaluations have impact upon self-esteem to the extent that these domains are important to the individual.

School experiences

Research has attempted to identify the causal direction in relationships between academic self-concept and academic achievement, asking whether students lack confidence in their ability because of their poor attainments, or whether their low achievement is a consequence of the anxiety, reluctance to face challenges and failure to persist at difficult tasks that are usually associated with low self-esteem. The existence of subject-specific self-concepts suggests that self-esteem is associated with particular educational outcomes but this is, at most, indirect evidence. More direct evidence is difficult to obtain, and two approaches have been taken. One is to measure self-esteem and achievement at different times in students' careers and to apply statistical models to identify the influence of earlier measures upon later ones. The second approach is to try to change students' self-concept, for example, by a programme of counselling, and to see if this has an effect on subsequent attainment. We look briefly at examples of each approach.

Marsh (1990b) studied a large, representative sample of 1500 American high school students, in tenth, eleventh and twelfth grades, and one year following graduation. He administered standardised tests of ability at grade 10, and took measures of academic self-concept at grades 10 and 11 and then following graduation. Participating students were asked to report their grade scores on school attainment tests at grades 10, 11 and 12. Correlations were computed between all these measures and Marsh attempted to fit different causal path models to the pattern of relationships. The trends in the results were for academic self-concept to have a signifi-cant influence upon subsequent school grades but for prior grades to have much less influence upon self-concept measured on later occasions.

These findings offer support for the hypothesis that academic self-concept has a causal influence on achievement and is not simply its consequence. This conclusion must be regarded as tentative, because this study has several limitations. Academic self-concept was chosen as the measure of self-esteem, and we have seen that better predictions of grades can be made by subject-specific measures. Students' grades were assessed by asking them to report their own average grade for the year and this is not a very sensitive measure of school achievement and, as a single score, it does not permit evaluation of its reliability. Marsh suggests that school attainment measures might be more sensitive to the influence of self-esteem than standardised test scores, and this is a further reason for trying to assess attainment with reliable measures. The span of time over which the study takes place is also very short in relationship to the school careers of these students. The results are also an average of the relationships for a very large number of people, and may mask different kinds of relationships for different groups of students; for example, the pattern might be different for students of extremely low self-esteem compared to others. These criticisms are not specifically addressed to this study, which seems particularly well designed, but apply more generally to this kind of investigation. There is, indeed, very little evidence on causal relationships between self-esteem and achievement.

The second approach attempts to change self-esteem. Lawrence (1988) reported a series of experiments that compared different approaches to improving the reading skills of 48 primary school children with reading difficulties. In a typical example of these studies, one group of children were given direct help over a period of 20 weeks using a reading programme. A second group followed this programme and also received one hour of counselling each week from non-professional counsellors. A third group attended drama sessions aimed at enhancing self-esteem in addition to the reading programme. A fourth group received no special attention and served as the control group. The two groups receiving self-esteem enhancement showed significant gains in reading relative to the other two groups.

A similar design was employed by James *et al.* (1991), who involved peer counselling in an attempt to improve the spelling and reading performance of 12 secondary school pupils attending special classes in the same school. Pupils were trained in counselling over three 1-hour periods and then worked with those who had learning difficulties in a weekly meeting for 20 weeks. At the end of this period, the group had made significant gains in reading and spelling relative to a control group. The sample sizes in these intervention studies are necessarily small, but the trends do seem encouraging, and support the findings from large-scale statistical studies that self-esteem has a causal influence on achievement.

The experience of school presents boosts and threats to self-esteem, perhaps with a directness that is unique in children's lives. Success and failure outcomes become salient and children are compared with one another. The language and gestures that teachers use when talking to children communicate their views of their pupils and their expectancies of them, and most writers on the self suggest that these have a formative influence on self-esteem. The organisation of schooling and the predominant forms of assessment also contribute, in that there is an emphasis upon comparing children's abilities to reach common standards, rather than encouraging them to improve on their personal standards. However, children's self-conceptions are not simply passive reflections of other people's evaluations and they actively seek to construct a coherent view of themselves.

One source of information is comparisons with peers. There is considerable evidence that, from an early age, children do seek out information about the abilities and attainments of other children. Meisel and Blumberg (1990) studied the preferences of children from second grade to ninth grade who had an opportunity to see the points obtained by other children in a scheme where pupils earned points for good work and behaviour. Children asked to see the points of children of the same gender and ethnic group; they were not more likely to look at their friend's scores but they did tend to look at those obtained by the more popular children. Ruble *et al.* (1980) suggest that this information is only used to make self-evaluations from about 8 years old. Younger children seek the information but do not use it to make judgements about their own performance.

Indirect, but telling evidence about social comparison comes from research that shows that the relationship between attainment and academic self-concept is influenced by the overall attainments of the school. Pupils compare their own ability with the abilities of other students in their class or school. Hansford and Hattie (1982; cited by Marsh and Parker, 1984) found that at the level of individual students, achievement and academic self-concept were positively correlated, but at the school level, average school attainment was negatively correlated with average academic self-esteem. Students in higher achieving schools tend, on average, to have lower self-esteem than those in lower achieving schools.

Marsh and Parker replicated this finding in a study of sixth grade students in five schools in Australia. The schools varied in the socio-economic status (SES) and achievement levels of their students, but there was no streaming of pupils within schools. Students completed self-concept inventories and attainment tests; teachers rated their students' academic ability and (what they estimated to be) their self-concepts. Students' ratings of their own self-concepts were higher in the low-SES schools although, *within* any school, SES was positively correlated with self-concept. However, this pattern of results was not predicted by the teachers. Although their ratings correlated moderately highly (and statistically significantly, r = 0.47) with students' self-reports, teachers in the high-SES schools rated their students' self-concepts more highly than did teachers in the low-SES schools. Marsh and Parker suggest that this difference is because the two groups are using different frames of reference in their ratings. Students are comparing themselves with the other pupils in their school. Teachers are drawing upon their more general knowledge of the influence of socio-economic status on academic achievement.

Parent and teacher attitudes and expectancies, students' evaluations of their own accomplishments and social comparison information are all potential sources of information about the self. Although these can be analysed into different influences, they must interact with each other and comparable information is evaluated in different ways according to the individual's level of self-esteem. We now turn to this question of how self-esteem affects students' interpretations of information about their performance.

Self as process

We have introduced the notion that high self-esteem students hold a particular set of beliefs about the causes of their successes and failures, attributing the former to their ability and the latter to external factors for which they are not responsible. This pattern is an example of a more pervasive kind of thinking that psychologists have labelled *self-serving bias*. This takes several forms where the individual perceives him- or herself as responsible for good outcomes and blameless for bad outcomes (Greenwald, 1980). It involves a bias towards recalling successful experiences rather than failures. People also tend to exaggerate their personal contributions to shared undertakings, particularly successful ones. Although this bias entails an inaccurate perception of the self, it does seem to have beneficial consequences for psychological functioning. An example of this is provided by an experiment conducted by Lewinsohn *et al.* (1980) where observers rated participants in small-group discussions on a number of desirable attributes, such as their social skills and assertiveness, and the participants also rated themselves on the same attributes. Depressed participants rated themselves less positively on these attributes than non-depressed participants, as might be expected, but their self-ratings were more similar to the ratings made by observers – they were more 'accurate' in their self-perceptions.

On the basis of their review of a number of studies like this, Taylor and Brown (1988) argued that it is the non-depressed person rather than the depressed person who has a distorted perception of the self: 'the mentally healthy person appears to have the enviable capacity to distort reality in a direction that enhances self-esteem, maintains beliefs in personal efficacy, and promotes an optimistic view of the future' (p. 204).

Baumeister *et al.* (1989) argued along similar lines about self-esteem. Their concern was less with correlational studies of the kind we have been concentrating upon, and more on studies that contrast two groups of subjects, those with high self-esteem and those with low self-esteem. They wished to understand why such studies typically show that high self-esteem subjects are more likely to show self-serving bias. Inspection of the mean self-esteem scores obtained by subjects in these experiments revealed that the 'low self-esteem' subjects tended, in fact, to be of moderate self-esteem, in the sense that they tended to endorse items towards the mid-point of self-esteem scales rather than endorse extremely low scores. This implies that these studies are effectively contrasting high self-esteem with moderate self-esteem subjects, and Baumeister proposed that the question to be addressed is why high self-esteem subjects hold the beliefs that they do, as opposed to the usual research question that focuses on people with low self-esteem. Baumeister argued that moderate and low self-esteem subjects have realistic views of their strengths and shortcomings whereas high self-esteem subjects are susceptible to self-serving bias and exaggerate their strong points rather than take a realistic view of them.

The approach that Baumeister takes is derived from the *self-presentation* or *impression management* perspective, that assumes that the individual is motivated to create a positive identity in the eyes of other people. This perspective was introduced by the American sociologist Goffman in, for example, his book, *The Presentation of Self in Everyday Life*, published in 1959, where he argued that self-presentation motives were fundamental to society. Goffman's ideas were taken into social psychology, to influence a class of 'mini-theories', as researchers emphasised different points that he had raised. Baumeister (1982) distinguished between the motive to create an impression on a specific audience and the motive to become one's ideal self, that is to present a generally good impression.

Goffman's notion that people adopt strategies and tactics in order to promote their identity has been particularly influential. Strategies are actions that aim to set up and maintain identities in the long term, whereas tactics are situation-specific responses improvised to cope with particular dilemmas or threats to the identity one seeks to create. The pupil who has been daydreaming during a lesson and who is suddenly asked a question by the teacher has to quickly invent some tactics to cover up his or her lack of attention.

A pupil who arrives late at school has to have an excuse ready and even a transparent excuse will be better than no excuse at all, for if you cannot create the impression of being a punctual, if accident-prone student, at least you can show that you are prepared to show to the teachers that you recognise the legitimacy of their demand for an excuse, that you are not outside the moral order of the school. As Goffman argues, 'society is organized on the principle that any individual has a moral right to expect that others will value and treat him in an appropriate way' (1959: 24). The excuse recognises the teacher's moral right; in return, the teacher is under an obligation to deal appropriately with the excuse that has been offered. On the other hand, the defiant pupil will try to make it all too obvious that he is late, there will be no sneaking in or excuses in his case, for these would weaken the impression that he is trying to make. A pupil who is studious but who wishes to be accepted by his or her less studious peers has to take a strategic approach in order to avoid the reputation of swot or teacher's pet, on the one side, and of the able student who doesn't try, on the other.

Jones and Pittman (1982) distinguished between assertive and defensive strategies: assertive strategies seek to establish a particular identity, whereas defensive strategies seek to protect an identity that has been established but has been threatened. They also offered a classification of specific strategies and their goals (see Table 6.1).

Self-handicapping

The goals of all these strategies are to present an acceptable image to other people, and this is interpreted by theorists in terms of the motives to enhance and protect self-esteem. Self-handicapping looks at first sight an improbable means of enhancing self-esteem. Why should anyone try to set up obstacles to make success more difficult to achieve? Self-handicapping can take one of two forms (Baumeister and Scher, 1988).

The first is to set up obstacles to success so that any failure can be attributed to these obstacles. Thus, an individual may suspect that failure

Table 6.1 Assertive and defensive self-presentation strategies

Assertive		Defensive	
Strategy	Goal	Strategy	Goal
Ingratiation	To be liked	Excuses	To minimise responsibility
Intimidation	To be feared	Justifications	To accept responsibility but provide overriding reason for action
Supplication	To be viewed as weak, dependent	Disclaimers	To offer an explanation before one's predicament
Self-promotion	To be respected for one's abilities	Self-handicapping	To set up obstacles to success
Exemplification	To be respected for moral worthiness	Apologies	To admit guilt and responsibility; to express remorse and guilt

Source: Based on Jones and Pittman (1982: 249) and Tedeschi *et al.* (1985: 70).

in an examination is likely and so decides not to revise for it. Should the individual fail, as he or she expected (and this outcome is now, of course, more likely), then this can be attributed to the lack of revision. This explanation will make it less likely that failure will be attributed to the person's lack of ability. Alternatively, the individual might actually pass the examination and, in these circumstances, the fact that he or she did not revise will contribute in a positive way to his or her image. To succeed in the absence of effort would be regarded as more convincing evidence for the person's high ability than success following effort. This is a risky strategy and involves what Baumeister and Scher (p. 8) describe as a 'tradeoff that sacrifices one's chances for success in exchange for attributional benefits'.

The second form of self-handicapping is to put forward excuses that will offer an explanation of actual or anticipated failure by drawing attention to factors that interfere with performance. 'This won't be a very good lecture because I have been ill.' Again, if the lecture turns out to be poor then no one will think badly of the speaker: 'She did very well under the circumstances'. If the talk is a success, then the audience's impression of her is even more positive: 'Think how good she would have been if she had not been ill!' Speakers making a presentation at a conference will often preface their talk with an excuse of one kind or another: 'I am sorry that I haven't had much time to prepare this talk; I have had to rush from the operating theatre'; 'I feel embarrassed, as a mere psychologist, speaking to you, an expert audience of midwives'. It is my experience that excuses also figure prominently in the nervous conversations that take place among candidates preparing for an examination or waiting to be called in for an interview. Claims like 'I haven't done any revision for this examination' or 'I have only prepared two questions' are commonly heard.

Excuses don't, of course, interfere with performance in themselves, but simply aim to shape the attributions made by other people. They tend to be used when failure is predicted or if the individual has little confidence in him- or herself. They can become self-defeating and provide actual obstacles to success if the individual puts into practice some of the factors that are alluded to in the excuse, for example through inadequate preparation. Are excuses mere forms of words or does the person actually engage in self-defeating behaviours?

Self-worth theory

Covington and Beery (1976; see also Covington, 1992: 74–82) have advocated self-worth theory. This takes as its basic premise that students' primary motive is not to be successful but to protect their own sense of self-worth. In an educational system worth and self-worth are linked to academic success and to attributions of ability. Failure reflects badly on the individual and can produce low self-esteem and feelings of shame. Thus, students are strongly motivated to avoid failure and any implication that their failure has been brought about by any lack of ability. An individual's level of ability is beyond his or her control, but the amount of effort that is invested in a task can be controlled. Effort is the focal concept in the theory.

Effort is usually necessary to achieve academic success but, in attributional terms, as we have seen, there are risks associated with effort. The student who tries and fails will be regarded as less able than the one who has not tried. Someone who has not tried and succeeds will be regarded as more able than the student who has tried. On balance, there seems to be some advantage in not trying too hard, if the goal is to maintain self-worth. This perspective is not shared by teachers, who place a positive value on effort and disparage the student who doesn't try. From their point of view, students who try and fail are more worthy than those who haven't made the effort. The able student who doesn't try is also likely to be censured for failing to make the most of his or her potential.

An alternative approach is to choose either very easy tasks where success is more likely or to choose very difficult tasks where failure can safely be attributed to the nature of the task rather than to ability. However, this strategy is not always available as the choice of educational tasks is not typically under the student's control. Finally, the student can seek to shape the attributions made by others through the use of excuses.

These ideas have been studied empirically. Covington (1992) confirmed that teachers attached more importance to effort than to ability in responding to students' success and failure. Teachers were significantly more likely to punish students for failure and less likely to reward them for success when they had made no effort compared with when they had made an effort. Covington and Omelich (1979) established that teachers and students held different perspectives on effort and that their views were modified by excuses. The participants in their study were asked to rate how ashamed they would be if they failed in one of four different ways: fail without effort, and with no excuse; fail without effort and with an excuse (illness); fail after effort, no excuse; fail after effort, but with an excuse (through no fault of their own, the student had revised the wrong material). They were also asked to rate the extent to which failure under each of these conditions would reflect on the person's ability. Finally, they were asked to adopt a teacher's point of view and to suggest how punitive the teacher would be in each of these conditions. Students reported most shame and believed their performance was indicative of low ability when they had made the effort and less shame when they had not tried. Shame and the attribution to lack of ability were strongly correlated. They believed that teachers would be most punitive when the student had not tried and when there was no excuse. They did not think teachers would be punitive in any of the other three conditions.

Chaplain (1996) interviewed a sample of teachers about secondary school boys in years 8 and 9 whom they identified as 'disengaged' from learning. Common themes in teachers' understanding were that these boys were trying to protect self-esteem and to maintain an identity of being 'macho' and having 'street credibility'. Some teachers also surmised that this attitude reflected anxiety about leaving school, particularly when pupils were conscious that they were still having difficulty with basic skills of literacy and numeracy. No teacher mentioned that any negative messages they might be communicating contributed to pupils' disengagement.

Thompson (1993) examined the influences of low self-esteem and self-worth protection on performance on a test of creativity. The first administration of the test established a baseline for performance. In the second presentation of the test the items were made very difficult to ensure that participants would fail. In the third presentation of the test, this failure was, or was not, followed by a face-saving excuse. Finally, the test was completed once again.

Self-worth protection was defined as deterioration in performance following failure but subsequent improvement when an excuse was available so that failure would not have to be attributed to lack of ability. A group of 'self-worth protection' participants was identified on the basis of this procedure. This group (some 20 percent of the participants in the study) scored significantly lower than other groups on measures of academic self-esteem (but not global self-esteem) and test anxiety. On an attributional style questionnaire, self-worth protection subjects tended to attribute success to external factors rather than take credit for them. On the other hand, they did not differ from other groups in their attributions for failure. Thompson (1993: 482) sees this pattern of attributions as characteristic of 'the perpetual fear of failure driving the achievement behaviour of the high achiever . . . namely a failure to fully internalise success and regard it as anything more than specific to the occasion'. This provides a close description of the behaviour of Plath at college that we discussed above. Covington (1992) describes this pattern as 'overstriving', a combination of high ability and intense effort and setting very high goals, and he argues that it characterises students with exceptional academic achievement but low self-esteem.

Do people of low self-esteem have different motives from those of high self-esteem? Some psychologists have argued that individuals with low self-esteem are more concerned with *protecting* their image than with seeking opportunities to enhance it. Arkin (1981) introduced a distinction between acquisitive self-presentation and protective self-presentation motives. The underlying motivation in the latter case is to avoid social disapproval, and this encourages the person to adopt strategies of appearing innocuous, to hold uncontroversial attitudes, to be conformist in appearance, and to avoid situations where he or she might be in the position of being evaluated by others.

Although these strategies can often seem to be effective in the short term, they do have costs. Other people may take the individual at face value and he or she may have little opportunity to create a positive impression, to be liked or to gain promotion. The individual with low self-esteem also denies him- or herself the opportunities to acquire skills of communication and self-assertion. Ultimately, defensive behaviours are restrictive and can create a vicious circle where the individual becomes trapped in an identity that is unfulfilled. Covington makes a similar point about self-worth protection strategies which ultimately lead students to accept failure and cease to make any effort. Their attempts to find excuses and to attribute failure become progressively less plausible. Their defensive behaviour isolates them from success experiences.

This pattern of reactions seems similar to learned helplessness, which we discussed in Chapter 5. However, there is an important difference between the two accounts. According to self-worth theory, the lack of effort is not because students see no point in trying because they believe they cannot succeed, whatever they do; rather, lack of effort is the long-term consequence of withholding effort in order to protect self-esteem in the short term.

An alternative to the position that the predominant goal is to enhance the self is that people are primarily motivated to hold a *consistent* view of themselves. This notion has a long history in psychological explanation; for example, cognitive dissonance theory proposed that holding contradictory views of the self gives rise to psychological conflict, and this conflict is a powerful source of motivation to reconcile these views. Self-verification theory (e.g. De La Ronde and Swann, 1993) proposes that people learn that their relationships run more smoothly when there is a match between how they see themselves and how others see them, and this provides a means by which 'people come to associate self-verifying evaluations with feelings of authenticity and non-verifying evaluations with feelings of uneasiness or bemusement' (p. 149).

The theory gives rise to the prediction that people seek out information that is congruent with their view of themselves. We have seen that people with high self-esteem seek information that is consistent with their view of themselves, that is, they seek positive feedback. However, the prediction is also that people with low self-esteem seek out information that is congruent with their view of themselves; that is, they look for *negative* feedback to confirm their low opinion of themselves and they discount or feel uncomfortable with positive information about their accomplishments.

De La Ronde and Swann argue that there is a great deal of evidence to support this prediction, particularly from studies of partners in social relationships. Swann *et al.* (1992) found that subjects of low self-esteem who had received praise for their performance subsequently preferred to seek out unfavourable feedback information. Shrauger (1975) argued that this tendency holds for factual information about performance; because people of low self-esteem expect to fail they are more comfortable with feedback that is consistent with their expectation. However, they seek praise and are averse to criticism just like those with high self-esteem.

CONCLUSION

Bandura's research into self-efficacy has teased out the contributions that ability and self-confidence in one's ability make to academic success. Studies of motivation have shown that neither ability nor success is sufficient to generate self-confidence. The academic career of Sylvia Plath provides an example of the treadmill that can ensue when past success is not taken as an indication of future success. She lacked efficacy expectancies, in Bandura's terms, rather than outcome expectancies, since she perceived that academic work could produce success. What are the origins of these expectancies, if they are not to be found in academic experiences? Why are they so strong that they can outweigh the evidence from academic outcomes?

In terms of attribution theory, the student achieves success but attributes this to effort and not to ability, and believes that future success can only be brought about by renewed effort. What self-efficacy adds to our understanding of this pattern of beliefs and behaviour is, I think, a recognition of the importance of perceptions of lack of control. Academic success requires performance on tasks where the outcome is never entirely within the student's control. For example, no candidate can predict with confidence how the marker will respond to an essay, what questions will be included in an examination or whether he or she will perform well on the day. From an outside perspective, the teacher develops confidence in the student because the student tends to do well whenever he or she is examined. If the student lacks efficacy beliefs, then she will reflect on her experience and reach the conclusion that she succeeded because she worked hard, and because of the particular questions asked, the material revised, and so on. This combination of effort and outcome offers a plausible interpretation of academic success. Positive feedback and teachers' compliments are acknowledged but reinterpreted.

An alternative approach to explaining relationships among ability, effort and academic outcomes emphasises the individual's need to establish and maintain an identity. In order to achieve this, the individual makes use of self-presentation strategies of various kinds. Within school, ability is positively valued and the lack of ability derided, and there is plenty of available information on which to make evaluations of one's own and others' abilities. Students try to influence the attributions that others make, for example, by adopting self-handicapping strategies. The recurring bouts of illness suffered by Plath are presumably a consequence of the high stress and exhaustion she experienced in pursuit of excellence; alternatively they might have elements of self-handicapping, making an excuse available for the failure that would inevitably occur at some point. Self-worth theory regards excuses and withholding effort as strategies for influencing attributions for failure in terms of lack of ability.

Psychologists who adopt a self-presentational perspective explain patterns of attributions in terms of self-serving bias. This gives rise to the question why those with low self-esteem do not share this bias or choose to present themselves in a positive light. Baumeister (1993: viii) outlines the 'puzzle' of low self-esteem:

> But why do these people say bad things about themselves on a questionnaire? Do they really believe themselves to be inferior and inadequate? Are they trying to manipulate the reader into feeling sorry for them, or into something else? . . . After all, it is unclear what one can hope to accomplish once one portrays oneself to others as inept and unattractive.

This quotation captures the logic of the self-presentation approach – self-descriptions must be strategic, so what strategy is being used? One solution to the puzzle is to argue that there are other motives at work, for example, to be consistent. Self-verification theory suggests that those with low self-esteem are more comfortable with, and attach more weight to, information that is compatible with their view of themselves. They can seize upon one critical remark in an otherwise laudatory report.

Another solution to the puzzle is to propose that many people 'really believe themselves to be inferior and inadequate', at least in specific domains, and are characterised by a deep-seated and persistent lack of confidence in themselves that is resistant to change. Evidence for this proposition needs to go beyond self-report questionnaires to develop a comprehensive theory of the self in academic performance. The theories we have reviewed in this chapter offer a beginning to this endeavour.

Chapter 7

Shyness

A school is an inherently social place, and the pupil will perhaps have as intense a social experience there as at any time in his or her life. School is distinctive in many important respects in comparison with the life of the family and the local community. Most schools are large institutions that provide an environment that is sometimes highly structured – the classroom with its rules for who can say what to whom, and when – and at other times less structured, like the playground or the time spent between classes or going to and from school.

Personal relationships play a salient part in children's experience of school. This is illustrated in a study by Jones (1995), who presented primary school pupils with a projective test that involved a set of rather ambiguous line drawings of adults and children, and asked them to pick out pictures that represented good and bad schools, liked and disliked schools, and sad and happy schools, and to explain their choices. Her respondents made more frequent mentions of relationships between pupils than of teachers or academic work, and this was the case whether the school was perceived in a positive or negative light. In a further test, participants were invited to nominate characteristics of good and bad schools. The principal characteristic of a good school was 'friends' and the principal characteristic of a bad one was 'bullying'. When participants were subsequently asked to rate their own school alongside these different kinds of hypothetical schools, friendship and bullying emerged as the most important factors in distinguishing good from bad schools.

MATTERS OF DEFINITION

Our concern in this chapter is with students who are shy and withdrawn, who perhaps have few friends and who are susceptible to social isolation and loneliness. Such students present few problems to the school in comparison with, say, those who are disruptive, but research suggests that this pattern of behaviour may be maladaptive and can be a precursor to psychological difficulties later in life. However, we recognise that there are many reasons why a child might appear withdrawn that do not necessarily reflect specific difficulties with social relationships. As we discussed in Chapter 5, a child might be disengaged, lacking interest in school and becoming detached from its activities. Or perhaps a child is preoccupied with worry about problems at home or about bullying.

Pye (1989) has explored these aspects of school life through examination of case studies of 'invisible' children, pupils who have adjusted to the demands of school and to the attitudes of teachers by adopting a self-protective strategy of passive withdrawal. They try to avoid attracting the teacher's attention and do the minimum amount of work to make this possible, they never volunteer their participation in any activities, and respond to any approach or question by the teacher in ways that are intended to discourage further interaction. Pye's research led him to conclude that this pattern of behaviour was common in the schools he studied, and he labelled this experience of school, 'Nomansland'. The students who inhabit Nomansland, like anyone who maintains a defensive or protective strategy for any length of time, find a way of coping that seems to be effective in the short term but that isolates them from the potential benefits of education in the longer term and that denies them the experiences that would increase their self-confidence and foster more assertive coping skills.

Pye argued that the typical organisation of schools and the ways in which teachers behave towards pupils are instrumental in creating the conditions for the adoption of this strategy. He arrived at this conclusion partly from observations of classroom practice and interviews with the students, partly from reflection on his own teaching experiences, and partly from the recognition that 'invisible' children often behaved in very different ways outside school or when they were pursuing extra-curricular interests. Outside the constraints of school these children could be active, interested and engaged.

Other studies, however, suggest that students may be reluctant to participate in class because they are shy, anxious and lack confidence in themselves, and they wish to avoid being the centre of attention. Jones and Gerig (1994) interviewed a sample of children who had been identified as 'silent' on the basis of systematic observations of their behaviour in class. These students considered themselves shy and lacking in self-confidence and feared being embarrassed in front of others. They liked working alone and preferred classes where it would be unlikely that they would be asked questions or otherwise be the focus of attention.

We shall see that these concerns are widespread among children and adults. This chapter focuses on social difficulties, and we examine psychological research into withdrawn behaviour. This research regards this behaviour as problematic, because it has an impact upon children's social relationships and also because it predicts future difficulties. However, Pye's study should serve as a reminder that we must be cautious in attributing withdrawn behaviour that is seen in one context, like school, to a personality trait or habitual way of interacting with other people, when it might be better understood in terms of the environment that confronts the child.

Considerable research has been directed at children who are less sociable in social situations as this is widely believed to be a potential indication of psychological problems. Renshaw and Asher (1982) argued that a tendency to be less popular in childhood, that is, to be either neglected or rejected in sociometric analysis, is predictive of later social adjustment problems. The *Diagnostic and Statistical Manual of Mental Disorders* (American Psychiatric Association, 1987) included a number of disorders that are closely related to withdrawn social behaviour. 'Avoidant disorder of childhood or adolescence' was partly defined in terms of 'excessive shrinking from contact with unfamiliar people . . . that interferes with social functioning in peer relationships' although the person exhibits a 'Desire for social involvement with familiar people . . . and generally warm and satisfying relations with family members and other familiar figures' (p. 62). In the fourth edition of the *Manual* this disorder had been subsumed under 'social phobia', defined as 'A marked and persistent fear of one or more social or performance situations in which the person is exposed to unfamiliar people or to possible scrutiny by others. The person fears that he or she will act in a way (or show anxiety symptoms) that will be humiliating or embarrassing' (American Psychiatric Association, 1994: 416). This is distinguished from 'avoidant personality disorder', defined in terms of 'A pervasive pattern of social inhibition, feelings of inadequacy, and hypersensitivity to negative evaluation, beginning by early adulthood and present in a variety of contexts' (p. 664).

Other approaches to withdrawn behaviour focus on reticence and lack of communication. 'Communication apprehension' is defined as 'an individual's level of fear or anxiety associated with either real or anticipated communication with another person or persons' (McCroskey and Beatty, 1986). The concept of reticence takes the relative absence of speech as the salient aspect of withdrawn behaviour. 'Selective mutism' is defined in terms of 'the total lack of speech in at least one specific situation (usually the classroom), despite the ability to speak in other situations' (Dow *et al.*, 1995).

Avoidant personality disorder seems to have much in common with what is called, in everyday life, *shyness*. This seems to refer to an individual's sense of discomfort in social situations. It does not have a precise meaning, although it has connotations of timidity and implies behaviour that is awkward, inhibited or withdrawn. It is often used to describe someone's personality – 'She's very shy'; 'Underneath that exterior he's really a very shy person'. The plethora of terms has been taken by many commentators to indicate conceptual confusion, and studies can be difficult to compare because of inconsistency in terminology. Nevertheless, research has converged on a trait of wariness and inhibited social behaviour, and suggests that this has consequences for children's adjustment.

STUDYING WITHDRAWN BEHAVIOUR

One way of bringing order to the research is to consider the methods that have been used to define withdrawn behaviour. One approach relies upon children's perceptions of their peers and defines withdrawn behaviour in terms of their social relationships. A second approach defines it in terms of categories of observed behaviour in social situations. Finally, other studies have relied upon self-report questionnaires, particularly reports of shyness. Of course, any research programme draws upon more than one method, and ratings by teachers and parents have been widely used. Our primary concern is with how the trait is defined.

Peer choice and nomination

One of the most widely used techniques has been sociometry, a form of 'social measurement' that attempts to capture the pattern of social choices made within a group. In a typical application, students would be asked to nominate three other students with whom they would wish to work on a project and three students with whom they would not want to work. Among older children who do not stay with the same class for all their lessons, lists of classmates can be generated by the researcher and presented to the children as the basis for choices.

The choices can be depicted on a sociogram, a graphical network that displays choices as connecting lines, and this would display characteristics of the structure of the group; for example, the presence of reciprocal friendships and the existence of cliques, or sets of students who choose one another. The procedure can also identify individuals with specific roles in the group. The 'star' is a popular individual attracting a number of choices; the 'rejectee' is frequently chosen as someone with whom the others would not like to work; the 'neglectee' receives neither positive nor negative choices; the 'isolate' neither makes nor receives choices (it may not be possible to distinguish neglectees from isolates if the procedure requires that children only make choices); the 'controversial' child is both frequently chosen and frequently rejected. The wording of the question implies that the measure is one of social acceptance; however, the wording can be changed to assess other aspects of popularity – for example, children can be asked to nominate their three best friends in class.

A variation on this is the method of peer nomination, where children are asked to identify others who occupy specific roles or who display particular characteristics. For example, Boulton (1995) asked pupils in the course of an interview to give the names of pupils in their class who were bullies and those who were the victims of bullying. On the basis of the nominations provided by all members of the class, bullies and victims were defined as those children who were identified as such by a given percentage of the class. In order to establish whether this peer nomination measure had validity, the children were subsequently observed in the playground. Children nominated as bullies carried out significantly more acts of aggression than both victims and children who were not mentioned as bullies or victims.

Withdrawn behaviour has also been assessed by peer nomination techniques. Rubin (1993: 301) reports research where some of the peer nomination items related to withdrawn behaviour – children were asked to nominate someone who would rather play alone than with others; someone whose feelings get hurt easily; someone who is very shy; someone who is usually sad.

It seems important to distinguish between forms of withdrawn behaviour. Children might be withdrawn because they have little interest in interacting with others; they prefer their own company and to engage in solitary forms of play. Alternatively, they might seek the company of others but are unable to achieve this, either because they lack the necessary social skills or because they are timid and reluctant to engage in boisterous or adventurous activities. A child might be withdrawn because he or she has been rejected by other children. This too could be for many reasons, including the possibility that the child was initially withdrawn and this has influenced the group to reject him or her.

The most relevant categories in sociometric analysis are the rejectee and the neglectee. Although these are both types of unpopular children, we shall see that, psychologically, they are very different. It should also be recognised that it could be misleading to identify the neglectee with the withdrawn child. On the one hand, there are many ways in which children can obtain the status of neglectee that are not necessarily related to withdrawn behaviour. On the other hand, a child might be withdrawn without having a distinctive profile in a sociometric analysis. For example, Rubin (1982) found that children defined as withdrawn on the basis of observed solitary behaviour were not less popular than their peers according to sociometric analysis. Identification of withdrawn behaviour requires methods in addition to sociometry. One approach has been to use peer nomination techniques where the items refer to withdrawn behaviour, or to obtain ratings from teachers. Another method is to observe and record the frequency of solitary activities in the social behaviour of children. We begin with consideration of studies of neglected and rejected children.

Wentzel and Asher (1995) examined the school experiences of students aged 12 and 13 years who were identified on the basis of sociometric status as either neglected, rejected, controversial, average or popular. Peer nomination techniques were also applied in order to identify rejected students who were perceived as aggressive or submissive. Neglected students had significantly more *positive* experiences than average students on a range of measures of academic performance, motivation and classroom behaviour. They expressed themselves more satisfied with school and more committed to work. They were rated by teachers as better motivated, as more independent in their work and less impulsive, and as more helpful and considerate in class. There were few overall differences between rejected and average students, but when aggressive–rejected students in particular were looked at, it was found that they were rated by teachers in predominantly negative terms, and were seen as more impulsive, more likely to start fights, less independent, less considerate of others, and less likely to follow rules.

These findings reinforce the importance of maintaining a distinction between the different ways of being unpopular, between neglect and rejection. Renshaw and Asher (1982) reported that neglected children were more likely than rejected children to adjust to a new group whereas children who were rejected in one group also tended to be rejected when they joined a new group. Observation of the rejected children's behaviour showed a high frequency of over-possessive behaviour and verbal and physical aggression. Asher *et al.* (1990) found that rejected children obtained significantly higher scores on a questionnaire measuring loneliness and difficulties in making friends than neglected children, whereas the latter group had scores comparable to those of average children.

Renshaw and Brown (1993) also found that loneliness was positively correlated with teachers' ratings of children's withdrawn behaviour and negatively correlated with psychometric scores of friendship nominations and peer acceptance. Their study had a longitudinal design taking measures on three occasions, at intervals of 10 weeks and one year after initial testing. Withdrawn behaviour at first assessment was predictive of loneliness at the two subsequent assessment periods. Perceived lack of friends was correlated with loneliness, but peer acceptance seemed to modify this relationship. Children who lacked friends but who were generally accepted by their peers were less lonely than friendless children who were less well accepted.

French (1988, 1990) applied the statistical technique of cluster analysis to ratings and test scores obtained from samples of children aged from 8 to 10 years who had been identified as either rejected or popular on the basis of a sociometric technique. Two different sub-groups were identified among the rejected boys and girls. The contrast seemed broadly to be between those children who were rejected–withdrawn and those who were rejected–aggressive–withdrawn. Relative to popular boys, rejected boys classified as withdrawn were nominated by their peers as more withdrawn; were rated by teachers as more anxious and less cooperative; and were observed to spend more time in solitary activities. Rejected–aggressive–withdrawn boys exhibited more antisocial behaviour and were assessed by their teachers as significantly more aggressive, hostile and anxious, less motivated, and having less self-control than the other groups of boys. They were nominated by other boys as both more aggressive and withdrawn than other boys; as French points out, their withdrawn status might have been a consequence of their antisocial behaviour.

Two groups also emerged from a similar analysis of rejected girls. One group comprised girls who were nominated as extremely withdrawn by their peers, and were seen by their teachers as having a range of problems including anxiety, hostile isolation, poor academic achievement and low academic motivation. The second group were nominated by other girls as more aggressive and withdrawn than popular girls, but were seen by their teachers as having few distinctive problems.

Each study identified a group of students who were rejected and 'deviant'. The main gender difference was that aggression figured more strongly among the deviant boys, but this needs to be placed in the context that nominations of aggression were much more common among all groups of boys, including popular boys, than they were among girls.

Several studies reviewed by Hymel et al. (1993) have shown that rejected–aggressive students have more conduct problems than average children. In comparison with withdrawn students, rejected–aggressive–withdrawn students have more academic difficulties, are more impulsive and easily distracted, and show more conduct problems.

Their own study of children aged 10 years compared three groups of 'unpopular' children: aggressive, withdrawn, and aggressive–withdrawn. They defined unpopularity in terms of the number of nominations received on a peer acceptance measure; therefore these children are not rejectees, in the sense of being actively rejected by others. All three groups were viewed in negative terms by their peers although the withdrawn children were not seen in such negative terms as the other two groups. Withdrawn children were perceived as less attractive and lacking in athletic competence relative to the average group, but they were not perceived as having academic or conduct problems. The aggressive–withdrawn children were perceived as least academically competent, were least well liked and were rated as having most behaviour problems. The aggressive children were perceived as poor academically, less well behaved, and less socially competent with adults and peers, but they were not rejected by their peers as often as the aggressive–withdrawn group. There were few differences between groups on measures of self-esteem, although the withdrawn group scored less than average children on measures of self-perceived athletic and social competence.

There is evidence that children think in different ways about the meaning of withdrawn behaviour as they grow older. Younger and his associates have used two tasks, a peer nomination procedure and a test of memory for information about hypothetical children, to provide support for the hypothesis that there are changes with age in children's schemas for withdrawn behaviour. Younger *et al.* (1985) asked first grade, fourth grade and seventh grade children to nominate classmates who were aggressive, withdrawn, or likeable on the Pupil Evaluation Inventory. A multidimensional scaling technique was applied to the similarities and differences among items in the pattern of nominations. Two items, say, 'too shy to make friends' and 'not noticed much', would be classified as similar to each other if the same children tended to be nominated as representative of both items, and would be scored as different if children who were seen as representative of one were seldom chosen as representative of the other. The analysis showed that whereas the aggressive items formed a cluster at all three ages, items referring to social withdrawal only produced a coherent grouping among the older children. The judgements of the younger children could be explained in terms of one underlying evaluative dimension, that contrasted aggression with likeability. Among the older respondents, a second dimension emerged, that contrasted active with passive behaviour.

Younger and Piccinin (1989) also explored children's understanding of withdrawn and aggressive behaviour through examination of their performance on memory tasks. The rationale here is that when children listen to the accounts of aggressive and withdrawn behaviour they draw upon a relevant mental schema in order to interpret and store the incoming information. There is extensive evidence that schemas do aid memory performance; for example, children who are expert at chess have superior recall for the positions of chess pieces on a board, and students who are more knowledgeable about football have superior recall for the scores of football matches. The hypothesis is that if children lack a schema for withdrawn behaviour then they will find it more difficult to organise and retrieve information about that kind of behaviour.

The results showed significant age improvements in recall and recognition memory for descriptions of withdrawn behaviour relative to descriptions of aggressive behaviour that did not change much with age. The researchers also asked participants to rate hypothetical aggressive and withdrawn children in terms of how much they would like to have them as friends. The ratings revealed trends towards expressing more negative attitudes towards withdrawn behaviour that coincided with improvements in performance on the memory task. This research focuses on the structure of children's understanding, proposing that there is greater cohesion of withdrawn items with age and also that children's judgements come to reflect a second, active–passive dimension that is added to the evaluative, aggression–likeable dimension that dominates the judgements of younger children.

Observations of behaviour

Children's solitary play

Rubin (1982) identified a category of *passive–withdrawn* behaviour children on the basis of observations of young children's free play activities. He observed social participation during the classroom play activities of samples of pre-school and reception class children. Withdrawn children, or 'isolates', were defined as those children whose observed social behaviour was significantly less frequent than the average for the group; they were involved with fewer conversations with other children and spent much of their time looking on, rather than joining in.

The different kinds of play pursued by withdrawn children were investigated. Behaviour was observed and coded using a classification scheme originally constructed by psychologists studying the development of play. There were five categories of activity: functional–sensorimotor play; dramatic play; constructive play; exploratory play; games-with-rules. Each of these five categories was also coded in terms of the type of social activity: whether the child was engaged in solitary, parallel or group activities.

Drawing upon the findings of developmental research, these types of play were placed in rank order of their level of cognitive maturity. Solitary functional play and solitary dramatic play were regarded as least mature. Solitary constructive play was regarded as more mature. Social dramatic play and games-with-rules were regarded as the most mature. Findings from this study showed that age differences in the frequency of types of play were compatible with this assumption. Rubin found that isolates were involved 'in less mature forms of play; in particular they participated in less social dramatic play and there were no instances at all of playing games-with-rules.

On the basis of this pattern of results, Rubin distinguished two types of solitary activity. *Active solitude* was based on the categories of solitary functional and solitary dramatic play. *Passive solitude* (or passive withdrawn behaviour) embraced the categories of solitary constructive and exploratory play. Active–solitary play is less common and more problematic from an early age. It is an immature form of behaviour that can be associated with impulsiveness. The observed frequency of active–solitary behaviour was significantly correlated with mothers' ratings of the child's impulsiveness ($r = 0.26$) within the sample of pre-school children studied by Coplan *et al.* (1994).

On the other hand, passive–withdrawn play is common in early child-hood and tends to be regarded by parents in a positive light, as time usefully spent in learning. It is not at that stage an indication of social difficulties. For example, it is not associated with either reticence or shyness. Coplan *et al.* (1994) found that within their sample of 4-year-old pre-school children, mothers' ratings of their child's shyness were significantly correlated with a measure of reticence (r = 0.50) but were not correlated with passive–withdrawn play (r = 0.03).

However, passive–withdrawn play becomes more problematic in later childhood when a range of social opportunities becomes available to the child and more social demands are made upon him or her. Rubin *et al.* (1989) reported that measures of passive–withdrawn play taken in reception class and in grade 2 were correlated with low self-esteem, loneliness and unsatisfactory peer-group relationships at grades 4 and 5, and with measures of depression and teacher-rated shyness at grade 5. Rubin argues that passive withdrawal merges with reticence from about 7 to 9 years to become a single trait of wariness, fearfulness and social anxiety.

Inhibition

Kagan and his colleagues at Harvard University have been studying a temperament that they label inhibition, which displays itself in infant behaviour as timidity and fearfulness in novel situations. In their initial studies, children at the age of 21 months were observed in unfamiliar situations such as meeting a strange adult or being exposed to novel toys and objects, and were classified as inhibited on the basis of their tendencies to avoid or escape from the situation, to cry, show distress, or cling to the mother. Longitudinal studies have shown that inhibition at 21 months is predictive of shyness at age 4 years and beyond. The Fels Research Institute longitudinal study (see Kagan *et al.*, 1986) found that inhibition in infancy predicted later behaviour in school, college and adult life. For example (p. 55), inhibited children

> avoided dangerous activities, were minimally aggressive, conformed to parental requests, and avoided unfamiliar social encounters. As adolescents, they avoided contact sports and other traditional masculine activities, and the four boys who were most inhibited during the first 6 years chose intellectual careers as adults (music, physics, biology and psychology).

Further psychological and physiological assessments of the children provide strong evidence of the biological basis of this behavioural tendency. Thus, for example, inhibition is correlated with measures of heightened stress reactions to a psychological test, including a higher recorded heart rate and greater variability in heart rate, greater motor tension, and increased dilation of the eye pupil when taking the test. Subsequent research has followed a group of infants from the age of 4 months, and has established that infants of that age who are classified as 'high reactive', in the sense that they cry a lot and are very active, are more fearful in novel situations at 14 months and have similar profiles on heart rate measures to inhibited children (Kagan *et al.*, 1993).

Studies of family resemblance in shyness suggest a significant heritable component. Plomin and Daniels (1986) review a large number of investigations of shyness in infancy, childhood, and adulthood, drawing upon studies of identical and fraternal twins, comparisons between parents and their children, and comparisons between adopted children and their biological and adoptive parents. We focus here on studies of twins up to 5 years old. Scores of infants and young children are based on parental ratings on scales devised to measure temperament. Correlations between identical (MZ) twins range from 0.47 to 0.69; correlations between fraternal (DZ) twins range between –0.13 and 0.24 with an average close to zero. These statistics suggest a clear heritable basis for shyness.

This research suggests a continuity between infant inhibition and adult shyness, and also supports the position that temperament has a biological, possibly inherited, basis. This continuity is maintained despite the obvious differences between inhibition and shyness; for example, shyness in adulthood tends to be accompanied by the shy person's extensive set of beliefs about the self and his or her responsibility for awkwardness in social encounters, and is also associated with strategies that people develop to cope with their shyness. Some people who appear confident and outgoing nevertheless consider themselves to be essentially shy.

Longitudinal research has shown that there are discontinuities in inhibition, but it is children who are most strongly inhibited whose inhibition persists. For many reasons, one would predict that comparison of a sample of inhibited infants with a sample of shy adults would show both continuities, where inhibition had persisted into adulthood and found its expression there in shyness, and discontinuities, with some inhibited children who were not subsequently shy, and shy adults without any apparent history of inhibition. Individuals may strive to overcome their inhibition. Parents may arrange different experiences in an attempt to modify it, and they may react differently to signs of shyness in their male and female children (Kerr *et al.*, 1994, found greater stability of inhibition into adolescence among girls who had been extremely inhibited in early childhood in comparison with boys and with less inhibited girls). Children might be labelled by parents or teachers as shy and come to adopt this label. Specific learning experiences might have a role to play. Children might learn that certain behaviours, like quietness or solitary interests, are regarded as signs of shyness and, because they think they demonstrate those behaviours, they label themselves as shy. People might attribute the anxieties that are widely experienced in novel social situations as due to their personal qualities rather than to elements in the situation.

Self-reported shyness

A fresh approach to shyness was instigated by Zimbardo and his associates who administered a questionnaire, the Stanford Shyness Survey, where the first item simply asked respondents whether or not they regarded themselves as shy (see Pilkonis and Zimbardo, 1979). Some 40 percent of respondents described themselves as shy, and over 80 percent claimed to experience shyness in at least some situations. Subsequent studies by other researchers in different countries have replicated these statistics. There is some evidence of cultural variation, but there is no doubt that a substantial number of respondents in all the countries that have been surveyed are prepared to describe themselves as shy, and a sizeable proportion of these regarded their shyness as a severe problem. Nearly all respondents view their shyness in negative terms, as an impediment to their social life.

The next stage in shyness research was based on the development of personality questionnaires, for example, the Cheek and Buss scale (Cheek and Buss, 1981). A substantial number of studies showed that shyness could usefully be construed as a personality trait. This approach made a number of points about shyness.

First, shyness was defined in terms of three components (Cheek and Briggs, 1990). These are cognitive processes, including self-consciousness; somatic symptoms like blushing, perspiring and increased heart rate; behavioural tendencies including gaze avoidance, reticence, and a reluctance to initiate conversation or to express an opinion. No single component in itself is sufficient to define shyness.

Second, feeling shy is accompanied by self-consciousness, and the person is preoccupied with what others might think of them. Self-appraisal, and consciousness of how one's behaviour might appear to others, seem fundamental to shyness, and this raises the question of the stage at which this develops. It does not seem a requirement of inhibition, since this is apparent at an age when it seems unlikely that the young child has the cognitive capacity to make evaluations of the self or to anticipate being evaluated by others. Crozier and Burnham (1990) asked children during the course of individual interviews what shyness meant. There were clear age trends, with the youngest children associating shyness with concerns about meeting new people and older children concerned with both meeting new people and being evaluated. A strong element of embarrassment was apparent in the older children's responses. Crozier (1995) found that children in the age range 9 to 12 years produced both kinds of situations in equal measure when asked to nominate words or phrases that were associated with shyness. Shyness most commonly implied being scared or nervous, hiding, crying or being sad, being quiet or not talking, and going red, blushing, and being embarrassed. These findings are compatible with research that suggests that two classes of situations elicit shyness; novel situations, and those where the individual believes that he or she will be evaluated (Asendorpf, 1989); and that there is a developmental progression towards an emphasis on evaluative situations.

Third, there is a strong element of conflict, with the person eager to contribute but inhibited from doing so. Thus, shyness is distinguished from lack of sociability, where someone has little interest in socialising with others. This aspect of shyness is often observed in the child who 'hovers' on the fringes of group activity, hesitant about participating but reluctant to leave.

Finally, research consistently shows that shyness is associated with low self-esteem (Crozier, 1995). Correlational studies leave unresolved the causal direction of the relationship. Is low self-esteem a consequence of shyness or its cause? Contemporary society places a premium on social adroitness, and the media present countless images of attractive and popular people, particularly, perhaps, in the area of sexual relationships. If these images are internalised as the 'standard', then individuals who believe themselves to be shy will feel devalued and lacking in self-worth. Preoccupation with what others think makes a person vulnerable and unable to discount the adverse experiences that are an inevitable part of social life, as no one is immune to criticism or can altogether control whether they are disliked or rejected by others.

Alternatively, shyness might be a consequence of low self-esteem. Doubts about one's ability to contribute effectively to social encounters and the anticipation that one will be negatively evaluated by others may contribute to the inhibited behaviour and social anxieties that characterise shyness; social withdrawal and defensive behaviours that are associated with negative self-evaluations may in turn reduce self-esteem or else shape a social environment that provides few opportunities for rewarding experiences or boosts in self-confidence.

THE EDUCATIONAL EXPERIENCE OF SHY STUDENTS

Shyness and language development

Despite their social difficulties, there is no evidence that shy students do less well in education than their peers. The silent sixth-grade students tested by Jones and Gerig (1994) had school attainments comparable to those of their non-shy peers. Call *et al.* (1994) found no correlation between shyness and grade point average scores among a sample of children from grades 4 to 6. Gough and Thorne (1986) reported correlations that were close to zero between self-described shyness and scores on the Scholastic Aptitude Test among a sample of American university students.

It has been argued that shyness is associated more specifically with language difficulties, and there is some evidence that shy children perform less well on tests of verbal fluency and vocabulary. One of the earliest studies to report this was undertaken by Gewirtz (1948) testing pre-school children with an average age of 5 years. This involved a test of word-fluency, where the children had to generate as many words as they could within a fixed time interval in response to target questions, for example giving words that rhymed with the target word, providing descriptions of their home, or producing the names of children and adults. The children's teachers rated them on a set of personality trait rating scales, the Fels Child Behavior Scales. The scale measuring shyness, 'social apprehensiveness', correlated significantly with scores on all seven sections of the word fluency measure, the correlation coefficients ranging from –0.25 to –0.58, with a median coefficient of –0.47.

Some more recent studies, reviewed by Evans (1993), show that shy children within the age range 3 to 11 years perform more poorly than their non-shy peers on standardised language assessments including tests of both expressive and receptive vocabulary. The Expressive One Word Picture Vocabulary Test (EOWPVT) is a test of expressive vocabulary where the child has to name line drawings. The Peabody Picture Vocabulary Test (PPVT) is a test of receptive vocabulary; the child hears a word and simply points to which of four pictures illustrates it. Evans (1989; see Evans, 1993: 197) administered these tests to a sample of American first grade children who had been identified by their kindergarten teachers as either 'very quiet' or 'very verbal' in class. The reticent group obtained significantly lower scores than the verbal group on the expressive test (EOWPVT) but there was no significant difference on the test of receptive vocabulary (PPVT).

Vriniotis and Evans (1988) found that reticent children from grades 2 to 6 obtained lower scores than verbal children on the verbal fluency sub-scale of the Clinical Evaluation of Language Functions Test, although there was no difference between groups on the 'vocabulary' scale of the WISC intelligence test. Other studies report mixed findings with the PPVT. They either find no differences or, where withdrawn children obtain lower scores than average children, their scores are in line with the norms for their age (Rubin, 1982). The trend seems to be for sociable children to obtain vocabulary scores significantly higher than their age norms, rather than withdrawn children performing poorly.

To summarise, tests of verbal fluency and of expressive vocabulary present a more consistent picture of differences between shy/reticent and non-shy/reticent children than do tests of receptive vocabulary. The Evans (1989) study is particularly suggestive in that two tests presented the same subjects with pictures: reticent children performed more poorly when naming the pictures but not when responding by pointing to the appropriate picture.

This implies that the difference between shy and less-shy children cannot simply be a matter of testing per se; it is what the child has to do that is important. Evans' interpretation of the poorer performance of shy children is that they lack communicative competence, that is, she assumes that these tests make valid assessments of shy children's abilities. She suggests that they lack competence relative to their peers because their reticence has impeded the development of communicative skills. It is possible that reticence, in turn, is linked to characteristics of the shy person's home that are less conducive to the development of vocabulary, for example, less social stimulation, less conversation, or a smaller social network of friends and acquaintances. These links would be more plausible if one accepted that shyness had a genetic basis, as a shy parent might not only pass on genes to their child but would also provide conditions within the family that foster shyness.

In interpreting these results it is essential to distinguish between competence and performance. An alternative explanation to the view that shy children lack competence is that shyness is triggered by the assessment process. Most of the studies assess linguistic performance through face to face testing. It is evident that encounters with strangers and situations where they are being assessed are the most common causes of shyness in childhood. It is not clear whether variation in test performance reflects relative differences in competence in expressive and receptive vocabulary, or whether the first kind of test is more susceptible to the influence of shyness in that the test subject is required to make verbal responses. This effect might be examined by comparing performance under different test conditions, contrasting face-to-face with group or written forms of the tests.

There are also several possible mechanisms by which shyness could influence performance. This might be through attention processes. Crozier (1990: 24–5) argued that shyness produces anxious self-preoccupation which, in parallel with well-established findings in the field of test anxiety, results in attention being self-focused rather than task-focused. This could interfere, for example, with the generation of responses in vocabulary tests. Alternatively, shy children might set a more rigorous criterion for response selection, fearing the embarrassment of giving a wrong answer. Here shyness would produce hesitation or reluctance to respond at all, a phenomenon that is often encountered in testing children. These alternative hypotheses imply that the tests underestimate children's abilities. Evans (1993: 203) has explicitly rejected this interpretation, arguing that shy children's deficits are also evident in tests which require no or minimal verbal responses and are not apparent in assessments on non-verbal tasks.

These alternative hypotheses should not be interpreted as a denial of the importance of the influence of shyness upon assessment or of its educational implications. Formal assessment of language has come to occupy a pivotal role in the education of even quite young children; less formally, effective teaching depends on successful evaluation of children's strengths and weaknesses which are typically assessed through conversation between teacher and pupil, asking questions of individuals, inviting participation from the whole class, setting group tasks, and so on. There is a clear need to be aware of temperamental characteristics of children that may be influencing these appraisals.

When we move from formal tests of language to investigations of communication in the classroom, the differences between shy and less reticent children are sharper. Evans (1987) has recorded the language of children during 'sharing time' sessions in kindergarten classrooms, where individual pupils take turns to tell the teacher and classmates about things they have done or seen. Shy children introduced fewer topics, spoke fewer words about each topic, and their mean length of utterance was shorter. Their contributions were simpler and tied to objects that they had brought with them and they were less likely to develop a story about the object. Shy children volunteered less information. They were more likely to offer no response or only a minimal answer to teachers' questions and this tended to elicit further teacher questions and a stilted conversation.

Evans and Bienert (1992) suggested that teachers found the silences and minimal responses of shy children uncomfortable and coped with their discomfort by producing further questions; however, this had the effect of producing yet more minimal responding as the teacher began to control the conversation rather than create the conditions for dialogue. In general, children were less fluent when the teacher asked direct questions (those that could be answered yes or no, and those prefaced with 'how' or 'wh-type' words – who, why, where, when, what). They were more fluent when the teacher adopted a more conversational style, elaborating upon the child's contributions and introducing his or her own observations. It is striking that these differences are apparent in settings like 'show and tell' and 'sharing time' since these are structured, in the sense that each child has his or her turn to speak and it is clear what is expected of them.

Asendorpf and Meier (1993) found that children rated by their parents as shy spent as much time in conversations as those rated for sociability when the situation was familiar, but participated less in unfamiliar situations. Other research has shown that shy people have greater difficulties when they have to initiate conversation, when they have to interrupt others or find the appropriate moment in which to speak, and when they have to think what to say, rather than following a 'script'. I recently heard an example of this in a radio interview with the chairperson of one of the country's leading financial institutions who had had an outstanding career as a barrister, but who recalled that he had never been able to overcome his shyness to speak in the university debates that he regularly attended as a student. He believed that he was less shy in the courtroom because he knew when it was his turn to speak and he did not have to interrupt others – he had a brief, a clear role to play.

There are substantial individual differences in the contributions that children make to class. Studies of primary and secondary school children suggest that some 30 percent of pupils remain silent in class, and silent children initiate seven times fewer interactions than their peers (Jones and Gerig, 1994). A similar trend is apparent in higher education. Seale (1980) found that 50 percent of students provided only 5 percent of contributions to university seminar discussion. Reticence may have long-term consequences for students as it makes it more difficult to develop self-confidence and it can also create a negative impression among teachers. Much current thinking about learning emphasises the value of collaboration and shared understanding in cognitive development, and the shy student can isolate him- or herself from these benefits. The study by Evans also suggests that it creates problems in the short term, as reticence can produce interactions with teachers that are uncomfortable and mutually unsatisfactory. It would not be surprising if these experiences only served to reinforce the shy student's lack of self-confidence and led him or her to approach further situations with shyness. We now turn to consider the kinds of situations that elicit shyness.

Shyness and adjustment to university

Shy people believe that they often fail to realise their potential because their reluctance to speak up, their avoidance of controversy, and their tendency to be reserved and keep in the background mean that their qualities are often overlooked. Their abilities may be under-estimated, they may be less likely to be invited to join in activities or to take responsibility. Their reluctance to participate can create a vicious circle, where they have restricted opportunities to develop important skills or to receive positive feedback from others and this will make their non-participation more likely in the future. Self-consciousness may result in an inability to think clearly and to communicate effectively. Making a contribution to a discussion, following the line of an argument, being able to formulate an answer to a question – all require attention to the topic under consideration; and this is more difficult if the shy person's thoughts are self-directed, preoccupied with their own appearance and performance and fearful of what others might think.

There was consensus in the Stanford study among respondents, whether or not they regarded themselves as shy people, about the kinds of situations that tend to elicit shyness. The most common situations were: (a) other people – strangers, authorities by virtue of their knowledge or of their role, members of the opposite sex; (b) social situations: where they are the focus of attention in large groups, as when giving a speech, where they are of lower status, where assertiveness is required, new situations, and where they are being evaluated. Russell *et al.* (1986) found that shyness was most frequently elicited by strangers (reported by 79 percent of student respondents), authority figures (such as talking with a lecturer – also 79 percent), and public performances like giving a speech (46 percent). Also frequently mentioned were new situations such as a new job or school (25 percent), and evaluations (oral examinations and interviews; 23 percent). There seem to be two broad classes of situations that produce shyness: new situations and unfamiliar people; and the anticipation of social evaluation.

These can be illustrated by one of our own studies, where we interviewed mature students about their experience of university (Crozier and Garbert-Jones, 1996). Clearly, entering higher education is for adult learners an experience likely to involve both classes of situations. Universities are invariably large, impersonal places where students are frequently faced with novel social situations and where their written work and contributions to seminars are evaluated, both formally and informally. All those taking part in our study reported feeling shy, often extremely shy, in university, particularly when they had first entered the course. There was consensus about the situations that elicited shyness: speaking to lecturers, participating in seminars, and feeling conspicuous because of their status, that is, they were older than almost all other students and they lacked the qualifications of younger students.

> I looked around and saw all these people and I felt like hiding away – I mean I felt very shy and I used to hate going into the library because I'd see all these young people around me and they probably think what on earth is someone like that doing here.
>
> (p. 196)

Interacting with authority figures was frequently mentioned as a source of shyness, and, in university, this can take the form of speaking to lecturers. The students explained this reaction in terms of what they saw as the superior knowledge of lecturers. To quote one student:

> I feel they've got more knowledge than me – so I'd feel shy about questioning them on something unless I was really sure they'd made a mistake or something – I wouldn't dream of – I'd argue a point but I wouldn't dream of saying they were wrong in any way because they – I'd say they were superior to me.
>
> (p. 195)

One student recalled that during the early part of her college career her shyness with lecturers caused her to avoid approaching them to obtain information, and she preferred to remain in ignorance rather than seek help. However she eventually overcame this, realising that she needed to have certain information in order to complete her studies successfully. She would now initiate conversation with lecturers even though she admitted to feeling shy and awkward still.

The situation that had the greatest potential for shyness was the academic seminar. Seminars seem to hold particular anxieties, as they require the student to speak on academic issues in front of their fellow students and a tutor, and there is a strong implication of evaluation. One respondent described seminars as 'some of the most horrific social situations you'll ever come across'. The concerns these students expressed reveal the core characteristics of shyness: fear of making a contribution in case one appears foolish, remaining quiet and trying to keep in the background. This inactivity is accompanied by intense mental activity including rehearsing possible answers to questions but being inhibited from uttering them, because they believe they would be inappropriate or of an inadequate standard. The student feels self-conscious, very aware of him- or herself in the situation.

CONCLUSION

Shyness and withdrawn behaviour are hidden problems in school. Shy students cause few difficulties to their teachers and their attainments are comparable with those of their peers. However, shyness should be of concern to schools if they recognise that the social and emotional development of children is one of the goals of education. Evidence suggests that withdrawn behaviour in childhood does predict internalising difficulties of anxiety and low self-esteem. The self-reports of shy adolescents and adults reveal their beliefs that they have never developed their potential and these are supported by more objective indicators. For example, longitudinal research by Caspi *et al.* (1988) has shown that shyness assessed in childhood predicts the timing of subsequent significant life events such as age of entry into a settled career.

One of the problems in studying shyness is that it is difficult to provide a satisfactory definition that ties it to observable behaviour. Children can be solitary or withdrawn for many reasons. Observations of behaviour do not closely match sociometric status or peer nominations, and there are many reasons why a match should not be expected. Ratings of shyness and self-ratings do not always correspond. However, research that takes various approaches converges upon the notion of someone who is wary and inhibited about social situations and where there is a contrast between overt passiveness and intense cognitive activity. This pattern is not peculiar to shyness, and has been described by Kuhl (see Chapter 6), in different contexts, as state orientation.

Finally, shyness illustrates many of the strengths of taking a trait perspective on personality that is prepared to accommodate a dynamic interaction between personal and situational factors, such as Bandura's

(1978) concept of reciprocal determinism. Shyness is produced by the interaction of an individual's reflections on his or her own behaviour, observations of the apparent effects of this behaviour on others and their responses to it, together with the person's beliefs about him- or herself. Shyness cannot be reduced to any one of these. For example, an individual's observations of his or her own behaviour, both overt behaviour and cues of anxiety and self-consciousness, help to shape expectancies about future social interactions. These expectancies influence the environment to which the individual exposes him- or herself and also the behaviour that he or she exhibits there. Thus, the shy student has many responses already primed when she anticipates a seminar. Anxiety and lack of participation during the seminar function to maintain the state orientation, and the student's reflection on her own mental, physiological and overt activities provide an explanation of her predicament.

References

Abramson, L. Y., Seligman, M. E. P. and Teasdale, J. (1978) 'Learned helplessness in humans: critique and reformulation', *Journal of Abnormal Psychology*, 87: 49–74.

Achenbach, T. M., McConaughy, S. H. and Howell, C. T. (1987) 'Child/adolescent behavioral/emotional problems: implications of cross-informant correlations for situational specificity', *Psychological Bulletin*, 101: 213–32.

Achenbach, T. M., Howell, C. T., Quay, H. C., and Conners, C. K. (1991) 'National survey of problems and competences among 4 to 16 year olds: parents' reports for normative and clinical samples', *Monographs of the Society for Research in Child Development*, 56: v–120.

Allport, G. W. (1937) *Personality: A Psychological Interpretation*, New York: Holt.

American Psychiatric Association (1980) *Diagnostic and Statistical Manual of Mental Disorders, 3rd edn*, Washington, DC: American Psychiatric Association.

American Psychiatric Association (1987) *Diagnostic and Statistical Manual of Mental Disorders, 3rd edn, Revised*, Washington, DC: American Psychiatric Association.

American Psychiatric Association (1994) *Diagnostic and Statistical Manual of Mental Disorders, 4th edn*, Washington, DC: American Psychiatric Association.

Andrews, B. and Brown, G. W. (1995) 'Stability and change in low self-esteem: the role of psychosocial factors', *Psychological Medicine*, 25: 23–31.

Archer, J. (1991) 'The influence of testosterone on human aggression', *British Journal of Psychology*, 82: 1–28.

Arkin, R. M. (1981) 'Self-presentation styles', in J. T. Tedeschi (ed.) *Impression Management Theory and Social Psychological Research*, New York: Academic Press.

Arnkoff, D. B., Glass, C. R. and Robinson, A. S. (1992) 'Cognitive processes, anxiety, and performance on doctoral dissertation oral examinations', *Journal of Counseling Psychology*, 39: 382–8.

Arntz, A., Rauner, M. and van den Hout, M. (1995) '"If I feel anxious, there must be danger": ex-consequentia reasoning in inferring danger in anxiety disorders', *Behaviour Research and Therapy*, 33: 917–25.

Arthur, W., Jr and Day, D. V. (1991) 'Examination of the construct validity of alternative measures of field dependence/independence', *Perceptual and Motor Skills*, 72: 851–9.

Asendorpf, J. (1989) 'Shyness as a final common pathway for two different kinds of inhibition', *Journal of Personality and Social Psychology*, 57: 481–92.

Asendorpf, J. and Meier, G. H. (1993) 'Personality effects on children's speech in everyday life: sociability-mediated exposure and shyness-mediated reactivity to social situations', *Journal of Personality and Social Psychology*, 64: 1072–83.

Asher, S. R., Parkhurst, J. T., Hymel, S. and Williams, G. A. (1990) 'Peer rejection and loneliness in childhood', in S. R. Asher and J. D. Coie (eds) *Peer Rejection in Childhood*, Cambridge: Cambridge University Press.

Ashton, P. (1984) 'Teacher efficacy: a motivational paradigm for effective teacher education', *Journal of Teacher Education*, 35: 28–32.

Atwood, M. (1989) *Cat's Eye*, London: Bloomsbury.

Baddeley, A. D. and Hitch, G. J. (1974) 'Working memory', in G. H. Bower (ed.) *Recent Advances in Learning and Motivation, vol. 8*, New York: Academic Press.

Bandura, A. (1973). *Aggression: A Social Learning Analysis*, Englewood Cliffs, NJ: Prentice-Hall.

Bandura, A. (1978) 'The self system in reciprocal determinism', *American Psychologist*, 33: 344–58.

Bandura, A. (1986) *Social Foundations of Thought and Action: A Social Cognitive Theory*, Englewood Cliffs, NJ: Prentice-Hall.

Banister, P., Burman, E., Parker, I., Taylor, M. and Tindall, C. (1994) *Qualitative Methods in Psychology: A Research Guide*, Milton Keynes: Open University Press.

Barkley, R. A. (1994) 'Impaired delayed responding: a unified theory of attention-deficit hyperactivity disorder', in D. K. Routh (ed.) *Disruptive Behavior Disorders in Childhood*, New York: Plenum.

Baron, R. A. (1977) *Human Aggression*, New York: Plenum.

Bates, J. E. (1986) 'The measurement of temperament', in R. Plomin and J. Dunn (eds) *The Study of Temperament: Changes, Continuities and Challenges*, Hillsdale, NJ: Erlbaum.

Baumeister, R. F. (1982) 'A self-presentational view of social phenomena', *Psychological Bulletin*, 91: 3–26.

Baumeister, R. F. (ed.) (1993) *Self-Esteem: The Puzzle of Low Self-Regard*, New York: Plenum.

Baumeister, R. F. and Scher, S. J. (1988) 'Self-defeating behavior patterns among normal individuals: review and analysis of common self-destructive tendencies', *Psychological Bulletin*, 104: 3–22.

Baumeister, R. F., Tice, D. M. and Hutton, D. G. (1989) 'Self-presentation motivations and personality differences in self-esteem', *Journal of Personality*, 57: 547–79.

Bebbington, A. and Miles, J. (1989) 'The background of children who enter local authority care', *British Journal of Social Work*, 19: 349–68.

Bennett, N. (1976) *Teaching Styles and Pupil Progress*, London: Open Books.

Berman, P., McLaughlin, M. W., Bass, G., Pauly, E. and Zellman, G. (1977) *Federal Prorams Supporting Educational Change, vol. 7: Factors Affecting Implementation and Continuation*, Santa Monica, CA: The Rand Corporation.

Besag, V. (1989) *Bullies and Victims in Schools*, Milton Keynes: Open University Press.

Betjeman, J. (1964) *A Ring of Bells. Poems of John Betjeman*, London: John Murray.

Beynon, J. (1985) *Initial Encounters in the Secondary School*, Lewes, Sussex: Falmer Press.

Beynon, J. (1988) 'A school for men: an ethnographic case study of routine violence in schooling', in J. Archer and K. Browne (eds) *Human Aggression: Naturalistic Approaches*, London: Routledge.

Biggs, J. B. (1978) 'Individual and group differences in study processes', *British Journal of Educational Psychology*, 48: 266–79.

Biggs, J. B. (1993) 'What do inventories of students' learning styles really measure? A theoretical review and clarification', *British Journal of Educational Psychology*, 63: 3–19.

Blankstein, K. R., Toner, B. B. and Flett, G. L. (1989) 'Test anxiety and the contents of consciousness: thought-listing and endorsement measures', *Journal of Research in Personality*, 23: 269–86.

Boekaerts, M. (1995) *Motivation in Education: The Fourteenth Vernon-Wall Lecture*, Leicester: British Psychological Society.

Boer, F. and Westenberg, P. M. (1994) 'Factor structure of the Buss and Plomin EAS Temperament Survey (parental ratings) in a Dutch sample of elementary school children', *Journal of Personality Assessment*, 62: 537–51.

Borkovec, T. D. and Inz, J. (1990) 'The nature of worry in generalized anxiety disorder: a predominance of thought activity', *Behaviour Research and Therapy*, 28: 153–8.

Borkovec, T. D., Robinson, E., Pruzinsky, T. and DePree, J. A. (1983) 'Preliminary exploration of worry: some characteristics and processes', *Behaviour Research and Therapy*, 2: 9–16.

Boulton, M. J. (1993) 'Proximate causes of aggressive fighting in middle school children', *British Journal of Educational Psychology*, 63: 231–44.

Boulton, M. J (1995) 'Playground behaviour and peer interaction patterns of primary school boys classified as bullies, victims and not involved', *British Journal of Educational Psychology*, 65: 165–77.

Boulton, M. J. and Smith, P. K. (1994) 'Bully/victim problems in middle-school children: stability, self-perceived competence, peer perceptions and peer acceptance', *British Journal of Developmental Psychology*, 12: 315–29.

Bowers, L., Smith, P. K. and Binney, V. (1994) 'Perceived family relationships of bullies, victims and bully/victims in middle childhood', *Journal of Social and Personal Relationships*, 11: 215–22.

Bowlby, J. (1988) *A Secure Base*, London: Routledge.

Brodzinsky, D. M. (1982) 'Relationship between cognitive style and cognitive development: a 2-year longitudinal study', *Developmental Psychology*, 18: 617–26.

Bromley, D. B. (1986) *The Case Study Method in Psychology and Related Disciplines*, Chichester, Sussex: Wiley.

Brown, G. W. and Harris, T. (1989) *Life Events and Illness*, London: Unwin Hyman.

Brunner, H. G., Nelen, M. R., van Zandvoort, P., Abeling, N. G. G. M., van Gennip, A. H., Wolters, E. C., Kuiper, M. A., Ropers, H. H. and van Oost, B. A. (1993) 'X-linked borderline mental retardation with prominent behavioral disturbance: phenotype, genetic localization, and evidence for disturbed monoamine metabolism', *American Journal of Human Genetics*, 52: 1032–9.

Buss, A. H. and Plomin, R. (1984) *Temperament: Early Developing Personality Traits*, Hillsdale, NJ: Erlbaum.

Byrne, B. M. (1984) 'The general/academic self-concept nomological network: a review of construct validation research', *Review of Educational Research*, 54: 427–56.

Call, G., Beer, J. and Beer, J. (1994) 'General and test anxiety, shyness, and grade-point average in elementary-school children of divorced and nondivorced parents', *Psychological Reports*, 74: 512–4.

Carey, W. B. and McDevitt, S. C. (1978) 'Revision of the Infant Temperament Questionnaire', *Pediatrics*, 61: 735–9.

Carlen, P., Gleeson, D. and J. Wardaugh (1992) *Truancy: The Politics of Compulsory Schooling*, Milton Keynes: Open University Press.

Carr, M., Borkowski, J. G. and Maxwell, S. E. (1991) 'Motivational components of underachievement', *Developmental Psychology*, 27: 108–18.

Caspi, A., Elder, G. H. and Bem, D. J. (1988) 'Moving away from the world: life-course events of shy children', *Developmental Psychology*, 24: 824–31.

Caspi, A., Henry, B., McGee, R. O., Moffitt, T. E. and Silva, P. A. (1995) 'Temperamental origins of child and adolescent behavior problems: from age three to age fifteen', *Child Development*, 66: 55–68.

Castellanos, F. X., Elia, J., Kruesi, M. J. P., Gulotta, C. C., Mefford, I. N., Potter, W. Z., Ritchie, G. F. and Rapoport, J. L. (1994) 'Cerebrospinal-fluid monoamine metabolites in boys with attention-deficit hyperactivity disorder', *Psychiatry Research*, 52: 305–16.

Cattell, R. B., Pierson, G. and Finkbeiner, C. (1976) 'Proof of alignment of personality source trait factors from questionnaires and observer ratings: the theory of instrument-free patterns', *Multivariate Behavioral Research*, 4: 1–31.

Cattell, R. B., Sealey, A. P. and Sweney, A. B. (1966) 'What can personality and motivation source trait measurements add to the prediction of school achievement?', *British Journal of Educational Psychology*, 36: 280–95.

Chaplain, R. (1996) 'Making a strategic withdrawal: disengagement and self-worth protection in male pupils', in J. Rudduck, R. Chaplain and G. Wallace (eds) *School Improvement: What Can Pupils Tell Us?*, London: David Fulton.

Chazan, M., Laing, A. F. and Davies, D. (1994) *Emotional and Behavioural Difficulties in Middle Childhood: Identification, Assessment and Intervention in School*, London: Falmer Press.

Cheek, J. M. and Briggs, S. R. (1990) 'Shyness as a personality trait', in W. R. Crozier (ed.) *Shyness and Embarrassment: Perspectives from Social Psychology*, Cambridge: Cambridge University Press.

Cheek, J. M. and Buss, A. H. (1981) 'Shyness and sociability', *Journal of Personality and Social Psychology*, 41: 330–9.

Chess, S. and Thomas, A. (1986) *Temperament in Clinical Practice*, New York: Guilford.

Cheung, Sin Yi and Heath, A. (1994) 'After care: the education and occupation of adults who have been in care', *Oxford Review of Education*, 20: 361–74.

Child, I. L. (1968) 'Personality in culture', in E. F. Borgotta and W. W. Lambert (eds) *Handbook of Personality Theory and Research*, Chicago: Rand McNally.

Colton, M. and Heath, A. (1994) 'Attainment and behaviour of children in care and at home', *Oxford Review of Education*, 20: 317–27.

Conley, J. J. (1984) 'Longitudinal consistency of adult personality: self-reported psychological characteristics across 45 years', *Journal of Personality and Social Psychology*, 47: 1325–33.

Coopersmith, S. (1967) *The Antecedents of Self-Esteem*, San Francisco: Freeman.

Coplan, R. J., Rubin, K. H., Fox, N. A., Calkins, S. D. and Stewart, S. L. (1994) 'Being alone, playing alone, and acting alone: distinguishing among reticence and passive and active solitude in young children', *Child Development*, 65: 129–37.

Corulla, W. F. and Coghill, K. R. (1991) 'Can educational streaming be linked to personality – a possible link between extroversion, neuroticism, psychoticism and choice of subjects', *Personality and Individual Differences*, 12: 367–74.

Covington, M. V. (1992) *Making the Grade: A Self-Worth Perspective on Motivation and School Reform*, New York: Cambridge University Press.

Covington, M. V and Beery, A. G. (1976) *Self-Worth and School-Learning*, New York: Holt, Rinehart & Winston.

Covington, M. V. and Omelich, C. L. (1979) 'Effort: the double-edged sword in school achievement', *Journal of Educational Psychology*, 71: 169–82.

Cox, C. M. (1926) *The Early Mental Traits of Three Hundred Geniuses*, Stamford: Stamford University Press.

Crozier, W. R. (ed.) (1990) *Shyness and Embarrassment: Perspectives from Social Psychology*, Cambridge: Cambridge University Press.

Crozier, W. R. (1995) 'Shyness and self-esteem in middle childhood', *British Journal of Educational Psychology*, 65: 85–95.

Crozier, W. R. and Burnham, M. (1990) 'Age-related changes in children's understanding of shyness', *British Journal of Developmental Psychology*, 8: 179–85.

Crozier, W. R. and Garbert-Jones, A. (1996) 'Finding a voice: shyness in mature students' experience of university', *Adults Learning*, 7: 195–8.

Daniels, D. and Plomin, R. (1985) 'Differential experiences of siblings in the same family', *Developmental Psychology*, 21: 747–60.

Darke, S. (1988) 'Effects of anxiety upon inferential reasoning task performance', *Journal of Personality and Social Psychology*, 55: 499–505.

Daugherty, T. K. and Quay, H. C. (1991) 'Response perseveration and delayed responding in childhood behavior disorders', *Journal of Child Psychology and Psychiatry*, 32: 453–61.

Deci, E. L. and Ryan, R. M. (1985) *Intrinsic Motivation and Self-Determination in Human Behavior*, New York: Plenum.

Deffenbacher, J. L. (1978) 'Worry, emotionality and task-generated interference in test anxiety: an empirical test of attentional theory', *Journal of Educational Psychology*, 70: 248–54.

Deffenbacher, J. L. (1986) 'Cognitive and physiological components of test anxiety in real-life exams', *Cognitive Therapy and Research*, 10: 635–44.

De La Ronde, C. and Swann, W. B., Jr (1993) 'Caught in the crossfire: positivity and self-verification strivings among people with low self-esteem', in R. F. Baumeister (ed.) *Self-Esteem: The Puzzle of Low Self-Regard*, New York: Plenum.

Diener, C. I. and Dweck, C. S. (1978) 'An analysis of learned helplessness: continuous changes in performance, strategy, and achievement cognitions following failure', *Journal of Personality and Social Psychology*, 36: 451–62.

Douglas, G. and Riding, R. J. (1993) 'The effect of pupil cognitive style and position of prose passage title on recall', *Educational Psychology*, 13: 385–93.

Dow, S. P., Sonies, B. C., Scheib, D., Moss, S. E. and Leonard, H. L. (1995) 'Practical guidelines for the assessment and treatment of selective mutism', *Journal of the American Academy of Child and Adolescent Psychiatry*, 34: 836–46.

Dubow, E. F., Tisak, J., Causey, D., Hryshko, A. and Reid, G. (1991) 'A two-year longitudinal study of stressful life events, social support, and social problem-solving skills: contributions to children's behavioral and academic adjustment', *Child Development*, 62: 583–99.

Dunn, J. and McGuire, S. (1994) 'Young children's nonshared experiences: a summary of studies in Cambridge and Colorado', in E. M. Hetherington, D. Reiss and R. Plomin (eds) *Separate Social Worlds of Siblings: The Impact of Nonshared Environment on Development*, Hillsdale, NJ: Erlbaum.

Dweck, C. S. and Leggett, E. L. (1988) 'A social-cognitive approach to motivation and personality', *Psychological Review*, 95: 256–73.

Dweck, C. S., Davidson, W., Nelson. S. and Enna, B. (1978) 'Sex differences in learned helplessness: II. The contingencies of evaluative feedback in the classroom and III. An experimental analysis', *Developmental Psychology*, 14: 268–74.

Easterbrook, J. (1959) 'The effect of emotion on cue utilization and the organization of behavior', *Psychological Review*, 66: 183–201.

Eisenberg, R. B. and Marmarou, A. (1981) 'Behavioral reactions of newborns to speech-like sounds and their implications for developmental studies', *Infant Mental Health Journal*, 2: 129–38.

Elig, T. W. and Frieze, I. H. (1979) 'Measuring causal attributions for success and failure', *Journal of Personality and Social Psychology*, 37: 621–34.

Ellis, L. (1991) 'Monoamine oxidase and criminality: identifying an apparent biological marker for antisocial behavior', *Journal of Research in Crime and Delinquency*, 28: 227–51.

Emde, R. N., Plomin, R., Robinson, J., Corley, R., De Fries, J., Fulker, D. W., Reznick, J. S., Campos, J., Kagan, J. and Zahn-Waxler, C. (1992) 'Temperament, emotion and cognition at fourteen months: The MacArthur Longitudinal Twin Study', *Child Development*, 63: 1437–55.

Entwistle, N. J. (1988) *Styles of Learning and Teaching*, London: David Fulton.

Entwistle, N. J. and Ramsden, P. (1983) *Understanding Student Learning*, London: Croom Helm.

Entwistle, N. J. and Wilson, J. D. (1977) *Degrees of Excellence: The Academic Achievement Game*, London: Hodder & Stoughton.

Erikson, E. H. (1968) *Identity, Youth and Crisis*, New York: W. W. Norton.

Evans, M. A. (1987) 'Discourse characteristics of reticent children', *Applied Psycholinguistics*, 8: 171–84.

Evans, M. A. (1989) 'Classroom reticence: what it looks like and what might account for it', paper presented to the American Educational Research Association, San Francisco.

Evans, M. A. (1993) 'Communication competence as a dimension of shyness', in K. H. Rubin and J. B. Asendorpf (eds) *Social Withdrawal, Inhibition, and Shyness in Childhood*, Hillsdale, NJ: Erlbaum.

Evans, M. A. and Bienert, H. (1992) 'Control and paradox in teacher conversations with shy children', *Canadian Journal of Behavioural Sciences*, 24: 502–16.

Eysenck, H. J. (1978) 'The development of personality and its relation to learning', in S. Murray-Smith (ed.) *Melbourne Studies in Education 1978*, Melbourne: Melbourne University Press.

Eysenck, M. W. (1977) *Human Memory: Theory, Research and Individual Differences*, Oxford: Pergamon.

Eysenck, M. W. (1992) *Anxiety: The Cognitive Perspective*, Hove, Sussex: Lawrence Erlbaum.

Eysenck, M. W. and Calvo, M. G. (1992) 'Anxiety and performance: the processing efficiency theory', *Cognition and Emotion*, 6: 409–34.

Eysenck, M. W. and Folkard, S. (1980) 'Personality, time of day and caffeine: some theoretical and conceptual problems in Revelle et al', *Journal of Experimental Psychology: General*, 109: 32–41.

Eysenck, M. W. and Van Berkum, J. (1992) 'Trait anxiety, defensiveness, and the structure of worry', *Personality and Individual Differences*, 13: 1285–90.

Fahrenberg, J. (1987) 'Concepts of activation and arousal in the theory of emotionality (neuroticism): a multivariate concept', in J. Strelau and H. J. Eysenck (eds) *Personality and Dimensions of Arousal*, New York: Plenum.

Farrington, D. P. (1986) 'Age and crime', in M. Tonry and M. Morris (eds) *Crime and Justice. vol. 7*, Chicago: Chicago University Press.

Farrington, D. P. (1987) 'Epidemiology', in H. C. Quay (ed.) *Handbook of Juvenile Delinquency*, New York: Wiley.

Farrington, D. P. (1991) 'Antisocial personality from childhood to adulthood', *The Psychologist: Bulletin of the British Psychological Society*, 4: 389–94.

Fauber, R., Rorehand, R., Thomas, A. McC. and Wierson, M. (1990) 'A mediational model of the impact of marital conflict on adolescent adjustment in intact and divorced families: the role of disrupted parenting', *Child Development*, 61: 1112–23.

Fergusson, D. M. and Horwood, L. J. (1987) 'The trait and method components of ratings of conduct disorder – Part I. Maternal and teacher evaluations of conduct disorder in young children', *Journal of Child Psychology and Psychiatry*, 28: 249–60.

Fergusson, D. M., Horwood, L. J. and Lynskey, M. T. (1993) 'The effects of conduct disorder and attention-deficit in middle childhood on offending and scholastic ability at age 13', *Journal of Child Psychology and Psychiatry*, 34: 899–916.

Feuerstein, R. (1980) *Instrumental Enrichment: An Intervention Program for Cognitive Modifiability*, Baltimore, MD: University Park Press.

Field, T. (1987) 'Affective and interactive disturbances in infants', in J. D. Osofsky (ed.) *Handbook of Infant Development*, New York: Wiley.

Flanagan, R. M. (1992) 'Teachers' attitudes to bullying as assessed by their responses to hypothetical incidents', Unpublished MEd thesis, University of Wales Cardiff.

Foster, P. and Thompson, D. (1991) 'Bullying: towards a non-violent sanctions policy', in P. K. Smith and D. Thompson (eds) *Practical Approaches to Bullying*, London: David Fulton.

French, D. C. (1988) 'Heterogeneity of peer-rejected boys: aggressive and non-aggressive types', *Child Development*, 59: 976–85.

French, D. C. (1990) 'Heterogeneity of peer-rejected girls', *Child Development*, 61: 2028–31.

Gadow, K. D. (1986) *Children on Medication, vol. 1*, London: Taylor & Francis.

Galton, F. (1869) *Hereditary Genius*, London: Macmillan.

Gergen, K. J. (1985) 'The social constructionist movement in modern psychology', *American Psychologist*, 40: 266–75.

Gewirtz, J. L. (1948) 'Studies in word-fluency: II. Its relation to eleven items of child behavior', *Journal of Genetic Psychology*, 72: 177–84.

Gibson, S. and Dembo, M. H. (1984) 'Teacher efficacy: a construct validation', *Journal of Educational Psychology*, 76: 569–82.

Goffman, E. (1959) *The Presentation of Self in Everyday Life*, Harmondsworth: Penguin, 1971.

Goldsmith, H. H., Buss, A. H., Plomin, R., Rothbart, M. K., Thomas, A., Chess, S., Hinde, R. A. and McCall, R. B. (1987) 'Roundtable: What is temperament? four approaches', *Child Development*, 58: 505–29.

Gopnik, M. (1990) 'Feature-blind grammar and dysphasia', *Nature*, 344: 715.

Götz, K. O. and Götz, K. (1973) 'Introversion–extraversion and neuroticism in gifted and ungifted art students', *Perceptual and Motor Skills*, 35: 675–8.

Gough, H. G. and Thorne, A. (1986) 'Positive, negative, and balanced shyness', in W. H. Jones, J. M. Cheek and S. R. Briggs (eds) *Shyness: Perspectives on Research and Treatment*, New York: Plenum.

Gray, J. A. (1982) *The Neuropsychology of Anxiety*, Oxford: Clarendon Press.

Greenwald, A. G. (1980) 'The totalitarian ego', *American Psychologist*, 35: 603–18.

Griffiths, R. and Sheen, R. (1992) 'Disembedded figures in the landscape: a reappraisal of L2 research on field dependence/independence', *Applied Linguistics*, 13: 131–48.

Hagerman, R. J. (1992) 'Annotation: Fragile X syndrome: advances and controversy', *Journal of Child Psychology and Psychiatry*, 33: 1127–39.

Hagerman, R. J., Jackson, C., Amiri, K., Silverman, A. C., O'Connor, R. and Sobesky, W. (1992) 'Girls with Fragile X syndrome: physical and neurocognitive status and outcome', *Pediatrics*, 89: 395–400.

Hampson, S. E. (1988) *The Construction of Personality, 2nd edn*, London: Routledge & Kegan Paul.

Hansard (1994) Weekly Hansard, 12 December 1994, vol. 251, no. 19, cols 469–70, London: HMSO.

Hansard (1995) Weekly Hansard, 26 June 1995, vol. 262, no. 125, col. 483, London: HMSO.

Hansford, B. C. and Hattie, J. A. (1982) 'The relationship between self and achievement/performance measures', Review of Educational Research, 52: 123–42.

Harter, S. (1983) 'Developmental perspectives on the self-system', in M. Hetherington (ed.) Handbook of Child Psychology, vol. 4: Social and Personality Development, New York: Wiley.

Harter, S. (1985) The Self-Perception Profile for Children: Revision of the Perceived Competence Scale for Children, Denver, CO: University of Denver.

Harter, S. (1989) 'Causes, correlates, and the functional role of global self-worth: a life-span perspective', in R. Sternberg and J. Kolligian, Jr (eds) Competence Considered, New Haven, CT: Yale University Press.

Heidensohn, F. (1996) Women and Crime, 2nd edn, London: Macmillan.

Heider, F. (1958) The Psychology of Interpersonal Relations, New York: Wiley.

Hesketh, D. (1987) 'Advice from the shop floor: pupils' views of disaffection', in T. Booth and D. Coulby (eds) Producing and Reducing Disaffection, Milton Keynes: Open University Press.

Hinshaw, S. P. (1987) 'On the distinction between attention deficits/hyperactivity and conduct problems/aggression in child psychopathology', Psychological Bulletin, 101: 443–63.

Hodges, J. and Tizard, B. (1989) 'IQ and behavioural adjustment of ex-institutional adolescents', Journal of Child Psychology and Psychiatry, 30: 53–75.

Home Office (1994) Criminal Statistics – England and Wales 1993, London: HMSO.

Horne, J. and Ostberg, O. (1976) 'A self-assessment questionnaire to determine morningness–eveningness in human circadian rhythm', Journal of Chronobiology, 4: 97–110.

Houston, B. K. (1977) 'Dispositional anxiety and the effectiveness of cognitive coping strategies in stressful laboratory and classroom situations', in C. D. Spielberger and I. G. Sarason (eds) Stress and Anxiety, vol. 4, Washington, DC: Hemisphere.

Howarth, E. and Eysenck, H. J. (1968) 'Extraversion, arousal, and paired-associate recall', Journal of Experimental Research in Personality, 3: 114–6.

Hughes, T. (1857/1994) Tom Brown's Schooldays, London: Penguin Popular Classics.

Humphreys, M. S. and Revelle, W. (1984) 'Personality, motivation and performance: a theory of the relationship between individual differences and information processing', Psychological Review, 91: 153–84.

Hunt, J. McV. (1961) Intelligence and Experience, New York: Ronald Press.

Hyde, J. S. (1984) 'How large are gender differences in aggression? A developmental meta-analysis', Journal of Psychology, 20: 722–36.

Hymel, S., Bowker, A. and Woody, E. (1993) 'Aggressive versus withdrawn unpopular children: variations in peer and self-perceptions in multiple domains', Child Development, 64: 879–96.

Jackson, P. W. (1968) Life in Classrooms, London: Holt, Rinehart & Winston.

James, J., Charlton, T., Leo, E. and Indoe, D. (1991) 'Using peer counsellors to improve secondary school pupils' spelling and reading performance', Maladjustment and Therapeutic Education, 9: 33–40.

Jenkins, J. M. and Smith, M. A. (1991) 'Marital disharmony and children's behaviour problems: aspects of a poor marriage that affect children adversely', Journal of Child Psychology and Psychiatry, 32: 793–810.

Jones, E. E. and Pittman, T. S. (1982) 'Toward a general theory of strategic self-presentation', in J. Suls (ed.) *Psychological Perspectives on the Self, vol. 1*, Hillsdale, NJ: Erlbaum.

Jones, M. G. and Gerig, T. M. (1994) 'Silent sixth-grade students: characteristics, achievement, and teacher expectations', *The Elementary School Journal*, 95: 169–82.

Jones, R. A. (1995) *The Child–School Interface*, London: Cassell.

Kagan, J., Reznick, J. S. and Snidman, N. (1986) 'Temperamental inhibition in early childhood', in R. Plomin and J. Dunn (eds) *The Study of Temperament: Changes, Continuities and Challenges*, Hillsdale, NJ: Erlbaum.

Kagan, J., Snidman, N. and Arcus, D. (1993) 'On the temperamental categories of inhibited and uninhibited children', in K. H. Rubin and J. B. Asendorpf (eds) *Social Withdrawal, Inhibition, and Shyness in Childhood*, Hillsdale, NJ: Erlbaum.

Kaplan, P. S. (1990) *Educational Psychology for Tomorrow's Teacher*, St Paul, MN: West Publishing.

Keise, C. (1992) *Sugar and Spice? Bullying in Single Sex Schools*, Stoke-on-Trent: Trentham Books.

Kenrick, D. T. and Funder, D. C. (1988) 'Profiting from controversy: lessons from the person–situation debate', *American Psychologist*, 43: 23–34.

Keogh, B. K. (1982) 'Children's temperament and teachers' decisions', in R. Porter and G. Collins (eds) *Temperamental Differences in Infants and Young Children: Ciba Foundation Symposium 89*, London: Pitman.

Kerr, M., Lambert, W. W., Stattin, H. and Klackenberg-Larsson, I. (1994) 'Stability of inhibition in a Swedish longitudinal sample', *Child Development*, 65: 138–46.

Kershner, R. (1996) 'The meaning of "working hard" in school', in J. Rudduck, R. Chaplain and G. Wallace (eds) *School Improvement: What Can Pupils Tell Us?*, London: David Fulton.

Krahé, B. (1992) *Personality and Social Psychology: Towards a Synthesis*, London: Sage.

Krapp, A., Hidi, S. and Renninger, K. A. (1992) 'Interest, learning and development', in K. A. Renninger, S. Hidi and A. Krapp (eds) *The Role of Interest in Learning and Development*, Hillsdale, NJ: Erlbaum.

Kuhl, J. (1994) 'A theory of act and state orientations', in J. Kuhl and J. Beckmann (eds) *Volition and Personality: Action Versus State Orientation*, Seattle: Hogrefe & Huber Publishers.

Kuhl, J. and Goschke, T. (1994) 'State orientation and the activation and retrieval of intentions in memory', in J. Kuhl and J. Beckmann (eds) *Volition and Personality: Action Versus State Orientation*, Seattle: Hogrefe & Huber Publishers.

La Fontaine, J. (1990) *Bullying: The Child's View*, London: Calouste Gulbenkian Foundation.

Lane, D.A. (1989) 'Violent histories: bullying and criminality', in D. W. Tattum and D. A. Lane (eds) *Bullying in Schools*, Stoke-on-Trent: Trentham Books.

Larson, R. (1995) 'Secrets in the bedroom: adolescents' private use of media', *Journal of Youth and Adolescence*, 24: 535–50.

Lawrence, D. (1988) *Enhancing Self-Esteem in the Classroom*, London: Paul Chapman Publishing.

Lee, C. and Bobko, P. (1994) 'Self-efficacy beliefs: comparison of five measures', *Journal of Applied Psychology*, 79: 364–9.

Leith, G. O. (1974) 'Individual differences in learning: interactions of personality and teaching methods', in *Personality and Academic Progress: Conference Proceedings*, London: Association of Educational Psychologists.

Leon, M. R. (1989) 'Anxiety and the inclusiveness of information processing', *Journal of Research in Personality*, 23: 85–98.

Lewinsohn, P. M., Mischel, W., Chaplin, W. and Barton, R. (1980) 'Social competence and depression: the role of illusory self-perceptions', *Journal of Abnormal Psychology*, 89: 203–12.

Licht, B. G., Kistner, J. A., Ozkaragoz, T., Shapiro, S. and Clausen, L. (1985) 'Causal attributions of learning disabled children: individual differences and their implications for persistence', *Journal of Educational Psychology*, 77: 208–16.

Lykken, D. T., McGue, M., Tellegen, A. and Bouchard, T. J. (1992) 'Emergenesis: genetic traits that may not run in families', *American Psychologist*, 47: 1565–77.

Maines, B. and Robinson, G. (1991) 'Don't beat the bullies!', *Educational Psychology in Practice*, 7: 168–72.

Marsh, H. W. (1986) 'Global self-esteem: its relation to specific facets of self-concept and their importance', *Journal of Personality and Social Psychology*, 51: 1224–36.

Marsh, H. W. (1990a) 'The structure of academic self-concept: the Marsh/ Shavelson model', *Journal of Educational Psychology*, 82: 623–36.

Marsh, H. W. (1990b) 'Causal ordering of academic self-concept and academic achievement: a multiwave, longitudinal panel analysis', *Journal of Educational Psychology*, 82: 646–56.

Marsh, H. W. (1992) 'Content specificity of relations between academic achievement and academic self-concept', *Journal of Educational Psychology*, 84: 35–42.

Marsh, H. W. and O'Neill, R. (1984) 'Self-Description Questionnaire III (SDQ III): the construct validity of multidimensional self-concept ratings by late-adolescents', *Journal of Educational Measurement*, 21: 153–74.

Marsh, H. W. and Parker, J. W. (1984) 'Determinants of student self-concept: is it better to be a relatively large fish in a small pond even if you don't learn to swim as well?', *Journal of Personality and Social Psychology*, 47: 213–31.

Marton, F. and Säljö , R. (1976) 'On qualitative differences in learning. I – Outcome and process', *British Journal of Educational Psychology*, 46: 4–11.

Mathews, A. (1990) 'Why worry? The cognitive function of anxiety', *Behaviour Research and Therapy*, 28: 455–68.

Matthews, G. (1989) 'Extraversion and levels of control of sustained attention', *Acta Psychologica*, 70: 129–46.

Mauger, P. (1972) 'Selection for secondary education', in D. Rubinstein and C. Stoneman (eds) *Education for Democracy*, Harmondsworth: Penguin.

May, C. P., Hasher, L. and Stoltzfus, E. R. (1993) 'Optimal time of day and the magnitude of age differences in memory', *Psychological Science*, 4: 326–30.

McClelland, D. C. (1987) *Human Motivation*, New York: Cambridge University Press.

McCord, R. R. and Wakefield, J. A., Jr (1981) 'Arithmetic achievement as a function of introversion–extraversion and teacher-presented reward and punishment', *Personality and Individual Differences*, 2: 145–52.

McCrae, R. R. and John, O. P. (1992) 'An introduction to the five-factor model and its assessment', *Journal of Personality*, 60: 175–215.

McCroskey, J. C. and Beatty, M. J. (1986) 'Oral communication apprehension', in W. H. Jones, J. M. Cheek and S. R. Briggs (eds) *Shyness: Perspectives on Research and Treatment*, New York: Plenum.

McKenna, F. P. (1984) 'Measures of field dependence: cognitive style or cognitive ability?', *Journal of Personality and Social Psychology*, 47: 593–603.

McKenna, F. P. (1990) 'Learning implications of field dependence–independence: cognitive style versus cognitive ability', *Applied Cognitive Psychology*, 4: 425–37.

McKinnon, D. W. (1962/1970) 'The personality correlates of creativity: a study of American architects', in P. E. Vernon (ed.) *Creativity*, Harmondsworth: Penguin, 1970. (Original publication in *Proceedings of the Fourteenth Congress on Applied Psychology, vol. 2*, 1962.)

Meents, C. K. (1989) 'Attention deficit disorder: a review of literature', *Psychology in the Schools*, 26: 168–78.

Meisel, C. J. and Blumberg, C. J. (1990) 'The social-comparison choices of elementary and secondary school students: the influence of gender, race, and friendship', *Contemporary Educational Psychology*, 15: 170–82.

Meyer, T. J., Miller, M. L., Metzger, R. L. and Borkovec, T. D. (1990) 'Development and validation of the Penn State Worry Questionnaire', *Behaviour Research and Therapy*, 28: 487–95.

Mischel, W. (1968) *Personality and Assessment*, New York: Wiley.

Mischel, W. and Peake, P. K. (1982) 'Beyond déja vu in the search for cross-situational consistency', *Psychological Review*, 89: 730–55.

Mockros, C. A. and Csikszentmihalyi, M. (1996) 'The social construction of creative lives', in R. Purser and A. Montuori (eds) *Social Creativity*, Creskill, NJ: Hampton Press.

Mogg, K., Bradley, B. P., Millar, N. and White, J. (1995) 'A follow-up study of cognitive bias in generalized anxiety disorder', *Behaviour Research and Therapy*, 33: 927–35.

Moss, H. A. and Shipman, E. J. (1980) 'Longitudinal study of personal development', in O. G. Brim, Jr. and Kagan, J. (eds) *Constancy and Change in Human Development*, Cambridge, MA: Harvard University Press.

Murray-Harvey, R. (1994) 'Learning styles and approaches to learning: distinguishing between concepts and instruments', *British Journal of Educational Psychology*, 64: 373–88.

Nolen, S. B. (1988) 'Reasons for studying: motivational orientations and study strategies', *Cognition and Instruction*, 5: 269–87.

Norem, J. K. and Cantor, N. (1986) 'Defensive pessimism: harnessing anxiety as motivation', *Journal of Personality and Social Psychology*, 51: 1208–17.

Olweus, D. (1978) *Aggression in the Schools: Bullies and Whipping Boys*, Washington, DC: Hemisphere.

Olweus, D. (1993) *Bullying at School*, Oxford: Blackwell.

Olweus, D., Mattsson, A., Schalling, D. and Löw, H. (1987) 'Circulating testosterone levels and aggression in adolescent males: a causal analysis', *Psychosomatic Medicine*, 50: 261–72.

O'Neill, G. W. (1985) 'Is worry a valuable concept?', *Behaviour Research and Therapy*, 23: 479–80.

Pajares, F. and Johnson, M. J. (1994) 'Confidence and competence in writing: the role of self-efficacy, outcome expectancy, and apprehension', *Research in the Teaching of English*, 28: 313–31.

Pajares, F. and Miller, M. D. (1995) 'Mathematics self-efficacy and mathematics performances: the need for specificity of assessment', *Journal of Counselling Psychology*, 42: 190–8.

Paramo, M. F. and Tinajero, C. (1990) 'Field dependence/independence and pérformance in school: an argument against neutrality of cognitive style', *Perceptual and Motor Skills*, 70: 1079–87.

Pelham, B. W. and Swann, W. B., Jr (1989) 'From self-conceptions to self-worth: on the sources and structure of global self-esteem', *Journal of Personality and Social Psychology*, 57: 672–80.

Peterson, C., Semmel, A., Von Baeyer, C., Abramson, L. Y., Metalsky, G. I. and Seligman, M. E. P. (1982) 'The attributional style questionnaire', *Cognitive Therapy and Research*, 8: 287–300.

Phares, E. J. (1984) *Introduction to Personality*, Columbus, OH: Merrill.

Phillips, D. A. (1984) 'The illusion of competence among academically competent children', *Child Development*, 55: 2000–2016.

Pilkonis, P. A. and Zimbardo, P. G. (1979) 'The personal and social dynamics of shyness', in C. Izard (ed.) *Emotions in Personality and Psychopathology*, New York: Plenum.

Pintner, R. and Lev, J. (1940) 'Worries of school children', *Journal of Genetic Psychology*, 56: 67–76.

Plomin, R. and Daniels, D. (1986) 'Genetics and shyness', in W. H. Jones, J. M. Cheek and S. R. Briggs (eds) *Shyness: Perspectives on Research and Treatment*, New York: Plenum.

Plomin, R. and Daniels, D. (1987) 'Why are children in the same family so different from each other?', *The Behavioral and Brain Sciences*, 10: 1–16.

Potter, J. and Wetherell, M. (1987) *Discourse and Social Psychology*, London: Sage.

Powys, John Cowper (1934/1967) *Autobiography*, London: Macdonald.

Powys, L. (1937) *The Joy of It*, London: Chapman and Hall.

Pruzinsky, T. and Borkovec, T. D. (1990) 'Cognitive and personality characteristics of worriers', *Behaviour Research and Therapy*, 28: 507–12.

Pye, J. (1989) *Invisible Children*, Oxford: Oxford University Press.

Quinton, D. and Rutter, M. (1988) *Parenting Breakdown: The Making and Breaking of Inter-Generational Links*, Aldershot, Surrey: Avebury.

Rathunde, K. and Csikszentmihalyi, M. (1993) 'Undivided interest and the growth of talent: a longitudinal study of adolescents', *Journal of Youth and Adolescence*, 22: 385–405.

Reber, A. S. (1985) *The Penguin Dictionary of Psychology*, Harmondsworth: Penguin.

Renshaw, P. D. and Asher, S. R. (1982) 'Social competence and peer status: the distinction between goals and strategies', in K. H. Rubin and H. S. Ross (eds) *Peer Relationships and Social Skills in Childhood*, New York: Springer-Verlag.

Renshaw, P. D. and Brown, P. J. (1993) 'Loneliness in middle childhood: concurrent and longitudinal predictors', *Child Development*, 64: 1271–84.

Revelle, W., Humphreys, M. S., Simon, L. and Gilliland, K. (1980) 'The interactive effect of personality, time of day, and caffeine: a test of the arousal model', *Journal of Experimental Psychology: General*, 109: 1–31.

Riding, R. J. and Cheema, I. (1991) 'Cognitive styles – an overview and integration', *Educational Psychology*, 11: 193–215.

Riding, R. J. and Pearson, F. (1994) 'The relationship between cognitive style and intelligence', *Educational Psychology*, 14: 235–60.

Riding, R. J. and Read, G. (1996) 'Cognitive style and pupil learning preferences', *Educational Psychology*, 16: 81–106.

Rosenberg, M. (1965) *Society and the Adolescent Self-Image*, Princeton, NJ: Princeton University Press.

Rubin, K. H. (1982) 'Social and social-cognitive developmental characteristics of young isolate, normal, and sociable children', in K. H. Rubin and H. S. Ross (eds) *Peer Relationships and Social Skills in Childhood*, New York: Springer-Verlag.

Rubin, K. H. (1993) 'The Waterloo Longitudinal Project: correlates and consequences of social withdrawal from childhood to adolescence', in K. H. Rubin and J. B. Asendorpf (eds) *Social Withdrawal, Inhibition, and Shyness*, Hillsdale, NJ: Erlbaum.

Rubin, K. H., Hymel, S. and Mills, R. S. L. (1989) 'Sociability and social withdrawal in childhood: stability and outcomes', *Journal of Personality*, 57: 237–55.

Ruble, D. N., Boggiano, A. K. and Feldman, N. S. (1980) 'Developmental analysis of the role of social comparison in self-evaluation', *Developmental Psychology*, 16: 105–15.

Rushton, J. P., Fulker, D. W., Neale, M., Nias, D. B. and Eysenck, H. J. (1986)

'Altruism and aggression: the heritability of individual differences', *Journal of Personality and Social Psychology*, 50: 1192–8.

Russell, D., Cutrona, C. and Jones, W. H. (1986) 'A trait–situational analysis of shyness', in W. H. Jones, J. M. Cheek and S. R. Briggs (eds) *Shyness: Perspectives on Research and Treatment*, New York: Plenum.

Rutter, M. (1972) *Maternal Deprivation Reassessed*, Harmondsworth: Penguin.

Rutter, M. (1989) 'Pathways from childhood to adult life', *Journal of Child Psychology and Psychiatry*, 30: 23–51.

Rutter, M. (1991) 'Pathways from childhood to adult life: the role of schooling', *Pastoral Care*, September, 3–10.

Rutter, M., Quinton, D. and Liddle, C. (1983) 'Parenting in two generations: looking backwards and looking forwards', in N. Madge (ed.) *Families at Risk*, London: Heinemann.

Rutter, M., Bolton, P., Harington, R., Lecouteur, A., Macdonald, H. and Simonoff, E. (1990a) 'Genetic factors in child psychiatric disorder: I. A review of research strategies', *Journal of Child Psychology and Psychiatry*, 31: 3–37.

Rutter, M., Macdonald, H., Lecouteur, A., Harrington, R., Bolton, P. and Bailey, A. (1990b) 'Genetic factors in child psychiatric disorder: II. Empirical findings', *Journal of Child Psychology and Psychiatry*, 31: 39–83.

Sandler, I. N. and Block, M. (1979) 'Life stress and maladaptation of children', *American Journal of Community Psychology*, 7: 425–40.

Sarason, I. G. (1984) 'Stress, anxiety, and cognitive interference: reactions to tests', *Journal of Personality and Social Psychology*, 46: 929–38.

Sarason, I. G., Sarason, B. R. and Pierce, G. R. (1990) 'Anxiety, cognitive interference, and performance', *Journal of Social Behavior and Personality*, 5: 1–18.

Scarr, S. (1993) 'Biological and cultural diversity: the legacy of Darwin for development', *Child Development*, 64: 1333–53.

Schachar, R. J. and Logan, G. D. (1990) 'Impulsivity and inhibitory control in normal development and childhood psychopathology', *Developmental Psychology*, 27: 710–20.

Schiefele, U. (1996) 'Topic interest, text representation, and quality of experience', *Contemporary Educational Psychology*, 21: 3–18.

Schiefele, U. and Csikszentmihalyi, M. (1995) 'Motivation and ability as factors in mathematics experience and achievement', *Journal for Research in Mathematics Education*, 26: 163–81.

Schmeck, R. R. (1983) 'Learning styles of college students', in R. Dillon and R. R. Schmeck (eds) *Individual Differences in Cognition*, New York: Academic Press.

Schmeck, R. R. (1988) 'Strategies and styles of learning', in R. R. Schmeck (ed.) *Learning Styles and Learning Strategies*, New York: Plenum.

Schmidt, R. A. (1982) *Motor Control and Learning*, Champaign, IL: Human Kinetics Publishers.

Seale, C. (1980) 'Two views of discussion groups', *Journal of Further and Higher Education*, 4: 51–9.

Sharp, S. and Smith, P. K. (eds) (1994) *Tackling Bullying in Your School*, London: Routledge.

Sharp, S. and Thompson, D. (1994) 'How to establish a whole-school anti-bullying policy', in S. Sharp and P. K. Smith (eds) *Tackling Bullying in Your School*, London: Routledge.

Sharp, S., Cowie, H. and Smith, P. K. (1994) 'How to respond to bullying behaviour', in S. Sharp and P. K. Smith (eds) *Tackling Bullying in Your School*, London: Routledge.

Shavelson, R. J., Hubner, J. J. and Stanton, G. C. (1976) 'Self-concept: validation of construct interpretations', *Review of Educational Research*, 46: 407–11.

Shrauger, J. S. (1975) 'Responses to evaluation as a function of initial self-perceptions', *Psychological Bulletin*, 82: 581–96.

Silverman, W. K., La Greca, A. M. and Wasserstein, S. (1995) 'What do children worry about? Worries and their relation to anxiety', *Child Development*, 66: 671–86.

Simensen, R. J. and Rogers, R. C. (1989) 'School psychology and medical diagnosis: the Fragile X syndrome', *Psychology in the Schools*, 26: 380–9.

Simon, R. J. and Baxter, S. (1989) 'Gender and violent crime', in N. A. Weiner and M. E. Wolfgang (eds) *Violent Crimes, Violent Criminals*, London: Sage.

Simonton, D. K. (1984) 'Artistic creativity and interpersonal relationships across and within generations', *Journal of Personality and Social Psychology*, 46: 1273–86.

Simonton, D. K. (1987) 'Developmental antecedents of achieved eminence', *Annals of Child Development*, 4: 131–69.

Simonton, D. K. (1990) *Psychology, Science, and History*, New Haven, CT: Yale University Press.

Singer, E. (1992) *Child Care and the Psychology of Development*, London: Routledge.

Skinner, B. F. (1948/1976) *Walden Two*, New York: Macmillan.

Sloboda, J. (1990) 'Combating examination stress among university students: action research in an institutional context', *British Journal of Guidance and Counselling*, 18: 124–36.

Spielberger, C. D., Gorsuch, R. and Lushene, R. (1970) *The State–Trait Anxiety Inventory Test Manual*, Palo Alto, CA: Consulting Psychologists Press.

Sroufe, L. A. (1978) 'Attachment and the roots of competence', *Human Nature*, 1: 50–7.

Swann, W. B., Jr, Wenzlaff, R. M. and Tafarodi, R. W. (1992) 'Depression and the search for negative evaluations: more evidence of the role of self-verification strivings', *Journal of Abnormal Psychology*, 101: 293–306.

Stahl, S. M. (1992) 'The current impact of neuroscience on psychotropic drug discovery and development', *Psychopharmacology Bulletin*, 28: 3–9.

Taylor, S. E. and Brown, J. D. (1988) 'Illusion and well-being: a social psychological perspective on mental health', *Psychological Bulletin*, 103: 193–210.

Tedeschi, J. T., Lindskold, S. and Rosenfeld, P. (1985) *Introduction to Social Psychology*, St Paul, MN: West.

Teigen, K. H. (1994) 'Yerkes–Dodson: a law for all seasons', *Theory and Psychology*, 4: 525–47.

Thomas, A. and Chess, S. (1982) 'Temperament and follow-up to adulthood', in R. Porter and G. Collins (eds) *Temperamental Differences in Infants and Young Children: Ciba Foundation Symposium 89*, London: Pitman.

Thompson, T. (1993) 'Characteristics of self-worth protection in achievement behaviour', *British Journal of Educational Psychology*, 63: 469–88.

Thorne, B. (1993) *Gender Play: Girls and Boys in School*, Milton Keynes: Open University Press.

Tizard, B. and Hodges, J. (1978) 'The effect of early institutional rearing on the development of eight-year-old children', *Journal of Child Psychology and Psychiatry*, 19: 99–118.

Turner, A. K. (1994) 'Genetic and hormonal influences on male violence', in J. Archer (ed.) *Male Violence*, London: Routledge.

Verhulst, F. C. and Akkerhuis, G. W. (1989) 'Agreement between parents' and teachers' ratings of behavioural/emotional problems of children aged 4 to 11', *Journal of Child Psychology and Psychiatry*, 30: 123–36.

Virkkunen, M. (1991) 'Brain serotonin and violent behaviour', *Journal of Forensic Psychiatry*, 3: 171–4.

Virkkunen, M. and Linnoila, M. (1993) 'Brain-serotonin, Type II-alcoholism and impulsive violence', *Journal of Studies on Alcohol*, S11: 163–9.

Vriniotis, C. and Evans, M. A. (1988) 'The development of children's social communicative competence and its relation to classroom participation', paper presented to the Canadian Psychological Association, Montreal, Quebec.

Wagner-Martin, L. W. (1990) *Sylvia Plath*, London: Cardinal.

Weiner, B. (1979) 'A theory of motivation for some classroom experiences', *Journal of Educational Psychology*, 71: 3–25.

Wentzel, K. R. and Asher, S. R. (1995) 'The academic lives of neglected, rejected, popular, and controversial children', *Child Development*, 66: 754–63.

Wheldall, K. and Glynn, T. (1989) *Effective Classroom Learning*, Oxford: Blackwell.

Whitley, B. E., Jr. and Frieze, I. H. (1985) 'Children's causal attributions for success and failure in achievement settings: a meta-analysis', *Journal of Educational Psychology*, 77: 608–16.

Whitney, I. and Smith, P. K. (1993) 'A survey of the nature and extent of bullying in junior/middle and secondary schools', *Educational Research*, 35: 3–25.

Whitney, I., Rivers, I., Smith, P. K. and Sharp, S. (1994) 'The Sheffield Project: methodology and findings', in P. K. Smith and S. Sharp (eds) *School Bullying: Insights and Perspectives*, London: Routledge.

Wilkinson, H. and Mulgan, G. (1995) *Freedom's Children*, London: Demos.

Wine, J. (1971) 'Test anxiety and the direction of attention', *Psychological Bulletin*, 76: 92–104.

Witkin, H. A. and Goodenough, D. R. (1981) *Cognitive Styles: Essence and Origin*, New York: International Universities Press.

Wolfe, R. N. and Johnson, S. D. (1995) 'Personality as a predictor of college performance', *Educational and Psychological Measurement*, 55: 177–85.

Wolkind, S. N. and De Salis, W. (1982) 'Infant temperament, maternal mental state and child behaviour problems', in R. Porter and G. Collins (eds) *Temperamental Differences in Infants and Young Children: Ciba Foundation Symposium 89*, London: Pitman.

Yates, C. and Smith, P. K. (1989) 'Bullying in two English comprehensive schools', in E. Roland and E. Munthe (eds) *Bullying: An International Perspective*, London: David Fulton.

Younger, A. J. and Piccinin, A. M. (1989) 'Children's recall of aggressive and withdrawn behaviors: recognition memory and likability ratings', *Child Development*, 60: 580–90.

Younger, A. J., Schwartzman, A. E. and Ledingham, J. E. (1985) 'Age-related changes in children's perceptions of aggression and withdrawal in their peers', *Developmental Psychology*, 21: 70–5.

Index

DATE DUE

APR 0 3			

#47-0108 Peel Off Pressure Sensitive